Frances Wright
Camilla Wright
Harriet Garnett
Frances Garnett
Julia Garnett Pertz
Frances Trollope

RESTLESS ANGELS

The Friendship of Six Victorian Women

HELEN HEINEMAN

OHIO UNIVERSITY PRESS
ATHENS, OHIO

Library of Congress Cataloging in Publication Data

Heineman, Helen, 1936–
    Restless angels.

    Bibliography: p.
        1. Women intellectuals—Biography.   2. Women
intellectuals—United States—Biography.
3. Women intellectuals—History—19th century.
4. Women intellectuals—United States—History—
19th century.   I. Title.
HQ1233.H44   1983   305.4'092'2   [B]   82-12421
ISBN 0-8214-0673-6
ISBN 0-8214-0674-4 (pbk.)

RESTLESS ANGELS

The Friendship of Six Victorian Women

To the memory of Cecilia Payne-Gaposchkin.   Her careful preservation of the letters of her great-grandmother's circle of women first inspired and then made this book possible.

TABLE OF CONTENTS

LIST OF ILLUSTRATIONS

ACKNOWLEDGMENTS

I wish to express my gratitude to several people who have made important contributions to this book.

Margaret Touborg made significant organizational suggestions. Dr. Alan Lawson made comments on the American sections. My husband, Dr. John L. Heineman, helped with the sections concerning German history and was a valuable editor in all sections of the book.

M. Lisa Phipps is responsible for drawing and designing the cover and frontispiece, which so beautifully convey the story and spirit of the book. George Damon supervised and Sue Grudzinski did the photographic reproductions at the Framingham State College Media Center.

Katherine Haramundanis has generously made available to me her collection of family documents and pictures. I am indebted to her, as I was to her mother, Dr. Cecilia Payne-Gaposchkin, who read this book in all of its many phases and who made invaluable comments and criticisms throughout the period of its composition. She saw the final version just before her death in December 1979.

A NOTE ON SOURCES
AND REFERENCES

THE NOTES which follow each chapter are intended to direct the scholarly reader to the sources I have used in writing this composite biography. To avoid filling the text with distracting footnotes, a page number and short phrase have been used to document those quotations and statements whose date and identification are not clear from the context. The principal *published* sources are found in the Bibliography, where abbreviated titles from the references are given in full.

Unpublished material to which I make reference comes from the following collections:

The Garnett-Pertz Collection (GPC), used with the kind permission of Dr. Cecilia Payne-Gaposchkin, the great-granddaughter of Julia Garnett Pertz, and currently owned by her daughter, Mrs. Katherine Haramundanis, and housed in the Houghton Library of Harvard University. This important collection contains weekly or bimonthly letters to and from the Garnett sisters and their wide circle of friends. It forms a unique historical record of the thoughts and actions of a group of women between 1820 and 1852. The collection consists of 842 letters, which can be broken down in the following manner:

	Letters from the six women	*Abbreviations*
Harriet, Mary and Frances Garnett	435	HG, MG or FG
Julia Garnett Pertz	167	JGP
Frances and Camilla Wright	33	FW, CW
Frances Trollope	29	FT
	Letters from other correspondents	
J. C. L. Simonde de Sismondi	27	S
Julia Smith	43	JS
Anna Maria Garnett Stone	11	AMS
General Lafayette (copies)	12	L
Robina Craig Millar	4	RCM
Sophia Hay	3	SH
Helen Martineau	8	HM
Assorted Correspondents	70	By name

The Garnett-Pertz Collection also contains the autobiographical memoir MS of Georg Heinrich Pertz, and the unpublished MS of Harriet Garnett's novel.

The late Dr. Gaposchkin and I transcribed this entire collection as faithfully as possible, and any irregularities of spelling, punctuation, and usage may be attributed to the original correspondent. Dr. Gaposchkin translated the Pertz memoir (from German) and the Sismondi letters (from French).

Other collections which contain material used in this biography include the following:

The Morris L. Parrish Collection, Princeton University
The Robert H. Taylor Collection, Princeton University
The Gates Collection, New York Historical Society (NYHS)
The Demarest Papers, Rutgers University
The Lafayette Papers, University of Chicago
Frances Trollope's Journal of a Visit to LaGrange, University of Illinois (UIU)

Woman is like the Archangel Michael as he stands upon Saint Angelo at Rome. She has an immense provision of wings, which seem as if they would bear her over earth and heaven; but when she tries to use them, she is petrified into stone, her feet are grown into the earth, chained to the bronze pedestal.

FLORENCE NIGHTINGALE, **"Cassandra"**

If men could see us as we really are, they would be a little amazed; but the cleverest, the acutest men are often under an illusion about women: they do not read them in a true light: they misapprehend them, both for good and evil: their good woman is a queer thing, half doll, half angel; their bad woman almost always a fiend.

CHARLOTTE BRONTË, **Shirley**

Frances Wright
Camilla Wright
Harriet Garnett
Frances Garnett
Julia Garnett Pertz
Frances Trollope

Whitehouse Farm New Brunswick, New Jersey

CHAPTER ONE

A Circle of Women: The First Utopia, 1798-1824

Upon the whole, is not Biography the most interesting of all reading? I never have had insight enough into History to find much interest in it. It is not to me, generally so much a picture of characters with their passions and their intellects working upon the fate of the passive millions, as it is a picture of events following one another, often without apparent connection. I enjoy reading History - but Biography is much easier to deal with. One can follow the history of one mind and one can in the commonest experience of life find a key and an interpretation to the most uncommon. I often think people cannot make a more valuable contribution to their age than their own memoirs truly told, with all their faults and follies. But how few would have the courage for it. Even the most insignificant eventless life has moral experience in it that would be precious to everyone, if only they could get at it genuine.

JULIA SMITH **to Julia Pertz, 20 July 1850**

WHY SHOULD anyone try to reconstruct the lives of six relatively obscure women of the early nineteenth century? The famous are often interesting, but only two of this group achieved any prominence in the public world; the others were surely among those "mute, inglorious females" who have long since been forgotten. Still, these women were striving to define themselves in areas women are still exploring: meaningful occupation, relationships with other women, and some kind of fulfillment in their more traditional roles as wives, daughters, sisters, and mothers, in a century as definite and restrictive about the parameters of women's lives as our own is groping and open-ended. Primarily, these six women were unusual in that we know of them: they left behind a rich record of their shared experience by means of which we can trace their individual quests and struggles, as well as their reliance upon a supportive circle of friendship. Scholars have tried to recreate the lives of such women by analyzing the plethora of manuals, magazines, and novels that poured forth from their century. In the admonitory strictures of Mrs. Ellis and Mrs. Craik, in the inner thoughts of Jane Eyre and Emma Woodhouse, some have tried to find the sound of real women's voices. Through the letters of Frances and Camilla Wright, Fanny and Harriet Garnett, Julia Garnett Pertz, and Frances Trollope, we can share an authentic

1

experience of womanhood in an age just beginning to define the boundaries of female life.

The single thread that unifies their otherwise disparate destinies is their lifelong quest for self-definition, which centered around finding some serious occupation, either in place of or coexistent with their domestic tasks and assignments. This need to fill their increased amounts of leisure time became their deepest bond with one another, and it would transform some of them into rebels, others into victims, and at least one into a woman who achieved the full potential of her nature.

There were, of course, other factors that brought this group of women together. Family ties were the first, as were their varying connections with the promise of the new world, where some began their lives, and others later sought human perfectibility or refuge. All of them found the men in their lives failures at some crucial point, and all sought bonding or sisterhood with other women as solutions. Some found their letters to one another the most important means to such bonding, while others enjoyed real female companionship or projected it in fiction. But their commitment to a mutual correspondence kept them sensitive to the quality of one another's experience and made them friends for life, though their futures were widely divergent. That we have these letters permits one solution to a crucial problem of women's history—how to explore the world of women who left no direct accounts, how to write a story about those who remained inarticulate in the public sphere. These familiar letters unlock the inner lives of women, moving the reader beyond the evidence of statistics or cultural artifacts in tracing the dawning consciousness of a shared female condition.

Their story begins in an atmosphere of new freedoms, twenty years after the Americans had broken off relations with their mother country to become themselves a nation. An Englishman also disenchanted with the repressive policies of his own land, believing that great disturbances were coming, emigrated to America, seeking "a good climate, rational society, and a field for honest industry." John Garnett sailed for the new world in August 1798, bringing with him his wife Mary and their five children: Anna Maria (13), Henry (11), Julia (4), Harriet (3), and Fanny (2), along with Sophia Hay, a "valuable and worthy young woman," the girls' governess for the past four years. Ironically, Garnett's money had come through his wife's family, Bristol sea-merchants, who leased their ships to slave traders, also headed for the new world on very different kinds of errands. And while Garnett found it pleasant and even easy to transform himself into a new world Adam, a self-reliant man living in harmony with nature in a paradise of intellectual excellence, his girls would later have greater problems in reconciling the heady freedoms of their youth with the ideals of the century in which they would reach their womanhood. Long after his particular version of paradise had disappeared, his daughters would, along with their friends, be drawn to locate other dreams in the vast spaces of America. But for now, his was the time, and the place was Whitehouse Farm.

For Julia and Harriet Garnett, life began in an atmosphere of open space, both mental and physical. Their surroundings offered them that kind of intellectual and natural freedom which Margaret Fuller later argued was necessary for a woman's proper education. The Garnett girls' informal education commenced in that roomy farmhouse in America, with its library of treasured books brought from England at the expense of furniture. The collection was full of *belles lettres* as well as scientific treatises (Garnett was an amateur mathematician with scientific tastes who made discoveries ranging from methods of finding altitudes to observations of double stars.). Upstairs there was even an observatory for Garnett's favorite study, the stars, with which his daughter Julia would eventually help him. Their brother Henry went to Princeton to study, but, of course, there were no comparable institutions for women. Still, this enlightened father designed a rigorous and complete course of study for his daughters, one which would later cause them to strain at the molds into which they were destined to cast their lives. Their governess did instruct them on the feminine accomplishments, like the art of fine copper-plate writing, but she also taught them the classics and French. Garnett himself was their teacher in mathematics and astronomy. The girls' lives revolved around their father's advanced ideas. Even conventional religious training was avoided in the interests of full intellectual freedom. Thus, the Garnett women grew up largely unaffected by those restrictive ideals of piety and submissiveness even then becoming popular for young women of their class and kind. Later, when Sophia Hay left the Garnetts to found a school for girls, she did not follow Garnett's plan, but modeled her curriculum on other existing models, training her charges in deportment and posture, music and dancing, for the feeling of the time was that the more difficult studies were the prerogative of men. If we can believe some contemporary reports, such attention was paid to graceful carriage for women, that the girl who failed to hold herself erect was strapped to a door and forced to study her lessons in that position. Fortunately, the Garnett daughters had escaped such practices, and thanks to the training of their father, learned the habit of independent thought, a rare one for women of this new generation. They had been trained to define themselves and to be masters of their fates. Whether they would actually be, was an individual matter, a combination of inner and outer forces too complex for easy analysis.

Of the Garnett sisters, no likeness has survived either of Harriet or Fanny, although both lived well into the age of the daguerreotype and the photograph. Once, when the daguerreotype was new, Julia, hoping to bring them closer despite the separating miles, arranged to have herself and her family photographed, but Harriet's reaction was less than pleased—and even fearful. She replied:

> I hope we shall think the daguerreotype *pretty,* —on this score I am more difficult than you are, & I own I do not like to see or allow to be seen an ugly likeness of those I love. I have said formerly I only wished to see my foes daguerrotyped, but yours will I hope reconcile me to the art. . . . I saw a lady lately who said her picture taken in that way none of her friends would accept, they thought it so hideous, so she gave it to her maid. . . . Do not send us an ugly family group, dear Julia, or we shall not like to look upon it.

When at length the awaited picture arrived, Harriet, predictably, asked her sister instead for a sketch of her drawing room. A sense of place might be transmitted, but never of people as they existed in the mind's eye. She told Julia sadly:

> I cannot bear to show any one the daguerreotype—you all look so very old. . . . But this is always the case in daguerreotypes. I was glad to hear lately they are very incorrect likenesses, owing to the light magnifying some features more than others. Now your muff is almost as long as your whole person, yet you call it a *little* muff. But I could not bear to show such an unpleasing representation of those I love.

Such distorted likenesses reported a kind of aging of which the spirit took no account. In rejecting this picture of her sister, Harriet rejected all depictions which failed to capture and record the elusive essence of people. To be drawn or photographed was perhaps like being possessed, and Harriet would ever retain her sense of privacy and distance from others. She and her sister Fanny were the only women of the group who did not marry, rejecting those intimacies even as they had the ones captured by camera or brush. All her life, Harriet, with her bright intellect, would be like one of the pretty birds she loved in later years: "I have a little canary bird that I have made quite tame; it perches on my finger and eats out of my hand." There were more: "I have birds in quantity,—tame canaries, linnets, a goldfinch, a starling, & I am to have a blackbird. . . . they are tame enough to go in the garden on my hand, and the starling passes the whole day there. No cat fortunately visits the garden, for I often leave the canaries in freedom there." Like some tamed wild creature, Harriet grew and flourished under her father's tutelage, beside her beloved sister Julia, who was equally clever, but not so reserved, more soft and gentle, and open to others.

In later years, Julia's bereaved husband would commission a memorial portrait of her, whose features and expression embodied the essence of her life. In it, the large eyes are placid. All in her glance is sedate. Lettered in fine hand beneath the oval frame stand her name and the epitomizing phrase, "She lives and loves." Enclosed within the elliptic circle, she seems the perfection of womanliness. Her hair, confined beneath her cap, lies neat, symmetrically parted. The lace encircling her soft shoulders announces gentility. Pearls and brooch bespeak her comfortable status. She seems a man's woman, all stateliness, all softness. From this memorializing moment, she looks out with an expressive note of understanding. She inclines toward us, as if to listen and to help. Service seems the very posture of her life. No trace remains here of her struggles or her restlessness, of the sense of uselessness and failure which ended her life. All has been rarified into the ideal woman. The engraver has completed the shaping process, transforming the real Julia at the last into a sedate matron. Perhaps Harriet was right, after all, to preserve her essence safe from the shapings of others. It is difficult to find in this portrait the young girl her mother thought a chatterbox and "a little too wild," who rode horseback and sailed her own boat on the Raritan River, who was loved by the scandalous Prosper Mérimée, and who almost ran off to join a utopian colony. Nothing is left of that Julia, and there are only her letters to help us balance this idealized portrait.

Julia and Harriet absorbed much of their father's advanced learning, cleaving all the more closely to each other, an inseparable pair, so close in age and alike in looks that they were often mistaken for each other. Anna Maria Garnett was a good deal older, and by the time her younger sisters were growing up, she had found the young man she would later marry, settling with him for good in America. Fanny, the youngest, was always strange, a shy, slow girl, increasingly valetudinarian as the years wore on, and distinctly anti-social. Julia and Harriet, thrown together by these defections, flourished precociously in their American home. Little beyond their ambitious educational program is known of the girls until 1818, when the attractive atmosphere of Whitehouse Farm drew into its orbit the visiting young Englishwomen Frances and Camilla Wright, who were just then traveling on a long visit to America. Affection soon blossomed among the quartet of girls: Julia and Harriet, Fanny and Camilla Wright swore eternal friendship and made a pact to remain close to each other for the rest of their lives. This vague but compelling plan for some permanent sisterhood among the women was to be accomplished when the Wrights could settle their affairs in England and return to establish permanent residence in America.

Even at twenty-one, Frances Wright was a striking woman whom people noticed. Upon this point, those who attempted her portrait in words agreed. A nineteenth-century historian of Memphis who knew her, her utopian co-worker Robert Dale Owen, and Frances Trollope's son Tom all subsequently described a woman with great "personal advantages," a "commanding figure," and withal, "very remarkable," indeed, "the most conspicuous person in all the country round." Tall, slender, and graceful, she had a kind of beauty which all three observers independently classified as "masculine." Keating noted her "masculine strides," and her habit of wearing a man's hat. Tom Trollope found her "very handsome in a large and almost masculine style of beauty, with a . . . superb figure and stature fully masculine." Owen, who knew her best, characterized her profile as "masculine rather than feminine, like that of an Antinous, or perhaps nearly typifying a Mercury." Each qualified the praise he proffered. Her posture was "strident," and her character full of "exceptional eccentricities." She sometimes affected the wearing of "Turkish Trousers." Her shoulders were "a little bit too high," and her large blue eyes were "not soft." Ignoring the female fashion of the day, she wore her hair clipped short. It curled naturally about her face, giving her a "modern" look. The French artist Hervieu drew her portrait once, placing her beside a tall and graceful horse, perhaps thus suggesting something of her unconventionality. Her body soars beside that of the horse, matching both his strength and naturalness. Surely the pose must be unique among female portraits of the time. A more popular representation shows her in ordinary dress, with large, flowing sleeves and a lace collar dipping demurely at the neck. While the face is pretty, the dreamer stares out from her eyes. Most unusual is the portrait which still hangs in the home of one of her descendants, showing Miss Wright in profile; with her determined look and careless curls, she might be a Renaissance prince, steely-eyed, contemplating some conquest, not counting the cost. Her heroic look is curiously at odds with the ornate oval frame, surely meant to enclose some softer female subject. The portrait makes a companion piece for the verses later carved upon her Cincinnati tombstone: "I have wedded the cause of human improvement, staked on it my fortune, my reputation, and my life." Spoken in 1829, those words epitomize her life. If ever she wedded in earnest, it was the "cause of human improvement," and she made no mere mortal man her mate.

It has often been observed, particularly of the lives of early nineteenth-century women, that marriage is the essential fact of a woman's life. "Marriage is destiny," pronounced the countless manuals and articulators of "Woman's Mission." But for Frances Wright, and for her sister Camilla, both of whom did eventually wed, marriage was an insignificant interruption in

Frances Wright

the essential urge of their lives, which for Fanny was her passion for reform, and for Camilla, her devoted sisterhood with Fanny.

Fanny and Camilla had been orphaned early. Separated by only a chronological year (they were born in 1795 and 1796 respectively), they had lived apart since their early orphaning, Camilla with her old nurse in Dundee, and Fanny with her Aunt Frances Campbell in London. When they were eleven and twelve, Cam came to stay with her sister for good and became at once her elder sister's admiring disciple, missing those important first ten years when she might have learned to strive and scrap with Fanny more normally, as such close siblings often do. But Cam swam into her sister's magic sphere and was soon ready to adore and live in the shadow of Frances forever.

Fanny, on the other hand, wanted to offer some passionate service to the world, not to individuals. When her decided beliefs caused tensions with Aunt Campbell, the girls went to live with their uncle, James Mylne, professor of moral philosophy at the University of Glasgow. At once, the Mylnes were more fond of Camilla, whom they believed to be overly influenced by the more independent Frances. For her part, Fanny would have loved to find an object to worship. In this desire to dedicate herself to the needs of the world, she resembles Dorothea Brooke, the heroine of *Middlemarch,* published twenty years after Fanny's death. But in spite of great strength of character, Dorothea married twice and in the end was cudgeled by her creator into submission. Frances Wright, despite her subsequent marriage, never renounced the search for greater goals.

Formal religion she had given up early. Some time between 1816 and 1818 she declared, "I think I have done with churches. When I can hear of one that does honor to God and good to man it shall have my presence and my love." Apparently, she never did. But what she did hear of, and what did eventually gain both her "presence and her love" was the new republic of the United States of America. One day, browsing in her uncle's large library, she came across Botta's history of the revolution in America which, she says, awoke her to a new existence. At last, she had found an adequate divinity. She described her feelings in an autobiography on which she was already at work: "Life was full of promise; the world a theatre of interesting observation and useful exertion. There existed a country consecrated to freedom, and in which man might awake to the full knowledge and exercise of his powers." The connection in her mind between America and the development of human potential stood out clearly.

But a docile younger sister, and an elderly uncle teaching moral philosophy were not the ones to sustain a devotee in such enthusiasms. For support in her growing worship of America, she turned to Mrs. Craig Millar, widow of a favorite brother of Mrs. Mylne. Mrs. Millar's dead husband had been

Fanny's own father's friend, sharing with him a radicalism that had made them both unpopular in English society. The Millars had gone to America, in a kind of self-imposed exile, and after her husband's early death, Mrs. Millar returned to Scotland to live in seclusion in Whitburn, where Fanny had visited her. Almost at once, the two women formed a deep sentimental attachment, the focal point of which was their love of the new world.

Then, by the spring of 1818, both Fanny and Camilla had come of age. Now they could use their considerable inheritance without consulting either relatives or courts. What Camilla might have done with her new freedom is unclear, for Fanny had already decided upon their future. In the summer of 1818, the two young women sailed for a long visit to America. The thirty-day voyage was gruelling, particularly for the frailer Camilla. But she could endure much to be with her sister. In all other matters yielding and hesitant, Camilla was tenacious in her attachment to Fanny. Soon, the rigors of the trip were past, and the girls were meeting their first Americans. In New York, they had letters of introduction from Mrs. Millar to Charles Wilkes, the prominent New York banker, through whom the Wrights were introduced to the Garnetts, since their family of four daughters seemed likely companions for the young Wright sisters.

After a prolonged stay at the Garnetts' Whitehouse Farm, the Wrights continued their journey to see America, through the northern and eastern states, ebullient accounts of which Fanny sent on to Mrs. Millar. These eventually became a book describing her trip, *Views of Society and Manners in America* (1823). As she herself admitted, her enthusiasm for the new republic knew no bounds and threw "a Claude Lorraine tint" over all she saw. Indeed, if anything, her new friendship with the Garnetts intensified her optimism about America. As Mrs. Millar told the Garnetts, "In the natural, moral, and political features of your great and growing country, [Frances Wright] has found objects to fill and gratify her capacious—her magnificent mind—and in you she has met objects of esteem and affection she hardly believed to exist!" The circle of women was almost complete, but several years were to pass before it included its fifth member, who would also one day join in the search for happiness in the new world.

Frances Trollope was still in England, only a family friend about whom the Garnett girls as yet knew little. After all, Frances was almost fifteen years older than the group, and by the time the Garnetts and Wrights had met, she was a Harrow matron, giving birth to the last of her seven children. Born in 1779, Frances was one of three children of the Reverend William Milton, whose first wife had died early, leaving her three children without a mother in their growing years. Very little is known in detail about the first twenty years of Frances Milton's life, but she acquired an impressive number of accomplishments—like a knowledge of French and Italian, the classics, and the plastic arts–from her father, a clever, eclectic-minded clergyman more interested in his amateur inventions than in problems of theology or philosophy. In 1801 Frances went with her father and his new wife to live at Heckfield, where he had taken up full-time residence in his fifty-eighth year. Brought up amid enlightenment ideas, there she read Dante and Moliere and rode horseback down the hedges and coppices of green Middlesex. But soon such scenes became somewhat stifling for a young woman whose mind had been enlarged beyond her rural environs. And so, in 1803, she went up to London with her sister to live with their brother Henry, who had just taken a position at the War Office. She spent the next five years visiting museums and theatres, and reading extensively; she enjoyed a full, remarkably free, and intellectual life. Then, at twenty-nine, in 1808, she met Thomas Anthony Trollope and was courted by the serious young barrister with whom she would share so many trials and tragic sorrows. But for now they read Miss Edgeworth's *Modern Griselda* together, approving of its moral that wives should not dominate their husbands. Frances was herself ready to marry in the pattern of her time. Yet she would never abandon the intellectual life, even during courtship days, when her husband-to-be remarked on her propensity to hem sheets and read Dante at the same time.

She bore her children rapidly. Thomas Adolphus came a year after her wedding, followed closely by Henry (1811), Arthur William (1812), Emily I (1813), Anthony (1815), Cecilia (1816), and Emily II (1818). Just as the Garnetts and Wrights were meeting in America, Frances Trollope, at the age of thirty-nine, had born her last child, the seventh in eight years. Because the family had grown so rapidly, the Trollopes decided to move out of London and their crowded Keppel Street home. They accomplished their transfer in two stages, first renting land in Harrow, upon which stood a large farmhouse which the family renovated to meet their needs. It was a fun-loving, intellectual household, and Mrs. Trollope was content with her life as mother and housewife. She enjoyed fixing up the house and managing domestic affairs, as Mr. Trollope spent long hours away from home in his London chambers or on the circuits. Then, on the strength of an eventual inheritance from his Uncle Meetkerke and his own barrister's salary, in 1818 Trollope erected a big new house under favorable leasing arrangements with his landlord, John Lord Northwick. Here again, Mrs. Trollope made most of the decisions about the style and spaces of the house, a stately brick mansion which they called Julians and which now rose on a corner of their Harrow land with a magnificent view of London. The home, graceful and splendid, became a focus for entertainment and hospitality. All seemed joyful, despite Trollope's realization that he had seriously underestimated his costs. In that magnificent house, high on the hills of Harrow, lay both the seeds of the ruin of Mrs. Trollope's present life and the creation of a future which no one could at the time have envisioned.

Catastrophe came quickly. Trollope's Uncle Meetkerke, from whom he expected a legacy, remarried in his old age and produced a healthy progeny which now would supplant Trollope. Realizing the economics of their now changed life, the family rented out their beautiful house, and, making the best of a bad destiny, moved back to their farmhouse, bravely naming it Julian Hill. They would live there for almost ten more years.

Mrs. Trollope, who continued to enjoy the life of the mind, was sometimes called a "bluestocking" by her friends. She was a champion of Lord Byron in the days of scandal about his illegitimate daughter Allegra, and even began to write a poem attacking the hypocritical Harrow headmasters who refused the little girl a burial in Harrow churchyard, lest her presence corrupt the schoolboys. But soon there were worries closer to home, financial problems, and her husband's deteriorating physical condition. Mr. Trollope began to be racked by terrible headaches, which drove him to inwardness and moroseness. Even further disasters, the death of four of her six children, lay ahead, though mercifully no one foresaw those tragic losses in these years.

Mrs. Trollope would soon encounter a phenomenon to be shared in some degree by all her subsequent circle of friends. Though everything in their backgrounds had promised them that men were pivotal in women's lives, sources of meaning and security, their own experience would tell another story. Each woman came to experience not men's oppression, but their ineffectuality. Their fathers, husbands, brothers, and uncles failed them, grew weak or ill, were cowardly or conventional. Mrs. Trollope's father had remarried, leaving her to settle her own future. Her busy Harrow household would soon begin its troubled decline, based largely on her husband's poor management and increasingly bad health. So, too, the new world paradise of John Garnett was about to be shattered. Only a few months after the Wrights had left for England—projecting a permanent return to America—John Garnett suddenly died. The dynamic man who had shaped his daughters' existence was gone. Suddenly, all the really strong figures of life were women: dependence upon men seemed a risky business at best. As the complexities of modern life increased, the ability of the male to guarantee stability and shelter, despite the contemporary rhetoric about the woman being the angel or priestess in the sacred temple of home, became highly uncertain.

Fanny Wright mourned the passing of John Garnett, "her best philosopher and friend." For her new friends, "misfortune has followed misfortune ever since I left you; each letter has spoken of some calamity sustained, or some hope abandoned." Now that the Garnett women were alone, an ambitious idea took root in Fanny's fertile imagination. She advised the Garnetts to arrange their financial affairs, while she would seek some place in America where all of them could live together, sharing mutual interests and working to build useful lives. Repeatedly, her letters struck the same theme. "We are yet all to be united. It is sweet at least to live in the belief of this." Even though the rest of the world might present a spectacle of "moral waste," there would always be such friends. Fanny asked the Garnetts: "The dearest hope of your souls—is it not to be reunited to your friend—to be in the same country with her & occasionally at least to possess her society? I say *occasionally,* for situated as you are at present, dependent more or less upon the will of others whose will is seldom yours, I dare scarcely indulge the expectation that you can be mine wholly & that without interruption, thro' the year's circle, ours can be the 'same board, same bed, same exercise'." Even Mrs. Millar, now an old woman, was briefly tempted by her memories of America and Fanny's rhetoric. As she told the Garnetts, the Wrights had returned to Europe "wholly American in all their sentiments and feelings! . . . *Light* is everywhere making rapid progress—and we *shall* yet all meet to rejoice in the approaching reason, virtue, and consequent happiness of Mankind."

In a letter to the Garnetts, Frances Wright had specifically outlined her plans to emigrate in late 1820:

> If you then continue in America, I shall seek you there and follow the bent of my heart in becoming a citizen of the only country to which I acknowledge an attachment. . . . Here all is *retrograde.* England had once public spirit, she had dignity, she had, to a certain degree, freedom. —Where is all this now? In the lower classes there is discontent because there is misery. There is a considerable body among the middling classes where you will still find principle; but these chosen bands seem to be forsaking their country in disgust, and planting their domestic hearths in the wilds of your America.

But her own visit to the United States had revealed a flaw even in that dream country: slavery.

> My Harriet I love your feelings toward your country. You may well be proud of it; you may well exult in its prosperity & its freedom, & you may well too sigh when you throw your eyes Southward, & see liberty mocked & outraged & that by a race of free men, who while they have her name in their mouths, ay and her energy in their souls, grasp the chain of oppression in their hands, denying to the wretched sons of Africa that holy birthright which they themselves declare man holds of God. When my thoughts turn to America the crying sin of her slavery weighs upon my heart; there are moments when this foul blot

so defaces to my mind's eye all the beauty of her character that I turn with disgust from her & in her from the last & only nation on the globe to which my soul clings with affection, pride & hope. From a misanthrope I then find myself a Cynic; my heart is at war with man, I loathe his nature & his name & attribute his creation to a malignant demon, rather than to a beneficent God.

Reflection, however, makes me draw back the curse with the acknowledgment of my own injustice. I remember that the better half of those great republics are unprofaned by this crying sin—this reconciles me to the name of the United States. I recollect that some of the *free* were once *slave* states—this reconciles me in part with my species, & makes me hope that other states will follow this example, & that all those republics, nay that all that great Continent, *North & South,* may exhibit the perfection of freedom.

These private feelings, temporarily contained, would soon ripen into a plan to help free the American slaves by means of a community also focused on female cooperation and occupation.

But Fanny's ambitious plan would have to wait. Almost at once, the Garnett family found to their distress that John Garnett's financial arrangements had not been sound enough to permit their maintaining the large home and farm in America and the type of free, intellectual life they had been accustomed to enjoy. In 1823, after two years of trying to hold their affairs together, they sold the property at a loss and returned to England through the assistance of Henry Milton, Fanny Trollope's brother. When they looked around them for a new home, their eyes turned to Paris, a city which seemed the only place that even remotely approached the liberal atmosphere of their old home.

Moreover, Fanny Wright was in Paris, temporarily distracted from the idea of forming a community in America both by the Garnett's problems in retaining their American home and by the events following the publication of her book describing her American trip. It had attracted the attention of the great and made her a minor celebrity, especially among advocates of reform. She had been summoned into the presence of Jeremy Bentham, who offered her the hospitality of his home; she stayed with him, calling him "my Philosopher." Bentham was old and infirm; Fanny found his attention exciting, but also exhausting. For one thing, he was growing deaf. "An hour's conversation with my Socrates leaves me more fatigued than does a walk of 6 miles." More important to her future was her meeting with General Lafayette, an emotional introduction which she subsequently described to Bentham.

I sent a note, early the following morning, to General Lafayette, who soon answered it in person. Our meeting was scarcely without tears (at least on my side) and whether it was that this venerable friend of human liberty saw in me what recalled to him some of the most pleasing recollections of his youth (I mean those connected with America) or whether it was only that he was touched by the sensibility which appeared at that moment in me, he evidently shared my emotion. . . . My sister, and all the rest of the family, were escorted to Beaujons, while I remained to receive General Lafayette. We had an earnest tête-a-tête until after midnight. The main subject of our discourse was America, although we wandered into many episodes and digressions.

And so it began, this May-December friendship which was so to shape the course of all the women's lives over the next several years. Almost at once, these two loved each other with a devotion both fatherly and lover-like, too. Soon she was calling Lafayette "the best and greatest man that lives . . . my friend—my father," and herself "the child of his affection, the child of his adoption." From the first, his family distrusted and resented Fanny, but there was nothing they could do immediately. For the next three years, Fanny and Camilla lived near Paris, at La Grange, while Fanny devoted herself to the task of writing Lafayette's life and being his secretary and confidante. Before long, the language of their letters was laced with the rhetoric of love and kinship. It would seem she had forgotten her dream of a community of women in the overwhelmingly passionate attachment to Lafayette, who now became the cornerstone of her life. Also, the Garnetts had meanwhile returned to Europe and settled in Paris. Thus Fanny could be close to them and Lafayette at the same time.

Despite the otherwise fierce independence of Fanny Wright, she shared with others of her sex a deep need to be submerged in some powerful masculine "other." Lafayette was her "most valued, most revered friend," next, her "kind, indulgent friend," and finally, her "best friend." From friend, he soon became "father." Within a month of their first meeting, she was telling him, "You know I am your child. The child of your affection—the child of your adoption. You have given me the title and I will never part with it. To possess this title was the highest of my wishes—to deserve it is my proudest ambition." She hoped confidently to merit the "friendship and parental fondness of the best and greatest man that lives." Six months later, her feelings had, if anything, intensified. Her dependence upon Lafayette increased, and the language of her letters to him during his absences from La Grange, where she was now staying with her sister, seems baldly lover-like and for Fanny Wright curiously submissive.

In truth, I don't know what to make of myself without my paternal friend. I look around for you, listen for your foot, and your voice twenty times a day, but . . . in vain. You are in Paris, and I am 40 miles from it. La Grange looks very lovely and all its inmates are kindness and goodness personified & my little Cam is sweetly affectionate & so is Harriet also, but still I am alone without you. . . . I do not ask if you sometimes think of me. . . . My friend, my father, & if there be a word more expressive of love, & reverence, & adoration, I would fain use it. I am only half alive when away from you. . . . You must continue to love me, however, in spite of my little worthiness, for in truth I love you very, very much.

Calling him "father" and "paternal friend" enabled her to express more freely her deep feelings, but the kind of devotion which lay submerged beneath such effusions soon became intolerable to his large family.

Then, in late 1823, Frances Trollope entered the web of these complicated relationships as she and her husband left Harrow for a Paris vacation. In part, she intended to visit her son Henry, apprenticed at a French counting-house, to oversee his progress which, on his own report, had not been good. She also looked forward to renewing her friendship with the Garnetts, whom she had not seen since her girlhood around Bristol. In this exciting atmosphere of the French salon, rich with literary and political notables, Frances Trollope was drawn powerfully by this group of friends who had seen the world and even, in the case of Frances Wright, written books. Always a "special friend of all the young girls at Harrow," she saw in these younger women (Julia Garnett was thirty, Harriet twenty-nine, the Wrights twenty-eight and twenty-seven) an exciting dimension missing from her own more sheltered life. She had reared five children and the youngest was now at school. She felt herself vaguely ready for something new.

All the women were united by old connections, family ties, and deep affection—but also by a common fascination with the possibilities of life in the new world. General Lafayette unwittingly became the catalyst, providing the beginning of a future which none of the principals could have even dimly foreseen as the Trollopes accepted his invitation for an extended visit at La Grange.

Mrs. Trollope kept a journal of those days—a whirl of aesthetic and cultural activity—perhaps sensing more than any of the others, the significance of what was happening. Her husband was a background figure during the visit, spending many days indisposed with the persistent headaches which were ruining his practice and which would eventually kill him. The circle expanded to include Washington Irving, Fenimore Cooper, Prosper Mérimée, Benjamin Constant, the Swiss Historian Sismondi, and Henri Beyle (Stendhal). Despite her lively hostessing at Harrow, Mrs. Trollope had no comparable friends at home. With Lafayette, who deeply impressed her, she spoke of Fanny Wright and the American revolution. He described a projected tour to the United States in the following year, and on his recommendation, she read Miss Wright's book, an eloquent defense of the United States. As Mrs.

Trollope wrote in the concluding lines of her revealing journal, "I know not where to find so intellectual, so amiable a set of beings as those I have been living amongst here." This new circle of friends and their mutual attraction for the new world would all combine to impel her toward America when other factors subsequently made her life in England intolerable.

The Garnetts, too, were bewitched by the convivial Parisian society, with its perpetual round of soirees and engagements, its prevailing custom "of choosing one evening in the week for being at home to such of your friends and acquaintances as may feel disposed to assemble at your house, take a cup of tea and chat, and come and go without ceremony," as Cam described her life to her Uncle Mylne in 1823. The list of regulars, shared by the friends, was a cross section of the most fashionable intellectuals of the time: the Hyde de Neuville family (Hyde was a cabinet minister); the elfin Mary Clarke and her mother; General Lafayette; Mme. de Segur; the Fenimore Coopers; Benjamin Constant, a pale thin man with snowy hair, in whose still-brilliant blue eyes could be traced the old hopeless passion for Madame de Stael. The social life was rich and varied. The Garnetts went with Mrs. Macready to see "her husband act his inimitable and very difficult part [Hamlet]. He looked beautiful in his deep black suit and acted with so much grace and feeling." The ageless Mme. de Récamier, eternally devoted to the god-like Chateaubriand, also made one of their circle. One of the most faithful was Prosper Mérimée, who was pining after Julia (almost ten years older than himself) and even eventually proposed marriage. Once, he made a dramatic entrance, his arm in a sling, the result of a duel with an outraged husband. Stendhal seemed attracted to Harriet who, with her characteristic reserve, kept him at a distance by exchanging cynical barbs with him. The French salon was an institution which enlivened the lives of women, providing them with a focus and the mental stimulation of talk on the important subjects of the day. For more than a year now, it had engrossed the Garnetts, and Mrs. Trollope had stayed long enough to feel its fascination.

But Fanny Wright's friendship with Lafayette now began to threaten an open break which would shatter these satisfying arrangements. For some time his family had accepted with graceful, if cool, cordiality his increasingly deep feelings for this bright young Englishwoman. But now she was hoping to become his legally adopted daughter. Orphaned from her earliest days, she now sought a formal, irreversible tie with this older man who had long called her "daughter"; now she wanted absolute right to that title. Whatever the sources of feeling which underlay such a connection, neither of them stopped to contemplate.

While the sixty-seven-year-old Lafayette was troubled by this sudden upheaval in his personal life, his political position was also deteriorating.

Discredited for his share in the military conspiracies (Carbonarism), defeated in the elections for the Chambre in his own constituency, and nearly bankrupt, he gladly accepted the invitation of the Congress and President of the United States to visit in the summer of 1824. Then, buckling under the stress of solving his problems both with Fanny and his family, he fell ill on the eve of his proposed American trip. Frightened by his collapse, his family sought a reconciliation with Fanny, and now even urged that she go to America with him.

Loving America as she had, she easily decided to join him. The crucial issue would be their travel arrangements. Given the attitude of the Lafayette family, should they travel to America together or apart? Fanny believed in openness, and wrote Lafayette accordingly.

> Should I give an opinion, it is this. If our union is to continue, it can do so with honor to you and without prejudice to us by your assuming openly and avowedly the air and character of a protector. You must be our father not in a doubtful and covert way, but in an open and manly one. I blush, my honest friend, at this seeming arrogance—but it is not to you but rather to our mutual friends & to your family that I address these arguments. Forgive me then if I say that if you and yours approve I will call my Camilla to me. I will place her under your protection—we will assume together the place of your children— we will call you father—If not this . . . we must part.

Clearly, Fanny longed for an openly avowed adoption, as she explained to Cam, "that complete union which appears to me alone consistent with dignity and comfort."

In all these deliberations, the silent and apparently forgotten person was Camilla. Indeed, when Fanny relayed the contents of this letter to Cam, she must have sensed the indelicacy and even indifference with which she had made momentous decisions without even consulting her sister. Guilt made her add a postscript: "You see, my beloved Camilla, how I have ventured to dispose of you. I know your generous heart . . . and that in venturing to consider you as part of myself I shall best consult your wishes."

Camilla's response betrayed both a submerged reluctance and her usual quick rationalization as she prepared herself to follow, as she ever had, her sister's lead. She explained these sudden travel arrangements to Uncle Mylne, who probably guessed the moving force behind the journey: "Much as I dislike the thought of another voyage across the ocean to which experience has only tended to increase my aversion, I cannot but anticipate much satisfaction from witnessing Lafayette's reception in the United States." The trip was to last about a year in all, after which Cam clearly anticipated a return to the Mylnes and their friends. Whether Fanny shared these ideas is not clear, but since she had invested 120,000 francs in the State of Louisiana at about this time, there is at least some reason to speculate she was again planning a more permanent arrangement in America.

While people "talked" about Miss Wright's boldness in following the revered Lafayette to America, the Garnett sisters, ever worshippers at the temple of Fanny, supported her, as they told their mutual friend, Mrs. Frances Trollope. Mrs. Trollope was now in West Cowes for a recuperative visit, having just lost her twelve-year-old son Arthur to tuberculosis (the disease which would eventually claim three more of her children) and her aged father, all in the same month. In responding to Julia's letter of condolence, Mrs. Trollope agreed with the Garnetts' defense of Miss Wright, although she had at first been somewhat critical of the joint trip.

> It *seemed* as if she had acted rashly, intemperately—but *data* were wanting. You waited not for these—but with the full entire confidence of undoubting affection, felt she must be right because she was Fanny—She *was* right, she *is* right now—& I shall not easily be led to doubt it again. Most singular in truth has been, and must be her position. The very acts that in all other women we should deem wrong—are in her a great, or overpowering duty.

But despite her devoted support of Fanny, Mrs. Trollope worried about the destiny of Camilla: "Young, lovely—most attractive in manner—most estimable in mind, most amiable in nature. I would have had her the heroine of her own tale." "The heroine of a tale"—the phrase was significant. Camilla's story should have ended happily in one of those eminently sweet and suitable marriages always achieved by Jane Austen's heroines. But alas, Camilla was a plant of different and delicate growth, who needed for her nurture, not a man, but Fanny. Mrs. Trollope reluctantly, but perceptively, concluded that Cam "*could* have no happiness distinct from her glorious sister. She lives in her light, and would droop, would perish, were she withdrawn from it."

So Camilla moved into the supporting role she would fill until the end of her life. The sisters made one concession to public opinion and sailed on a different vessel to America, in a forty-day-long crossing which had the expected effect upon the delicate Cam. She told Mylne: "I suffered most severely from seasickness and lost pounds of flesh in consequence." For several months they traveled in the wake of Lafayette's itinerary. There were balls, dances, and fêtes from New Orleans to Boston. Typical of these receptions for the great man was his landing in Cincinnati in 1825, where he was rowed across the Ohio River from Kentucky in an elegant six-oared barge, while twenty-four guns roared a general national salute. The ceremonies surrounding his reception lasted for two days. Through Lafayette, Fanny met Madison, Jefferson, John Quincy Adams, and President Monroe, and for a while basked in the doubly intoxicating lights of Lafayette's fame and the splendid new republic.

Then the dream turned sour. When she entered the South, the ever-present evil of slavery began to trouble her. From Richmond, Virginia, she wrote the Garnetts a letter revealing the strengthening of her strong feelings about slavery.

> I see already that we shall find here . . . much pleasing and polished society but my thoughts & feelings ever wander from it contrasting the condition of the proud and accomplished master with that of the debased and injured slave to whom the master's will is law. Amid all the politeness I see & attention I receive my heart is sick. I have not yet seen my fellow creatures sold in the market place & God forbid I should see it, for I really cannot answer for what I might say or do, but I have seen them manacled when sold on board a vessel bound for New Orleans. Our steamboat brushed past her swiftly which perhaps prevented my committing what could only have been a folly. But I cannot write on this subject & yet it preys so continually on my mind that I find it difficult to write on any other.

Moreover, the thrill of witnessing Lafayette's triumph was gone. Perhaps she wondered that he accepted tributes from a country grounded in such hypocritical contradictions. She told the Garnetts:

> The enthusiasm, triumphs & rejoicings exhibited here before the countenance of the great & good Lafayette have no longer charms for me. They who so sin against the liberty of their country—against those great principles for which their honored guest poured on their soil his treasure & his blood are not worthy to rejoice in his presence. My soul sickens in the midst of gaiety & turns almost in disgust from the fairest faces or the most amiable discourse. With all the intelligence and virtue which yet lingers in these states their present condition is wretched and their future prospects worse.

But despite her disillusionment, she stayed in America when Lafayette returned to France. Before he left, they met in Philadelphia to discuss the subject of their relationship, at which time he finally and definitively refused to adopt her and Camilla. For Fanny, the unhappy interview spelled yet another kind of hypocrisy. At any rate, following Lafayette's return, their close relationship was over. Afterwards, she hardly mentioned him in her letters; she was not with him during the closing days of his American visit, nor was she present when he sailed for home. And while he continued to think of her very fondly, she had found her male mentor radically inadequate. No doubt these altered feelings were an important factor in her decision to remain in America. For Cam, too, the parting would be irrevocable; Lafayette was one whom "we can never hope to see again on this side the grave. Alas! Alas!" she told the Garnetts. An important tie with the past had been severed; the old French chateau, where the girls had lived amid elegance and culture, would never again be their home. Among the utopias of their lives, White-house Farm and La Grange were gone forever. Another episode in the search for physical space in which to locate the dreams of occupation and sisterhood was about to begin.

REFERENCES

PAGE

1 Mrs. Sarah Ellis was the writer of domestic manuals: *The Women of England* (1839), *The Daughters of England* (1842), *The Wives of England* (1843). Mrs. Dinah Maria Craik wrote the influential *A Woman's Thoughts About Women* (1864). Jane Austen's *Emma* had appeared in 1816; Charlotte Brontë's *Jane Eyre*, in 1847.

2 "good climate . . . " John Garnett to Horatio Gates, 4 May 1796, NYHS.

3 Margaret Fuller, *Woman in the 19th Century* (1855).

3 "strapped to a door . . ." Susan Demarest, "Some Early New Brunswick Schools for Girls," Demarest Papers.

3 "Sophia Hay school . . ." Sophia Hay to Mrs. Horatio Gates, November 1798, January 1799, September 1799, NYHS.

4 "I hope we shall think . . ." HG/JGP, 3 January 1848, GPC.

4 "I cannot bear . . ." HG/JGP, 26 August 1849, GPC.

4 "I have a little canary . . ." HG/JGP, 20 August 1840, GPC.

4 "birds in quantity . . ." HG/JGP, 12 June 1842, GPC.

5 "a little too wild . . ." Mrs. Mary Garnett to Mrs. Horatio Gates, April 1799, NYHS.

6 "a striking woman . . ." Keating, *History of Memphis*, I, 130; Robert Dale Owen, *Threading My Way*, p. 297; and Thomas Adolphus Trollope, *What I Remember*, p. 106.

8 "Fanny and Camilla had been orphaned . . ." Frances Wright, *Biography, Notes and Political Letters* (1844); and Waterman, *Frances Wright*, pp. 26-27.

8 "Formal religion . . ." Wright, *Biography*.

8 "connection in her mind . . ." Waterman, *Frances Wright*, pp. 38-41.

9 "love of the new world . . ." RCM/HG & JGP, 21 June 1820; 21 December 1825; 2 September 1826; 2 June 1827, GPC.

9 "became a book . . ." Frances Wright, *Views of Society and Manners* (1823).

9 "natural, moral and political features . . ." RCM/HG & JGP, 21 June 1820, GPC.

9f. Biographical information on Frances Trollope is from Helen Heineman, *Mrs. Trollope* (1979).

11 "Fanny Wright mourned . . ." FW/HG & JGP, October 1820, GPC.

12 "her letters struck the same theme . . ." FW/HG & JGP, October 1820; 22 November 1820, GPC.

12 "Light is everywhere making rapid progress . . ." RCM/HG & JGP, 21 June 1820, GPC.

12 "If you then continue . . ." and "My Harriet I love . . ." FW/HG & JGP, October 1820, GPC.

13 "An hour's conversation . . ." FW/L, 15-18 February 1822, Waterman, *Frances Wright,* p. 56.

13 "I sent a note . . ." FW to Jeremy Bentham, *Works,* X, 526.

14 "the best and greatest man . . ." FW/L, 18 July 1822, Waterman, *Frances Wright,* p. 65.

14 "most valued . . ." FW/L, 16 July 1821; 29 December 1821, Lafayette Papers.

14 "In truth, I don't know . . ." FW/L, 18 July 1822, Waterman, *Frances Wright,* p. 65.

15 "Mrs. Trollope kept a journal . . ." La Grange Journal, UIU.

16 "The Garnetts too were bewitched . . ." CW to James Mylne, 17 February 1823, Waterman, *Frances Wright,* p. 67.

16 "The Garnetts went with Mrs. Macready . . ." MG/JGP, July 1828, GPC.

16f. "Fanny Wright's friendship with Lafayette . . ." Waterman, *Frances Wright,* p. 78.

17 "Should I give an opinion . . ." FW/L, 10 June 1824, Waterman, *Frances Wright,* p. 81.

17 "my beloved Camilla . . ." FW/CW, 10 June 1824, GPC.

17 "Camilla's response . . ." CW to James Mylne, September 1824, Waterman, *Frances Wright,* p. 85.

18 "It seemed as if she had acted rashly . . ." FT/HG & JGP, 6 August 1824, GPC.

18 "I suffered most severely . . ." CW to James Mylne, September 1824, Waterman, *Frances Wright,* p. 85.

19 "I see already . . ." and "The enthusiasm, triumphs & rejoicings . . ." FW/HG & JGP, 30 October 1824, GPC.

19f. "the unhappy interview . . ." Waterman, *Frances Wright,* pp. 90-91.

20 "For Cam, too . . ." CW/HG & JGP, 7 July 1825, GPC.

V SETTLEMENT OF NASHOBA

Hervieu's Drawing for *Domestic Manners*

CHAPTER TWO

Frances Wright and the Second Utopia, 1825-1827

We have seen that among early peoples the quite normal man is warrior and hunter, and the quite normal woman house-wife and worker-round-the-house; and it is quite conceivable that if no intermediate types had arisen, human society might have remained stationary in these simple occupations. But when types of men began to appear who had no taste for war and slaughter—men, perhaps, of a more gentle or feminine disposition; or when types of women arose who chafed at the slavery of the house, and longed for the open field of adventure and activity—women, in fact, of a more masculine tendency—then necessarily and quite naturally these new-comers had to find, and found, for themselves, new occupations and new activities. The intermediate types of human beings created intermediate spheres of social life and work.

EDWARD CARPENTER, ***Intermediate Types among Primitive Folk: A Study in Social Evolution*** **(1919)**

Take up some one pursuit or occupation with persevering determination. I can truly declare that I have never enjoyed tranquility but when my time has been steadily employed.

FRANCES WRIGHT **to Julia Garnett, 1 December 1825**

FANNY WRIGHT'S revulsion against slavery, always intense, now combined with her passion for reform and found a favorable growing climate in the atmosphere of radical hopes that were then sweeping across certain areas of the United States. Change, conversion, awakening—these were the watchwords of the time and the place. It seemed time for every human institution to be questioned. As Ralph Waldo Emerson subsequently noted, "In the history of the world the doctrine of Reform had never such scope as at the present hour." And so, after Lafayette's return to the old world, Fanny turned to find inspiration in transforming ideas of reform. Once again, she was attracted to a powerful man and his vision.

On New Year's Day 1825, when Robert Owen, the English industrial magnate and utopian reformer completed the purchase of the large Harmony community of George Rapp in western Indiana, it seemed as though anyone

23

who had ever dreamed a dream or hankered after an ideal was ready to make concrete what had hitherto been only a subject for conversation or debate. Owen believed things were in the best possible state for beneficial change. People were talking about the perfectibility of man and taking the subject seriously. Owen's intellectual friends argued that Chinese children could be made Indian, and vice versa, were they simply removed early enough from one situation to another. For centuries, man had wondered about limits and potentialities. "Know then thyself," Pope had cautioned, and now people like Robert Owen, George Rapp, and William MacClure were convinced that they did. They were ready to test their theories on the virgin soil of America, hoping to raise up a society such as the world had never seen—free, open, peaceful, intelligent, and harmonious. People were ready to leave comfortable homes and dear relatives and journey to New Harmony, which shone with the aura of a bright new planet. Into this quest for earthly perfection, like moths to a destructive flame, Frances and Camilla Wright were drawn. For Cam, the attraction had ever been Fanny herself. But Frances Wright was fascinated by utopian experiments because she saw in them a hope for ridding the world of a ruinous system of exploitation. She also saw the chance to shape her own life anew, to make her own story, to escape the impediments of social class and gender. In saving others, she would also save herself and her friends.

Increasingly, Fanny's thoughts revolved around the subject of slavery. She wrote the Garnetts:

> Alas, Alas! The more I consider this subject the more I shudder, the more I tremble. This plague spot so soils the beauty of the robe of American liberty that I often turn in disgust from the freest country in the world. . . . American industry—morals—enterprise—all is benumbed. The heart is hardened—the character depraved. Our course is still to lie through the benighted & guilty regions [i.e., the South]. I could hardly execute the project did I not propose to turn my observations to account.

As she had traveled, she had been struck by the awesome vastness of America. But she could take no pleasure in its beauty, when she thought of the blight of slavery. Emotionally, she wrote:

> I could have wept when gazing on the lovely face of nature in the state of Mississippi—such woods, such lawns, such gently swelling hills, such glorious trees, such exquisite flowers, & the giant river wafting the rich produce of this unrivalled land to the ocean. I could have wept as I thought that such a garden was wrought by the hands of slaves! But when following the course of these

mighty streams you traverse varying latitudes and climates marking an extent greater than the continent of Europe, and reflect that this plague is gradually spreading under the cover of the forests & along the track of the rivers over this huge territory, the heart truly sickens and curses the progress of cultivation.

But writing letters about the problem was not enough. For Fanny, thoughts and words must be translated into action. A specific plan took root as she prepared an article for the *Westminster Review* on the subject of American Negro slavery. Though the essay never appeared, the research permitted Fanny to gather her emotions into thought on the problem which continued to engross her. On a visit to New Orleans, she found slavery "in all its horrors," from the clank of chains to the "dark-eyed rich-complexioned damsels" of mulatto blood whose offspring could never be acknowledged by their white fathers. In the seven months she had spent in slave states, she had mulled over various modes of curing this great evil. But not until she had made her second visit to Harmony did specific ideas take shape. Curiously enough, the communities of New Harmony had made no provision for slaves, freed or otherwise. Blacks were absolutely excluded from Owen's experiment. Fanny Wright decided to try Owen's principles on a project of slave emancipation. Her first idea was "that the slaves on a plantation should be led to work from the incentive of working out their liberty with a view to their being afterwards employed as waged laborers." Then, at Harmony, "a vague idea" crossed her mind, "that there was something in the system of united labor as there was in operation which might be rendered subservient to the emancipation of the South." United labor would undersell the slave labor of the South, even as slaves worked out their freedom and became educated at the same time. Thus engrossed, Fanny rode about the country seeking advice and support of her plan for the amelioration and, eventually, the abolition of slavery in the United States of America. By April 1826 she had purchased the necessary tract of land, along with eight Negroes who would be the first laborers there. In all, to set up her colony, she would spend over $10,000 in expenses, more than a third of her total property. She was ready to start creating her world.

As ever, Camilla followed her sister's lead, content with a dependent and peripheral role, playing Miss Matty to Fanny's Deborah Jenkins. Camilla was the gentle, giving one, the sister always described as "feminine." She was ever loyal to persons, not to principles, as her sister was. When Fanny took on too much work, Camilla handled the less significant tasks, taking over Fanny's personal correspondence, especially to the Garnetts, describing, when the busy Fanny could not, "the great and important object," and rejoicing in her self-effacing way in "the new and glorious career thus opened to our heroic

Fanny by the energy of her own powerful intellect and indefatigable mind."
Cam, by contrast, hardly seemed present to her sister, except when her
physical indispositions impeded Fanny's progress. "Cam was seized yester-
day with a bad cold which altho' better today must detain us here some days
longer. This I fear will throw us into decided & naked winter so soon as we
shall have crossed the mountains." Unwittingly, Cam fed the flames of Fanny's unconscious egotism with her unswerving devotion.

Fanny was the "highly gifted one." As Cam once said, "I marvel not that
all should fall short in a comparison with her, for the more I see of life, and
above all of womankind, the more I am persuaded her equal never can, and
never will be found." Camilla's devotion was simply the most obvious and
extreme expression of what most of Fanny's circle of friends thought about
her. She had become their heroine, their ideal woman. Their intellectual roots,
put down in the climate of eighteenth-century Enlightenment thought, pre-
disposed them to admire such intellectual women—thinkers, as Frances
Wright had been. In their youth, ideas through writings and literature had
converted people to truth. A transitional figure, Fanny was the first of a new
generation of women who deserted the realm of pure ideas for that of action.
For a time the Garnett circle watched fascinated, circling the flame of her
all-consuming idealism as it worked upon the materials of life. Then, as she
turned increasingly activist, her old friends gradually would grow estranged
from the beloved Fanny, seeing her first as misguided, at the last as mad. She
seemed to have overstepped the boundaries of her sex.

But for Fanny, her womanhood was not an obstacle, but an advantage in
her new occupation. She believed herself the only individual "who could
enter on or carry through such an undertaking. . . ." "Against violence," she
wrote her friends, "my very sex might be a defense." Indeed, Fanny Wright
was one of the first to see that women were ideal reformers; they alone could
convert women's prescribed mission of service to others into a self-fulfilling
goal. The popular wisdom had seen as women's peculiar talent their unselfishness. "Their mission is the establishment of peace, & love, & unselfishness, to be achieved by any means, at any cost to themselves. . . ." Frances
Wright's interpretation of rhetoric like this would shock her contemporaries,
who saw the sphere for such action as the domestic one. Her supreme self-
confidence about her task and her qualifications for it contrasted starkly with
the more hesitant attitudes of Cam, who told the Garnetts: "Should all my
hopes regarding this interesting, this important experiment be realized, I shall
indeed bless the hour that we first crossed the Allegheny mountains." Fanny's
rhetoric would never have permitted the subjunctive mood.

In bringing her project to fulfillment, Frances Wright was gifted not only
in terms of intellect and will, but in constitution as well. By comparison,

Camilla fell short of her sister in the essential matter of physical stamina, so important a factor in women's success during this period. She lacked the strength to conquer, though she pushed herself hard, almost too hard at first. In the months before the plans for Nashoba were completed, the Wright sisters traversed the country looking for land and financial support for the colony. Riding across Pennsylvania, through Kentucky, "the beautiful and wonderful Ohio," Illinois, the whole of Indiana, New York, Connecticut, and Boston, the young women traveled 5,000 miles and upwards. In all these journeys, Cam was her sister's companion. Later, there had been a 600-mile ride on horseback which Cam claimed "entirely restored Fanny's health and in great measure her strength." How she felt herself after such rigors she did not say, unless by indirection: "The heat which appears to oppress and overpower every one else, imparts to Fanny new life and energy."

This veritable marathon eventually produced Cam's physical breakdown; when the sisters reached Boston to attend the opening of the Bunker Hill monument, Cam took immediately to bed, in severe pain from a boil on her back. For two weeks, she lay prone, while the usual devastating remedies were implacably applied, but even twenty-four leeches failed to give any relief. She told the Garnetts: "For five nights I got no rest save through the means of opium. The physician who attended me with unremitting care pronounced it the worst of the kind he had ever seen, approaching somewhat to the *carbuncle.*" He diagnosed the cause as being "occasioned by the pressure of my corset bone during our long ride on horseback in the western country." While the bolder Frances had long since abandoned such attempts to mold the female figure into acceptable form, Cam had still persisted in wearing dresses. Three weeks later, the wound in her back was "a running sore." Camilla's eventual martyrdom was underway.

During the period of her recuperation, Cam had time to formulate her own views about her sister's plan to establish a colony ameliorating the condition of American slaves. Lying alone on her back, she began to express what she really wanted from Nashoba—a quiet place to be happy with her beloved sister forever. Rather than contemplating the effect upon the slaves, Cam dreamed of "a prospect of future happiness to ourselves such as we might not otherwise have known for many years," and escape from a life of "constraint and endless solitude." In Europe, her desire to live with her sister and other women friends in a community would clearly be impossible and was certain to be misunderstood. Indeed, she once referred to the project as providing "the certain prospect of our being reunited and that in a manner far more desireable than ever could have been effected by a residence in Europe. . . ." Certainly England did not as yet boast even a fictional Cranford governed by "amazons." Life there must bring the inevitable marriage and painful separation from Fanny. Here in America, her fate could be different. Freed from the endless round of social activity which filled the hours of most women of her class and from the marriage which would bring the "servitude of domestic duty and childbearing," Cam hoped in a vague and somewhat unformulated way that Nashoba might provide a female haven of affectionate companionship.

Fanny's dreams had more clarity. They were twofold, the parts separate but hinged, like contrasting but connected pictures in a locket. Ever since she had watched Father Rapp leading his people out of the Promised Land and Mr. Owen establishing a harmonious new order there, Frances had longed to be part of some great work. For her, the first purpose of Nashoba was the abolishing of slavery, a problem her fellow reformers had thus far largely ignored.

But at the same time, she had hopes for those who would dedicate their lives to this purpose. They would find not the peaceful haven of Camilla's thinking, but useful, if strenuous occupation, for women who were proud and strong enough to grasp the opportunity. Fanny had watched the women of her acquaintance—the Garnett sisters, her dear friend Mrs. Millar, the Lafayette daughters, her own sister—and she had come to some painful conclusions about the lives of women in general.

> Without some fixed and steady occupation of labor—of business, of study, something which keeps in habitual exercise our physical or mental energies— and the better when it is both—it is impossible to make our existence glide smoothly. We must know moments, nay hours of vexation and lassitude. It is this which makes the pretty universally marked difference between men & women, that gives to the former good health and good nerves, and fits them more or less to taste the enjoyments of life without being dependent upon any and to bear or brave its ills with a resisting spirit.

She recalled one of the observations of John Garnett, who had educated his daughters so well in the old days in America:

> Geometry had been his best friend and most consoling companion. Rousseau said the same of botany—Gibbon of his historical research and composition and every poet has said or sung the same of his muse.

Frances resolved that her physical and mental energy would be directed away from the conventional, life-consuming activities of women, and toward some more satisfying and independent work of her own. She admitted that such activity was for her an absolute necessity. "I can truly declare that I have never enjoyed tranquility but when my time has been steadily employed." While those interests with which most women filled their lives—"amusements, social intercourse, friendship, love"—were "the precious diamond sparks in the hourglass of human existence," she was sure that "the mass of the sand is composed of homelier materials." Unless she found whereof this latter material was made, she would become like her other women friends, distracted, her blood "fevered," and full of vague "disquietude." She had, after all, tried with painful consequences being the faithful daughter to Lafayette. Her sermons to her friends, lengthy and perhaps tedious, and surely perplexing, she could not forswear. She continued to sound the theme of occupation across the measures of her whole life.

Depositing the still weak Cam at New Harmony and Albion (George Flower's colony across the river), Fanny at once set out to find land that would provide the arena where she would shape her fate and, she hoped, that of America itself. She had already seen much of good and evil in the West. She had ridden through the forests of Indiana, en route to Tennessee, where the good land lay, and witnessed the cruel kidnapping of a poor hunted black boy. She had tried to rescue the boy, recovering him for a brief moment, only to lose him again. But such failures only increased her determination, despite the surrounding dangers, to start the work of abolishing the evil of slavery. The secret of her plans for an educational colony aimed at slave emancipation must be kept for at least a year, for in the southern states, news of her scheme would be a devouring flame, running from Virginia to Georgia, from Kentucky to Louisiana. Her ultimate goal was nothing less than a holy conversion of the entire country. Her friend Robert Dale Owen, son of Harmony's founder, was her fellow warrior. She saw him and herself as partners in a dramatic transformation of American society. "He is working miracles and promises fair to revolutionize a second time the North as I pray we may do in the South."

She was ready to work hard and pay much for the accomplishment of her own prospective miracle. After much negotiation and discussion, she purchased two hundred acres of land in Tennessee, on the Chickasaw bluffs near the Wolf River, about five miles from the Indian line. Hoping to avoid the American "fever," she chose a spot "dry and rolling and second rate only as to richness of soil." Tennessee was "one of the most favored" states, "abundantly watered by navigable streams flowing in all directions and affording all varieties of wood and many of climate." Its prevailing summer sun, she had heard, was "genial." Now Frances sent for Camilla and her new friends George and Eliza Flower. The great experiment was imminent. Mrs. Millar, who viewed these activities with apprehensive interest, believed Fanny had found what she had ever sought: that "constant occupation of mind and activity" which "will I think preserve her." Whatever fears she permitted herself to express were all for Camilla.

Cam had spent the late winter of 1825–26 in New Harmony and Albion, impatiently waiting for her sister to choose a location and then, for the waters of the Ohio to rise so that she could make the journey to Tennessee. Separated for a while from Fanny's magnetic influence, Camilla betrayed some tentative misgivings. Despite Fanny's compelling letters, "full of encouraging and sanguine expectations," Cam confessed to the Garnetts "forebodings of disappointment to come." Perhaps she shared the feelings of Charles Wilkes, the banker and friend of Mrs. Millar who had remained friendly with the Wrights and taken an interest in them. He had offered the troubled Cam the best encouragement he could muster. "I am assured you would not have rested in peace without making the experiment & though I have no belief whatever in its success, I sincerely wish you all the satisfaction your ardor and enthusiasm in a good though hopeless cause so well deserve."

Perhaps, too, her forebodings had been born as she observed the fate of the women who had come to New Harmony, where she had spent the long winter months alone, waiting for Fanny. Her sister's theories and those of her friends she knew very well; now she had had a backdrop of reality against which to view the ideal at work. Utopian socialism had from the start been permeated by ideas about transforming relations between the sexes and through the building of a larger community, releasing male and female members alike into greater personal freedom. But in these early nineteenth-century American utopias, women were finding more problems than solutions. They wanted so much more than men did, and hoped to win a kind of freedom which they had never enjoyed. Many found it difficult to merge their own desires into the new regime of the socialist group which in some cases was more rigid than that of their former lives. From among the accounts of these leveling and uniform communities, women emerge as striking individuals. Sarah Pears, for example, whose few collected letters to her Aunt Bakewell are a record of hopes deferred and woman betrayed, was a member of the New Harmony community whom Cam probably came to know.

Sarah's background, like that of the Garnett circle, made her suited to experiments in perfect living. Her family had been foes of intolerance in England and had come to America seeking whatever order of earthly perfection the new world could offer. They settled in Philadelphia, where Sarah met and married Thomas Pears, to whom in nineteen years of marriage she bore seven children. When they heard about New Harmony, they abandoned their comfortable life in May 1825 for the Indiana settlement which had just changed hands from the Rapps to Robert Owen. Three months later, Cam

Wright was deposited at New Harmony and Albion for safekeeping while her sister prepared the location of their proposed settlement.

Mr. Pears, though a devoted Owenite, was guarded in his earliest judgments of the new arrangements. "Tho' I believe it will be safely reached, the promised land is farther off than most of us anticipated," he wrote Mr. Bakewell. The climate was unfavorable and his wife was suffering during the extremely hot and dry summer of 1825, when mosquitoes, prickly heat, fever, boils, and sore eyes abounded. For the frail Camilla Wright, such conditions were difficult indeed.

Sarah Pears was quickly disappointed in everything. Though she hoped that "all will be right in the end," she could not help casting "many a long lingering look toward Pittsburgh and its kind inhabitants." The journey had been "most fatiguing and disagreeable," and it had taken many hard days to negotiate the terrible roads between the Ohio River port and Harmony.

In keeping with communal ideas, the Pears were assigned to share lodgings with another family. But the house was small, a tenement containing only three rooms and a tiny kitchen. There, the Pears family (with Maria eighteen, John Palmer sixteen, Sarah Ann thirteen, Benjamin eleven, Ellen Mary eight, and William De Witt Clinton, the one-year-old baby) crowded with the family of Mr. Pearson. Almost at once, sickness struck and the Pears' oldest daughter fell ill with fatigue and "a bad cold caught with washing."

But beyond these merely physical discomfitures, Mrs. Pears was quick to realize that a more serious disappointment awaited them: here, women's lives stood little chance of improvement. Instead, domestic work for women abounded, along with less of the influence and serious occupation they had come seeking. Mrs. Pears grieved to see her daughter so constantly ill and tired.

> All the hard work falls upon her, and it is more than she is able to bear. We had hoped she would have been rather relieved from her heavy labor than otherwise by coming here; but at present it is far from being the case.... However I hope that by degrees I shall be enabled to take a more active part in our family business, and then perhaps we may do better.

Instead of increased importance, Sarah Pears found more problems which, without the elements which had always sweetened life for women, seemed unbearable. She missed her circle of old friends and relatives. She told her aunt, "How often do I think of the circle around your comfortable fire, my dear Aunt, may you long enjoy it. The idea that I may never again join it is too melancholy to reflect upon, but so many things have come to pass that I will not think it impossible that I may again see you." The old ties, which had bound women together in loving family communities, seemed shattered by these rationally planned experiments in living.

When summer ended, the real discord in Harmony began. By September, a bleak Mrs. Pears could no longer find time or strength to answer her aunt's letters. As she explained, "Sick and debilitated in body, distressed and disappointed in mind, oppressed by extreme heat night and day such as I never before experienced, I felt utterly incapable of writing." Then, the first deaths of the colony were upon them. One was in the Pears' own house, the seven-month-old baby of Mrs. Pearson. The mother was prostrate with grief, and as Sarah described the scene, her own baby Clinton "has been in my arms kicking about almost all the time I have been writing." Clearly, utopian experiments had not altered the exigencies of child care for women, nor could they change the anxieties and griefs which seemed so particularly their lot. Sarah felt increasingly restricted and began to chafe angrily against decisions made without her consent. She told Mr. Bakewell: "It makes my blood boil within me to think that the citizens of a free and independent nation should be collected here to be made slaves of." New Harmony seemed the end of the world, in relation to Pittsburgh. "I feel so forlorn that I could say with Cowper, 'I am out of Humanity's reach.' But it will not do to look that way. My lot is fixed. I feel like a bird in a cage shut up forever."

She and her husband took heart in the thought that Owen (who was completing financial arrangements in Scotland) would return in the fall. Then, perhaps, all would yet be well. But even after his re-appearance, unrest and dissension persisted, especially among the women. Even fistfights were reported, concerning who should do the work in the various community boarding houses. The women's complaints of overwork finally reached Owen, but he was insensitive to their grievances. When the women objected to attending his evening forums because it would interfere with preparations for the evening meal, "He intimated mildly that they were spending time in talking that should be devoted to work." Eventually, all Sarah's hopes for improving her life vanished. Deprived of the strength of family ties, and now of the support of letters, she told her aunt: "We begin to feel like isolated beings forgotten by all the world, nay, even by our best friends. . . ."

Sarah grew increasingly bitter about the second-class treatment of women in the colony. She was pleased to receive a package of Pittsburgh newspapers, for "I hear very little more of the old world than if I were an inhabitant of a different planet. I believe there are papers at the reading room, but only the male part of the community have as yet assumed the privilege of reading them." More rebellious and despondent than ever, she told her aunt:

> There appears nothing cheering, nothing consoling on which to rest. Hope which had never before quite deserted me seems now to have taken her flight.

Mr. Owen has delivered several lectures here, but as I always return from them more unhappy than I went, I have half determined to go no more.

But because there was little else to do at Harmony, or, because she still half feared Owen, she relented: "I shall probably break my resolution tonight." Still, Owen's general treatment of women had radicalized Sarah Pears. Her letters are more and more the letters of a discontented and angry woman.

I am confident I shall never be able to perform what he appears to expect from the women. My strength, which never was great and is much diminished since I came here, is unequal to taking my turn in the kitchen, which I find it is required that all should do by turns for 6 weeks together.

Clearly, New Harmony was not a paradise for women. What Cam Wright thought of all she saw and heard we do not know, but she was not overly optimistic when she left these scenes to join her sister. In Sarah Pears' words, "I think the person who wrote that this was a terrestrial paradise must have very odd ideas of paradise, or it must be meant as a joke."

By March 1826, two months after Cam had left for Nashoba, Mrs. Pears was reduced to despair. She told Mr. Bakewell: "I seem indifferent about going or staying. My health and strength have received a shock in this place [from] which they will probably never recover. I fear that a premature old age and inability for usefulness will be the consequence. Only in the grave can I see my prospect of rest." She poured out her distress to Aunt Bakewell: "I have hitherto been able to do very little besides sew and take care of my baby; and my health is now, as well as my poor babe's, extremely delicate. How I am to go through cooking, washing, and scrubbing I really do not know. But I know were I to consider this world only, I would rather, far rather, that Mr. Owen would shoot me through the head." A paragraph later, realizing what she had said, she added: "I know not really how I can write such things and keep my senses."

A month later Mrs. Pears was in the same state. "You must excuse dullness and stupidity as I am almost worn out with fatigue and hard work. . . . I am unable to sustain the fatigue of hard work without such complete exhaustion of strength that I have no power to sew, and scarcely to read in the evenings, so that you see how very unsuitable a person your poor niece is for a place *where the worth of a woman is so much hard work as she can go through.*" There was the heart of the matter: what was the worth of a woman? In the New Harmony of 1825, it was not very high. Whatever problems or ideals had sent her there, she was ready to go home. Sometime in late April or early May 1826, Sarah Pears and her family returned to Pittsburgh.

In Owen's utopian schemes, women were to be guaranteed equal rights within the community and freedom from domestic drudgery. In a single stroke, the connection between social revolution and the liberation of women had been made, however tenuously. But did the interests of women who were seeking freedom for themselves necessarily have anything to do with emancipation either of workers or slaves? Sarah Pears had had trouble connecting the two at New Harmony. She had sought useful activity and a sense of personal purpose ("by degrees I shall be enabled to take a more active part in our family business"), but had found only the disappointment of increased domestic labor. While utopian socialism had eliminated the servant class, it had simply made servants' work into women's work, thus creating another hierarchical structure worse than the one Mrs. Pears had left with high hopes. Cam Wright, too, seemed more interested in personal goals of sisterhood than in submerging the self in the communal goal of slave emancipation. Even Frances Wright, as we shall see, used her colony to implement her own ideals of religious and sexual freedom, both of which eventually conflicted with the goals of the colony regarding the education and freeing of slaves. Eventually, the conflict would bring the colony down. For all these women who had thrown in their lots with utopian socialism, the conflict between their personal desires for freedom and expanded destinies and the broader reform issues would remain a great problem.

Five months before the Pears family finally left, Camilla Wright was on her way to Memphis in the last days of February 1826. She arrived "after a tedious and hazardous navigation" in a Mississippi flatboat to find her sister waiting for her. Now she would see for herself whether or not Nashoba would satisfy her personal dreams. She had put all doubts and hesitations behind her. But the enthusiastic rendering of Cam's arrival came from Fanny's pen, as she described the happy scenes to which she had brought the tired Cam, sending to the Garnetts greetings "from our log cabins around which the axes are ringing and all is stirring. . . . Thank heaven, after all our perils, disasters and delays, we are all assembled in safety."

Aware as she must have been of the recent troubles at New Harmony, Fanny Wright was still convinced that her colony would work. Part of her optimism stemmed from her faith in the people who now surrounded her. George Flower, who had helped found the English settlement at Albion, Illinois, was to be a resident trustee of Nashoba. Some had accused him of bigamy, saying that he had married two wives and divorced none. In England, the stories went, he and his first wife had separated by mutual consent. Then, "wounded in spirit and almost heartbroken," he had passed to America, where he found "the beautiful, the gay, the attractive Eliza Andrews," whom he had married, winning her away from her fatherly protector, Morris Birkbeck, who had also proposed to her. The resultant breach between the two men had damaged their hopes of colonizing land in Edwards County for English settlers, and also produced the luxuriant crop of gossip which Fanny Wright ignored in inviting the Flowers to become part of her colony. Cam, of course, supported her sister in this defense of the outcasts, calling Eliza Flower "one of the most noble, generous, and candid minds I have ever known in life," whose "affections are entirely centered in her husband and children." Still, Cam was not completely comfortable with Mrs. Flower, and told the Garnetts what she kept from Fanny: "While I admire and esteem her as my friend, I do not & shall never feel for her that species of affection which constitutes real friendship." Cam's rendition of the complicated relationship between the Flowers and Mr. Birkbeck reveals her loyal support of her sister's choices in the face of "all that the ill-nature and malice of a misjudging world can suggest. . . ." The fact that Flower was being called an "immoral man," and that he and his wife could find no place in "polite society," made them ripe to share the perils of the Nashoba experiment, although, as Cam admitted, Mrs. Flower had "not the least faith" in this new colony, having seen their own settlement collapse and the New Harmony venture almost in ruins. As she told Cam, "she feels, herself, that she will never again be equal to the unheard of exertions she has undergone since her first arrival in this country, and well may she dread entering a second time the difficulties and hardships of a new settlement." Mrs. Flower's disenchantment with utopian ventures, like that of Sarah Pears before her, was another example of the sharp conflict between personal hopes and the communal regimen which seemed starkest in women.

Still, recruits were quickly made among the ranks of other "promising" outsiders. Fanny picked up James Richardson, a Scotchman who had studied medicine at Edinburgh, in Memphis where he was "recovering slowly from a long and painful illness." Once again, Fanny's eloquence about finding a sense of purpose had produced a worker for Nashoba. "Our conversation and friendship," she wrote, "first cheered his spirits and the prospect of assisting in our undertaking seems to have supplied him with what he wanted—an object in life suited to his feelings and opinions." She told the Garnetts that he "unites to the invaluable qualities of trust, prudence & accurate attention to business, a finely cultivated mind with every liberal and generous opinion and sentiment." Money to outfit the store ($550 worth of goods) came from a wealthy Quaker merchant in New York. And so, with eight purchased Negroes, five men and three women, who had arrived by steamboat from Nashville, a family of a mother and six daughters from South Carolina, a carpenter, a blacksmith, and, she hoped, a shoemaker, Fanny, Cam, Richardson, and the Flowers were ready to begin. Another recent addition, also a trustee, should be mentioned. Richeson Whitby, a Shaker, formerly resident of New Harmony and director of the commissary there, had early become disenchanted with Owen's experiment, leaving Harmony in December 1826 for Nashoba. Ironically, his position had been filled by Thomas Pears. Whether his intention was solely to make another try at living by utopian principles, or whether he felt already that attraction for the Wright sisters which would ultimately end with his marriage to Camilla Wright, is unknown. Nevertheless, he became part of the new world at Nashoba. It had not been difficult to attract male workers to Fanny's colony.

The only ingredient missing was the community of female friends, in particular, the Garnetts, who still lagged behind in Europe. Fanny chafed with resentment to think that her dearest friends still lived the old, outworn conventional life. When Julia and Harriet begged her for news and descriptions of Nashoba, Fanny's answer was a pointed reminder of what they were missing:

> Remember dear loves that we are not ladies of leisure with nothing to do but to follow up the correspondence of friendship. I wish I knew you engaged in some pursuit that could call forth your energies and prevent your indulging in melancholy and vain regrets.

When Fanny Wright spoke of calling forth the energies of her female friends, she had in mind that kind of imagination which can envision a self and a society as yet unformed in the given world. She herself had found both energy and will enough to abandon home, family, and religion to brave the social taboos which sought to confine her within a limited female sphere. She was ready to do yet more in her slave emancipation colony, testing the world's resistance to the society she envisioned for others and the self she was fashioning for herself. The Garnetts, too, had energies, and clearly, Miss Wright feared they would ultimately turn them inward by "indulging in melancholy and vain regrets," and be finally destroyed.

And, by the spring of 1826, Harriet and Julia were longing to join the Wrights. Still holding back the commitment of self, still not ready to exert their wills and join, they tried to gain a vicarious involvement by offering some of their money to Fanny as an investment in the colony. With her characteristic generosity, she refused their offer, even though she could not resist the opportunity to lecture: after all, money was not the issue, as they all knew. "Sometime hence, but I fear not in this generation, money may be done away with. . . ." The Garnetts centered their reluctance to come around their aging mother, for whom the rigors of Nashoba seemed excessive. Fanny had countered with a plan to have Mrs. Garnett stay at Harmony, but the unrest there had made that arrangement temporarily impossible. She had to advise them to wait until Harmony stood on a sure enough foundation to provide their mother with a home. But once the work of clearing and farming was over, she wanted Julia and Harriet to come, and "assist us here usefully."

Then, that summer, the guiding spirit of Nashoba was struck down with a severe attack, probably of malarial fever, which for ten days kept her sister trembling with anxiety and alarm. At almost the same moment, Mrs. Flower fell ill, too, with what Cam called "the effects of a milk fever that followed the weaning of her child." These events left Cam on her own, as she watched day and night by her sister's side. In the end, she credited Richardson with Fanny's recovery. He thus achieved great ascendancy in the affairs of the colony. But a frightened Cam now began to think with increasing longing of the Garnetts, of how they could succor their friends in time of need. Contrasting sharply with Fanny's cautious note, Cam's letters were filled with desperate pleadings for her friends to come. Her language became insistent, her rhetoric intense and heartfelt, as she proposed that Harriet come ahead without her mother and sisters.

> Yet think not, my sweet and tenderly loved friends, that my heart mourns not at our prolonged separation. Night and day do Fanny & I hold counsel together how we shall best meet to part no more on this side the grave. . . . In our last . . . we urged that our dear Harriet should lose no time in coming to us,—that she should sail from Havre by the 1st October after the equinox was passed. . . . This will be towards the end of November when she will be sure to find either F. or myself . . . awaiting her at Harmony which I should like her to see that she might judge of its advisability for your Mother and Fanny, & from there we should return together to our present and future *home,* for such I feel every day more persuaded this will be, & here, dear loves, you can be of *invaluable* service in forwarding the object that will engross the remainder of our life, however long or short it may be.

Towards year's end, the sisters' letters revealed a growing divergency in attitudes. For Fanny, Nashoba remained what it had ever been: an effort at slave emancipation and an occupation out of which she hoped to fashion a new world and a new self. But for Cam, whose world and self merged in Fanny, the colony promised a circle of women friends whose lodestar was Fanny, and with whom she could live in peaceful and harmonious cooperation forever.

Fanny had severed all her ties to Europe, and rarely mentioned General Lafayette anymore, although he continued to write and to mourn her prolonged absence. In one note to Julia, he added with ill-concealed bitterness:

"They [Fanny and Cam] love us dearly, I know, white as we are, but when shall we be blessed with the happiness to see them again?" He still loved Fanny, in spite of his refusal to adopt her legally. He told Julia, "I most cordially admire, cherish, and love the high-minded, devoted, philanthropic spirit of the angelic girls more than ever, if possible, dear to me."

Then, all at once, Cam's letters stopped, and three months of silence ensued, during which she, too, fell seriously ill of fever. Unequal to exertion of any kind, she was too unsteady even to write letters. Fanny, of course, insisted on attending to her sister; inevitably, a relapse followed, one "far more formidable in its effects than her previous illness." Later, Cam described the scene to the Garnetts.

> For three months have I seen her—precious life in imminent danger while I the greater of the time lay powerless beside her (a low & obstinate fever having succeeded my first attack), a sad spectator of her sufferings which before were chiefly in the head and from the effects of which she will probably be yet some time in recovering, for tho' now able to join me in a daily ride on horseback during the delicious season, the attempt to write or even look in a book is instantly succeeded by pain in the head and a weakness of sight that obliges her to forego almost the entire use of her eyes, nor can she ride out without a shade over them—this weakness time alone can remove. . . .

Cam still hoped for help from the Garnetts, to whom she continued her imploring letters.

> I have yet to state my other reason for still wishing to see you inmates of our future home—that even admitting the risk to your health being all & more than many will represent to you, I have that perfect belief in your affection for us and your inability to enjoy happiness at the distance that now separates us, that I would rather you incurred this risk than be as you are at present.

Now, too, the Flowers were talking about leaving Nashoba for good. His father was returning to England: no doubt his son would follow him, "in which case," wrote Cam, "we shall lose them as assistants in our undertaking." With Fanny debilitated, and Richardson, Cam, and Whitby in charge, the Flowers had decided to move on, and had already left for Illinois, "from whence," wrote Cam, "there is little probability of their return here." Although she had no criticism for the man, Cam's remarks about the beautiful Eliza reveal profound disappointment in the important matter of female companionship at Nashoba. "Our anticipations with regard to his wife have not been fully realized. She is not in any way suited to fill any situation in this establishment nor does she possess a mind calculated to enter into the views connected with it. I need not add that this observation is for yourselves alone." Mrs. Pears and Mrs. Flower had proven unequal to the task. Mrs. Millar, like the Garnetts, was still hanging behind in Europe. Where could the women be found to help the Wright sisters populate the wilderness with the utopian female paradise which they had so long envisioned?

But by Christmas, there could be no more talk about the Garnetts coming. Fanny Wright's health was now fearfully delicate. She was, as Cam described her, in "a state of emaciation such as I never before beheld." She still suffered frequent attacks of chills and fever, and the strain of any light upon her eyes was so great that she wore colored glasses, so that she could read and write. She relied totally upon Camilla, who sat for long hours writing to her sister's dictation, which still was full of joyful anticipations of the millenium. In spite of her illness, she felt "reconciled . . . with life" and full of "hopes for the human race as high as my former despair had been deep." But her bodily health was failing and now plans were underway for a spring visit to Europe. Richardson had strongly recommended a sea voyage, but it would be impossible for both Fanny and Cam to be absent from Nashoba for any length of time. The problem lay with the management of the slaves. Robert Dale Owen, who was a frequent visitor and resident, later described the state of affairs at the colony: "Slaves released from fear of the lash, working indolently under the management of Whitby, whose education in an easy-going Shaker village had not at all fitted him for the post of plantation overseer." Whitby himself had declared "that if both the sisters left Nashoba, he despaired of being able to manage the slaves: they would obey either, as their owner and mistress, and himself only when he had their authority to back his orders." Professing herself content to remain behind and escape the "horrors of a sea voyage," Cam was ready to help manage the colony in Fanny's absence. Perhaps, too, Fanny's recuperative trip could serve two purposes. Maybe her presence would re-animate those who were still afraid to commit themselves to the task of changing the world and recreating the self. Cam's commitment to her tragic destiny had long ago been made: only its fulfillment hung suspended.

Meanwhile, in Europe, events had already transpired which would make impossible the Garnetts' participation in the colony. In May 1827, Fanny had sent a paper to be printed in England, setting forth the principles of Nashoba. Frances Trollope, also a devoted admirer of Fanny, was distressed by the paper, which (as she wrote the Garnetts) both she and her husband agreed "would be utter madness to print . . . here. Contempt, ridicule, and reprobation would be the result. Believing this, I *cannot* cause it to be printed unless I receive from you a positive order to do so—and I shall be grieved to receive this order. Dear, noble, single-hearted Fanny dreams not of the light in which her declared opinions against religion would be viewed." Clearly, at this point, only religious opinions were at issue. Sismondi, cousin by marriage, friend, and male mentor of the Garnett sisters, counseled them against the "imprudence, the inconvenience, the impossibility of a journey to join them" at Nashoba.

> It would be especially impossible to take your mother. It is not at her age that one is able to go to look for death in the savannahs of the Mississippi, in the midst of flood, and mosquitos, in a miserable hut made of tree trunks, deprived of all the sweetness of life, of all society of her own age, of all medical care, even of furniture and common utensils, of food and drink of which long habit have made necessities. I would not believe that my dear friends, whom I have come to love in so short a time, would allow their mother to abide with strangers, either at New Harmony, even should that establishment correspond to the brilliant dreams of your friends, or would dream to lead her into the deserts of Tennessee. . . .

While stressing his "admiration and attachment" to the Misses Wright, he knew his letters would not impress Fanny herself. "The only thing which would have struck her is a chagrin to see confirmed in a most positive manner that you will not go to join her in America." The Garnetts asked Mrs. Millar and Mr. Mylne to entreat their friends to return, but Mrs. Millar was not optimistic. "You know how much I should wish them to do so, but I have no hope, now that they are so far embarked in their undertaking, that anything friends can say, will have any influence in opposition to the actual circumstances in which they find themselves placed." The Garnetts had definitely decided against going. How difficult this resolve had been is clear in the letters of their friends. As Mrs. Millar noted, "I had been led to imagine that you had thoughts of going out to them, but now find you not only do not intend it, but that . . . you had even taken a *lease* of a house in Paris, that it might operate as an obstacle to your going to America, lest you should be tempted." Calling the Wrights' American enterprise "this temptation," Sismondi was nevertheless certain that "the Garnetts have begun to feel its uselessness."

Sismondi always regarded Fanny's experiment as the result of Mr. Owen's influence. He seemed reluctant to concede that Fanny could have spun such ideas herself, or put them into practice. Repeatedly, he blamed Owen. "They are deceived in Mr. Owen," he wrote. "If Mr. Owen has caused humanity to lose the fruits of the immense sacrifice of these two excellent beings, he would have done more evil by his extravagant theories than all that he might be able to do by his writings. . . ." "I tremble that she may be under the influence of Mr. Owen, and if it is so, I am convinced that the plan which he would have her adopt, will never carry through to the end."

Lafayette was similarly distressed about the reports coming out of Nashoba. He agreed with the Trollopes that it would be decidedly "inconvenient" to publish the prospectus in England, "even for the sake of the cause." Still, at this point, objections seemed mainly directed toward Fanny's expressed opposition to religion.

Since year's end, no letters had arrived from the sisters; considering their recent illnesses, their friends were understandably concerned. Lafayette complained to Julia about "this so very cruel silence," and invited the Garnetts to La Grange. Like fellow worshippers at a shrine, he suggested, "let us meet before dear Fanny's portrait, and write to the beloved girls all together from this place." But such ritual was to be unnecessary.

Fanny was already on the high seas, heading for Europe. She had sailed from New Orleans on May 31 in company with Robert Dale Owen and a female nurse. She was so ill that she had to be transported in a hammock, swung in a covered wagon. But two months later, in the English channel, she found herself "perfectly restored, and that so far from suffering any inconvenience from the heat of our delightful summer, it has most effectively put to flight my most formidable foe, the chill and fever, and has imparted to my frame a degree of vigor that I hardly expected again to experience." Cam had written ahead, to give notice of Fanny's imminent arrival:

> You will readily conceive, my loved friends, with what anxious solicitude I await the tidings of our loved Fanny's safe arrival amongst you. From the untoward delay of the vessel at the mouth of the Mississippi they can hardly reach Havre before the end of this month, nor indeed, should I regard a prolongation of the voyage otherwise than as favourable, as it is to the sea air I mainly look for the restoration of her health.

From on board the *New England,* Fanny wrote with eager expectation of being "six-seven days at farthest" from being "in your arms, my beloved friends. You have been long without letters, for I have been long on the sea—& long enough to have acquired new limbs, new head, new eyes, new everything. I come to you & come to you in health." Everything was roseate. Fanny had bathed regularly and been idle, both of which "have daily added to my strength, size, & color until now it would be hard to detect in me any trace of the invalid." She would stay with the Garnetts, and had already written to the General at La Grange. "I conclude him to be now there and thus he will wish me there also, which perhaps might suit better my health than the air of a city. But if so, you must accompany me. My angels. I now count the hours and minutes. Pray Heaven our present wind last for 40 hours more!" Harriet, too, was wild with "agitation and joy." But she, at least, briefly remembered the absent one. "But alas! dear Cam, my heart sickens when I think of her."

But Sismondi, able to see a woman's fate only as relative, was sure that Cam had remained behind, not out of principle or duty, but because she had found a prospective husband in America. He told Harriet:

> I cannot torment myself as much as you do about this solitude of her sister: Lovely, young, in America where the heart speaks even more warmly than with us, I cannot believe her to be really alone, & I persuade myself that Fanny has already told you of a marriage either made or impending.

Professor Mylne, however, who had seen some more recent accounts of Nashoba, saw Cam's position as a terrible abandonment by her sister. His source of information was the publication in an Edinburgh paper of the principles of the Nashoba system by James Richardson.

As the trustee in charge of correspondence at Nashoba, Richardson had sent to Benjamin Lundy, editor of the *Genius of Universal Emancipation,* extracts from the society's records, and given permission to publish them. One incident was particularly shocking. On June 1, 1827, one of the female slaves "laid a complaint against Redrick (another of the slaves) for coming during the night of Wednesday to her bedroom, uninvited, and endeavoring, without her consent, to take liberties with her person." For the next few sentences, the account proceeded as one would expect. But then, stepping out from between the lines, Camilla Wright spoke with matter-of-fact boldness of a forbidden subject, taking toward it a stance which would shatter both her own life and, eventually, that of her sister's colony. It is her one public statement, and it makes somewhat perplexing and indeterminate all the images of docility and sweetness we have associated with Camilla thus far. "Camilla Wright informed the slaves that, as the conduct of Redrick, which he did not deny, was a gross infringement of that view (of the sexual relation which had been repeatedly given to the slaves), a repetition of such conduct . . . ought in her opinion, to be punished by flogging. *She repeated that we consider the proper basis of the sexual intercourse* to be the unconstrained choice of *both* parties." The interview concluded with Camilla refusing Nelly's request for a lock to her room, it being "inconsistent with the doctrine just explained." The extracts concluded with an entry of June 17 noting that "James Richardson informed them that, last night, Mamselle Josephine (a quadroon daughter of Mamselle Lolotte, the colony's washerwoman) and he began to live together; and he took this occasion of repeating to them our views on color, and on the sexual relation."

At once, Mylne saw the shocking ramifications of Fanny's "liberal ideas." More important, he saw how her long devotion to a cause had made a stone of her heart. In coming to Europe to revive her health, she had selfishly left "her sister alone, dispirited, and broken hearted by her absence, to encounter all the horrors of a forest solitude, or a solitude abated only by the society of negroes in all the debasement of ignorance & slavery; or if of whites, of whites whose intellects seem to be destroyed & whose moral feelings are, I fear, ruined by the absurd principles of her system—left there to manage & control an establishment which she had set up on the outlines of community of property-non-responsibility, atheism & an intercourse of the sexes unrestrained except by choice of the parties." He told Julia:

> I have the most painful proof that the above is no exaggerated account of Fanny's establishment & of poor Camilla's wretched situation. Two days before I received her first letter I rescued from publication in one of our newspapers in this town a letter from one of the settlers at Nashoba & a trustee of her institution in which the writer states, with triumph and exultation the principles of her project as I have given them. The printer of this paper declined to insert the letter till he should first have my permission, as he knew my connection with Fanny & was unwilling to give publicity to any thing which by bringing disgrace on her character should be deeply disturbing to me.

Mylne soon learned that the letter "was written by a genuine & sincere admirer of her doctrines, full of insulting anticipations of the universal felicity which the practical adoption of them were to produce in the world." And, although Fanny had never outlined her ideas on sexual freedom to her uncle, and had expressed her other principles moderately, he saw that while "she has not ventured to acknowledge to me the full intent for her extravagance, she has not had the common sense to conceal it from James Richardson and others in America who were admitted to her confidence." Just two days earlier, Mylne had met with the elder Owen, "fresh from his Establishment at New Harmony, who represented Fanny as having gone to much more extravagant lengths than he himself who, as I have long known, has very little limit to his extravagances," and who, though he has but a very small share of knowledge, has yet enough to perceive that this "folly cannot fail to obstruct the very objects of a philanthropical kind she has in view, and to bring ruin upon her project and disgrace upon herself. This he acknowledged to me & professed deeply to lament."

At once, Mylne wrote to his niece, expressing himself "in that language of affection," which he professed to bear toward her, even while confessing to Julia that "it was not quite easy for me to throw it in. Had the love I feel for her been less strong I would have found it impossible." He was angered, enraged, felt himself personally disgraced, and regretted "that I should live to see one in whom I had flattered myself I should have ground to boast as a benefit to mankind, an ornament to her sex & pride of her connections, reducing herself to such a state." He had been able to tolerate her project, "however visionary it may have seemed . . . in some respects," because it was "fraught with philanthropy, a project which if wisely and sturdily conducted might go far towards curing or abating some of the greatest ills of human life." For that, he could have seen her sacrifice "her time, her fortune, her health," but to see her turning upon a course which would bring disgrace to its author, and wretchedness to those around her, would be too much. The doctrine of sexual liberty was "hostile to the universal consent and feelings of mankind." As for atheism, that was at least a respectable subject. There, "she had the whole field of superstition and priestcraft lying before her open to attack." But meddling with sex was too much. Mylne feared "the incipient disorder of her mind." He ended his letter to Julia claiming he had not time to meet Fanny in France. Notably absent was an invitation to visit him in Edinburgh. Instead, he asked Julia to speak with her. "You may communicate to her this letter or what you think fit of it. I wish much that you and Lafayette should see what I have written to herself." Leaving the task of bringing Fanny to her senses to others, Dr. Mylne retired from the scene, in effect disowning his niece if she did not renounce her views. Thus, he separated himself from her and Cam forever. And while Fanny made brief but courteous farewell of him in her autobiography, she never saw him again. She would not force her views, sexual or otherwise, upon anyone.

If she had ever made any remarks to her friends upon the proper relations between men and women, she had couched them in oblique terms, as when she read a Chinese novel at La Grange, in which she found, as she told Julia and Harriet, some "very curious and interesting" characters.

> If they (the Chinese) are irrational I think them rather less so than we. Poetry is there the road to honor, and men give battle with pens instead of swords. Two literary heroines in love with the same literary hero, instead of killing each other or dying of consumption, see in their mutual affection for the same object a bond of union, & join hands and hearts, house and husband. They drink a little too much wine, write too much incomprehensible poetry . . . yet are the Chinese I think a *little* more rational than we are.

It would be as if Jane Eyre and Bertha Mason had found their truest bonds to be, not to Mr. Rochester, but to each other. This vision of a world in which the real bonds are between women, for whom men are playthings and possessions, was too advanced for its time. Probably, the Garnetts made no comment, especially Julia, who was even now beginning a relationship with the rising young historian, Georg Heinrich Pertz.

As Fanny viewed the world to which she had temporarily returned, she recognized the decreasing probability that any of the women she knew would join her at Nashoba. Like the sensible woman she was, she began looking elsewhere for recruits. While there was always Cam, she was not the commanding equal Fanny could respect and admire. Mrs. Trollope had called Fanny Wright "the most interesting woman in Europe"; Fanny wanted a female companion at least equally fascinating. Her search began on August 22 with a letter to a total stranger. With all the exalted eloquence of which she was ever the master, Fanny Wright addressed the widow of Percy Bysshe Shelley.

> As the daughter of your father and mother (known to me only by their works and opinions), as the friend and companion of a man distinguished during life, and preserved in the remembrance of the public as one distinguished not by genius merely, but, as I imagine, by the strength of his opinions and his fearlessness in their expression;—viewed only in these relations you would be to me an object of interest and . . . of curiosity.

But Fanny had heard that Mary Shelley shared her father's opinions and her mother's generous feelings; thus, she was ready to travel far, just to see her. "It is rare in this world, especially in our sex, to meet with those opinions united with those feelings, and with the manners and disposition calculated to command respect and conciliate affection."

Excusing her bold intrusion, Fanny pleaded the rare opportunity of finding someone with whom she could share her dedication to "moral truth and moral liberty." Should she "neglect any means for discovering a real friend of that cause," she wrote, "I were almost failing to a duty." Briefly, she explained her determination to undermine a variety of slaveries: of color, of mind, of rank, of wealth, of instruction, and last, but not least, of sex. Her determination was to create an entirely new world order.

> Our circle already comprises a few united cooperators, whose choice of associates will be guided by their moral fitness only; saving that, for the protection and support of all, each must be fitted to exercise some useful employment, or to supply 200 dollars as an equivalent for their support. The present generation

will in all probability supply but a limited number of individuals suited in opinion and disposition to such a state of society; but that, that number, however limited, may best find their happiness and best exercise their utility by uniting their interests, their society, and their talents, I feel a conviction. In this conviction, I have devoted my time and fortune to laying the foundations of an establishment where affection shall form the only marriage, kind feeling and kind action the only religion, respect for the feelings and liberties of others the only restraint, and union of interest the bond of peace and security.

Such were her extensive goals, and fifteen months had placed her establishment in what she called "a fair way of progress." Come to Europe only for reasons of health, she was now ready to return to her "forest home." Whatever happened, Fanny concluded, "I wish to convey to Mary Wollstonecraft Godwin Shelley my respect and admiration of those from whom she holds those names, and my fond desire to connect her with them in my esteem, and in the knowledge of mutual sympathy to sign myself her friend."

Mary Shelley answered at once. She was, as Robert Dale Owen subsequently noted, "genial, gentle, sympathetic, thoughtful, and matured in opinion beyond her years." Fanny had touched upon "the right chord" to win her attention.

The memory of my mother [she wrote] has always been the pride and delight of my life and the admiration of others for her, has been the cause of most of the happiness I have enjoyed. Her greatness of soul and my father's high talents have perpetually reminded me that I ought to degenerate as little as I could from those from whom I derived my being. For several years with Mr. Shelley I was blessed with the companionship of one, who fostered this ambition & inspired that of being worthy of him. He who was single among men for Philanthropy —devoted generosity—talent—goodness—yet you must not fancy that I am what I wish I were, and my chief merit must always be derived, first from the glory these wonderful beings have shed around me; and then for the enthusiasms I have for excellence & the ardent admiration I feel for those who sacrifice themselves for the public good.

If you feel curiosity concerning me—how much more in the refined sense of the word, must I not feel for yourself—a woman, young, rich & independent, quits the civilization of England for a life of hardship in the forests of America, that by so doing she may contribute to the happiness of her species. Her health fails in the attempt, yet scarcely restored to that, she is eager to return again to the scene of her labours, & again to spend the flower of her life in arduous struggles and beneficent, self-sacrificing devotion to others. Such a tale cannot fail to inspire the deepest interest and the most ardent admiration. You do honour to our species and what perhaps is dearer to me, to the feminine part of it.—and that thought, while it makes me doubly interested in you, makes me tremble for you. Women are so particularly the victims of their generosity and their purer, & more sensitive feelings render them so much less than men, capable of battling the selfishness, hardness, and ingratitude which is so often the return made, for the noblest efforts to benefit others. But you seem satisfied with your success, so I hope the ill-fortune which too usually frustrates our best view, will spare to harm the family of love, which you represent to have assembled at Nashoba.

Having only Fanny's letter to tell her about Nashoba, she wondered about the settlement's real success.

Is it all you wish? Do you find the motives you mention sufficient to tame that strange human nature, which is perpetually the source of wonder to me? It takes a simpler form probably in a forest abode—yet can enthusiasm for public good rein in passion, motive benevolence, & unite families? It were a divine right to behold the reality of such a picture. Yet do not be angry with me that I am so much of a woman that I am far more interested in you than in (except as it is yours) your settlement.

She invited Fanny to England, and asked to hear from her again. "At least, I pray you, write again—write about yourself—tell me whether happiness & content repay your exertions. I have fancied that the first of these blessings can only be found in the exercise of the affections—yet I have not found mine there.—for where moral evil does not interfere, dreadful Death has come to deprive me of all I enjoyed. My life has not been like yours publicly active, but it has been one of tempestuous suffering."

Mrs. Shelley was here asking a crucial question, one which Fanny had already begun to answer. Could women find happiness in work or were they required to find their deepest satisfactions in the realm of the affections? Living in seclusion with her only surviving son and with a beloved female friend, Mary Shelley drew back before the risk of a call to work at Nashoba, even while she entreated Fanny to maintain their correspondence. "I fully trust that I shall hear from you again. Do not, public spirited as you are, turn from me, because private interests too much engross me. At least, tho' mine be a narrow circle, yet I am willing at all times to sacrifice my being to it, & derive my only pleasures from contributing to the happiness and welfare of others." Was ever the century's ideal for women better expressed?

But Fanny Wright had already differentiated between the kind of love demanded by men and that possible among women who were truly equals.

In an enigmatic letter of October 1827, Fanny referred to one of her relationships with men, a dashing young adventurer named Dutrone, who had gone to fight in the war of Greek independence and with whom she had been briefly and passionately involved. He had offered to follow her to Nashoba. She told Julia: "Always to support others has cost me too much. To hold in check the passions of others, if it has aided me in mastering my own, has too much used up my strength and my life. In the annihilation of self, one enjoys calm and an inner peace, but it is not happiness. There are moments when it takes effort not to give way, when one's self feels the need of sympathy and the support of a strong and understanding spirit. Am I able to make myself understood?" And while Mary Shelley probably did understand, since she had herself devoted her whole being to the needs of a powerful man, she was unable to rouse herself to the active life Fanny was now describing.

But since the gates of friendship and feeling had opened, Fanny freely articulated her more selfish motive in wanting Mary to come. Relationships with men had been demanding and debilitating. She was ready to restate the idea of sisterhood, inextricably associating it with the work ahead.

> I do want one of my own sex to commune with and sometimes to lean upon in all the confidence and equality of friendship. You see, I am not so disinterested as you suppose. Delightful it is indeed to aid the progress of human improvement and sweet is the peace we derive from aiding the happiness of others, but still the heart craves something more ere it can say, I am satisfied.

In Fanny's mind, sisterhood was connected with the goal of useful occupation. For her, they were the companion parts of a complete life, both necessary in her Faustian quest for satisfaction. She offered to come to Brighton, to Arundel, "anywhere you may name," to convince Mrs. Shelley that she, too, could achieve this dual goal.

The last section of her letter contained Fanny's compelling self-portrait, a heroic picture, somewhat masculine and even Arthurian, with its suggestion of a dangerous and vigorous search for moral improvement. The passage gives insight into the created self of Frances Wright—strenuous, spartan, alienated from the masses—above all, a leader. She had transformed Cam's quiet haven of kindred spirits into an amazonian circle of strong souls ready to change the world at any cost.

> A delicate nursling of European luxury and aristocracy, I thought and felt for myself, and for martyrised humankind, and have preferred all hazards, all privations in the forests of the New World to the dear-bought comforts of miscalled civilization. I have made the hard earth my bed, the saddle of my horse

my pillow, and have staked my life and fortune on an experiment having in view moral liberty and human improvement. Many of course think me mad, and if to be mad means to be one of a minority, I am so, and very mad indeed, for our minority is very small. Should that few succeed in mastering the first difficulties, weaker spirits, though often not less amiable, may carry forward the good work. But the fewer we are who now think alike, the more we are of value to each other. To know you, therefore, is a strong desire of my heart, and all things consistent with my engagements, which I may call duties, since they are connected with the work I have in hand, will I do to facilitate our meeting.

But Mary's daring days were clearly over. And for Fanny Wright, the eligible women were vanishing fast.

Julia Garnett was certainly no longer a candidate for Nashoba. In the summer of 1827, at one of General Lafayette's Tuesday evening soirees, she had met a serious young German historian, Georg Heinrich Pertz. With the exception of the language difficulties, it seemed almost like the old days in America. They played chess and talked, and soon the two were deeply attached. It seemed to Julia that she had found a love she could truly return. In later life, Dr. Pertz recalled how their relationship had begun.

December 1826 brought me also to Paris, whose rich material for the *Monumenta Germanica* was used by me during the whole winter. While I spent the days of my research in the archives of the library, in the evenings, I appeared in society circles which had been opened to me. One of the most attractive was that of Mrs. Clarke and her daughter, where the most eminent friends, savants, and artists were always to be found. . . . There I saw the Garnett sisters among the ladies, and the complete beauty of their appearance, the magic of their conversation, and Julia's noble, soulful eyes, seized upon my heart. I saw her in her own house, at Mrs. Clarke's house, and at that of General Lafayette. Thus she engraved herself upon my heart. A discussion at Lafayette's, in which I told something about the King of Rome . . . led us to discuss other political events, especially England and its king George III, about which our opinions were in lively disagreement and were vigorously expressed. She showed me her . . . satisfaction . . . in a written invitation to a meal before my departure for England, and my very affectionate answer, as well as my behavior in those days of parting must have showed her how dear she was to me. But before I could bind her to myself forever, I needed the free-from-anxieties position that I hoped to obtain from my presence in England. Duty carried me across the Channel, but the tender, invisible cares of love went with me. In the hour of parting, Julia gave me a letter which would introduce me to her friend Mrs. Trollope in

Harrow. I sent it off as soon as I arrived in London and received an invitation to Julian Hill.

The somewhat formal Pertz was immediately taken in hand by Frances Trollope, whose energetic, natural response to Julia's letter contrasts sharply with his halting proprieties. Mrs. Trollope had read between the lines and assured her younger friend, that should Pertz accept her invitation to Julian Hill, she would "treat him accordingly."

Don't be frightened. I will *not* seize his hand the moment I see him, and with a tender squeeze exclaim, "Lover of my Julia, welcome!" No—I will only pump his heart a little—and it shall be done so gently, that he shall not only feel no pain, but he shall not even be conscious of what I am at.

Seizing the role of matchmaker, Mrs. Trollope soon invited Julia to Harrow as well. There, while walking across the lovely hill where all of green Middlesex spreads out as far as St. Paul's, Julia and Georg Heinrich surmounted the difficulties of language, etiquette, and German prudence and, as Dr. Pertz later recalled, "poured out our innermost feelings." His recollection of his declaration seems stilted and excessively flowery, making it somewhat difficult to find the man underneath the rhetoric.

We had never spoken of love, but our hearts lay open one to another. Usually I came on Friday or Saturday from London and returned thither early on Monday. About three weeks after Julia's arrival, Mrs. Trollope had got up a dramatic evening entertainment, in which I had to marvel at Julia, in English speech and dress, in the role of Roscolana in *The Malade Imaginaire*. I had waited to declare myself until my position was decided, but as a powerful bud, illuminated by the sun of July, breaks its casing and unfolds its priceless blossom, so did my love break through this last boundary, and on the 3rd of August she made me the happiest man by acknowledging her love for me.

Moved by these dramatics, Pertz broke through his reticence and proposed. Almost at once, Julia confessed to fears of inadequacy, explaining,

I *think* he will make me as happy—as I hope—as I wish at least to make *him*. But—he is very superior to me in every respect. . . . He is now in England, detained by *historical duties*—collecting materials for his German history. I expect him in the course of next week, and soon after, I have promised to be his wife, to follow him, or rather go with him, to Hanover in October, where his lodging is already secured.

Julia seemed ready to live in her husband's shadow. In terms of their century's expectations, they were off to a typical start in life. Julia had chosen a decidedly dominant male in her German suitor.

Despite her decision to marry, Julia was nevertheless fearful when she thought of adapting herself to a new country and a new language, and of separating herself from the women who had for so long been her companions and friends. Marriage to Pertz would mean a wrenching from her mother and sisters and, most important of all, from her friend Frances Wright, who had "for 9 years been the sole object of my thoughts—almost the sole object of my love." Her letter concluded with a wistful broken phrase, whose incompleteness signalled a regret yet to be articulated: "such a change in my life. . . ."

When the announcements went out, many friends wrote to offer congratulations. From Frances Wright, about to set out for the new world and Nashoba once again, came instead a veiled warning. From all she could now see, she wrote, Julia would have "a sweet and tranquil life," and she expressed herself satisfied in general with Julia's choice.

> I have no sort of doubt respecting him, Love, either head, heart, or person. I shall like them all I know. That they have pleased you is a sure sign, & that they have preferred you an equally sure one. It is only *very* superior men who make choice of superior women—only those who are above jealousy & who love the praises of those they love better than their own.

Still, should anything mar Julia's future happiness, "you know where you have another home and another fond friend to share it with," she wrote. She was unsure of Julia's successful metamorphosis to German matron and offered a haven for the future. "Thou knowest thou hast only to write to thy Fanny, come and take me to thee, and she will come—were it from the end of the earth to its other farthest extremity. Do not hesitate my Julia to share the contents of this letter with your friend. He knows the old and sacred claims of my affection and if he be all my heart hopes and believes, he will rejoice that your fate has more than one anchor and yourself more than one friend willing and able to protect you. Confidence, my Julia, is the staff of affection; and I shall never write to thee aught that I wish not thy friend to share."

One wonders what Pertz thought of Miss Wright's invitation. After all, she had already publicly castigated the institution of marriage. Two months before the wedding, she wrote of "the marriage tie as irrational and pernicious and as a subtle invention of priestcraft for poisoning the purest source of human felicity." But Fanny Wright's voice was the only discordant one among the general chorus of praise for Julia's choice of mate and vocation.

Mrs. Garnett was annoyed by Miss Wright's bold statements and radical doctrines. Julia was thirty-four, and in her view, it was time her daughter married. Furthermore, Julia's character and temperament seemed suited for marriage. As Mrs. Garnett told her daughter,

> Affectionate disposition and generous feelings added to your own taste for domestic life, must insure to you and your husband all the happiness this life affords—I am not, you well know, of your friend's opinion who says she never knew a happy marriage—and should you have the unspeakable happiness of becoming a mother, you will agree with me that a married life is perfect. I know in married life, and speak from experience, there is but one head, one heart and mind, and you will subscribe to this I am sure.

Joining Mrs. Garnett in these opinions was Sismondi, who enthusiastically approved Julia's choice. He was also sure that her new life would bring happiness, but his thoughts were all for Mr. Pertz: "If you love him, his domestic happiness is assured; he will never know boredom or listlessness, he will have the best confidante, the best consoler in his griefs, the best adviser in his successes." Of what Julia might find by way of personal satisfactions, little was said.

Sismondi seemed the more anxious to convince Julia of her prospective good fortune because her situation so exactly mirrored that of his own wife, also an Englishwoman (a distant cousin of the Garnetts) who had left land, language, and family for him. He told Julia: "It seems to me that there is a great connection between our situations, and I can assure you that the life of a historian and an expatriated English wife is a very sweet one." Sismondi was a prolific, old-style historian. Assembling the archives of the past in his study, he composed scores of new volumes, while his wife sat quietly beside him. And, "even though she made it a rule never to interrupt," he spoke to her, pleased to "feel her near me." So devoted was his wife, he confided in closing his letter, that she had given him no children "for fear of distracting me." Humor was not intended, and what Julia thought of such prospects for happiness, we do not know.

The lively hostess Mary Clarke also approved of Pertz, whom she found "remarkably good, amiable, and delicate." She thought Julia's future life might resemble her own, commenting that Pertz "sees, I should think, the best society, which is better than a large fortune." Since for her, society had become a vocation, she envisioned Julia's life as centering on a large social circle in Germany. She had herself entertained many distinguished German scholars; she expected Julia to make of Pertz's drawing room an intellectual center and, by extension, an occupation for herself as well.

Julia had completely turned away from her Nashoba ideas, and confided her new disillusionment with Fanny Wright to Sismondi.

> Mr. Owen has much to answer for—& you said truly, that in misleading, in sacrificing such beings as Fanny and Cam Wright, he has done an irreparable wrong to mankind. Alas! what a mind has he ruined. What a loss to the world —to her friends. I believe that Owen worked upon her mind at a moment when she was incapacitated by fever from judging sanely—and now I question much, if a fever constantly upon her, does not still warp her judgment. It is a most painful subject—& one which I cannot get rid of for a moment.

Julia was sure that with a male guide like Sismondi, Fanny would have been saved.

> Oh! that you were here dear friend! that you could see Fanny—love her you would, for she is a creature that none may see without loving. But you would look upon her with an interest almost too painful—for you would feel that her very virtues—her sensibility—her humanity, her generous forgetfulness of self, have been her ruin. Had she earlier known you—had she been blessed with such a friend—such a guide—Fanny had been an ornament to her sex—the boast of her friends . . . their happiness. Alas! Alas! Now *her* friends are most unhappy —for they see and feel that her reputation must be tarnished, that probably her life will be sacrificed, & this to produce no one advantage—not even to those for whose sake she is giving up her friends, her country, I had almost said her respectability.

Sismondi had written directly to Fanny, but her answer, explaining her colony and its goals, did not encourage or impress. He told Julia: "I suspect a community of enthusiasts; I catch a glimpse of the vague and disordered spirit of Owen, without being able to say precisely what the trouble is." He had long been aware of her "pronounced hostility toward religion" which he found regrettable: "I have always known her as impassioned, and of a penetrating but not accurate spirit. I know that she throws herself wholly into extremes on matters that she regards as censurable and I could only have wished that from womanly modesty she could have avoided saying these things." But her views on sexual liberty were almost unmentionable.

> I see by your letter there is another matter, too, words which cannot fall from your pen by chance, and which are not explainable except on the supposition that she preaches likewise the doctrine of Owen against marriage. In this respect her illness and that of her sister has been a blessing, for it has limited them both

to mere theory. I am astonished, I am frightened, at the persuasiveness of an eloquent man in his folly who has succeeded in perverting her superior mind. I see a confirmation of the great gulf between the intelligence of men and that of women, who subordinate in their decisions reason to the imagination and to sentiment, rendering them wholly incapable of treating questions of religion.

In conclusion, Sismondi called Fanny "insanely religious," seeing her, in anticipation of George Eliot's description of Dorothea in *Middlemarch*, as "a new St. Theresa in whom the love of principle and usefulness moves, but not that of the soul or the love of God." He hoped she would stay quiet, discussing Owen's system with other philosophers so that she might in the end see the truth. "Let her return quickly," he wrote, "to an equilibrium which has been upset because the only man of spirit who has approached her for some time was a fool."

And so, despite Fanny's continued importunings, her friends, amid such powerful tutelage and rumors of scandal, were reluctant to join Fanny on her return to America. At the last, she tried once more to convince Harriet Garnett.

> I cannot bear to think of your solitude [with Julia's impending marriage] and yet I cannot but think of it, day and night. A whole year, my Harry! It is too long—too long. Why should you not go with me? You did not convince me by any of your reasons at the time and now when I look back to them I am still less convinced.

The hoped-for female companionship was proving increasingly elusive. These early Victorian women were finding it still difficult to translate individual goals into anything as specific as, say, an infamous slave emancipation colony thousands of miles away.

All the talk of eternal pacts and friendship forever was over. From now on, sisterhood would prove to be mainly an intellectual and emotional mainstay, based on the connections forged by language, not actions. Whenever the demands made by one or another of the women approached an area requiring tangible support—a move to Nashoba, or Hanover, the braving of convention to take someone in—the sisterhood faltered. Never concrete, it remained a compelling idea which provided a continuing, if often fragile bond among members of the circle, a force which the women could draw upon only in personal, inward ways.

The really permanent bond was still the marital one. On September 23, 1827, Julia Garnett and Georg Heinrich Pertz were married at the American Embassy in Paris. The setting was splendid in an old-world way. The embassy, housed in a superb residence owned and still partly occupied by the Duc de Castries, was beautifully furnished. The main rooms were hung with splendid tapestries of Gobelin manufacture. The ambassador's wife had done all the honors of the establishment like a lady bred at court, not the native born Virginian that she was. The ambassador himself, appointed by President Monroe in 1823, was the Honorable James Brown, now serving under President John Quincy Adams, who described him as "a man of large fortune, respectable talents, handsome person, polished manners, and elegant deportment." The embassy had seemed the proper setting for Julia to accommodate with both economy and dignity her many friends, some of whom were surely among the world's luminaries.

The guest list was impressive, and included General Lafayette, the American author Fenimore Cooper and his wife, St. Leger, nephew of the statesman Hyde de Neuville, and Mary Clarke, later to become Madame Mohl. There were other notables, like Sismondi, the authors Washington Irving, Prosper Mérimée, and Stendhal, and political heroes like General Pepe. But of greatest importance to the bride was her circle of dear women friends who had gathered for this occasion. Frances Wright and Frances Trollope were there, and only Camilla was missing, of that original group who once swore eternal friendship.

Frances Trollope had come over from Harrow for Julia's wedding, even though it was a time of great trouble for the Trollopes, who found themselves enmeshed in the severe agricultural depression of 1827. Mr. Trollope's law practice had dwindled, and the farm he had bought to rescue himself was failing. There were still five children to find their places in the world, and a big house they stood in imminent danger of losing. She had enjoyed life at her big house, Julian Hill, but now the hard times had come, and it had really been quite wonderful and a measure of Mrs. Trollope's affection for Julia, that she managed at all to make the trip to Paris to see her younger friend married.

Although their enlightenment backgrounds had been remarkably similar, the six women of Julia's inner circle of friendship were to have markedly different marital fates. Julia would be married all her adult life. Harriet and Fanny Garnett would remain single. Frances Wright would later divorce the man she married, and Camilla Wright would be separated from her mate. Frances Trollope would be widowed during a significant part of her professional life. This happy occasion of Julia's wedding was the last time her circle of friends would be together in the same place. Although their deep ties of friendship and mutual regard made them sure that life would hold other meetings for them, it did not. The plot lines of their lives were about to diverge, and the wedding at the embassy marked an end of their old mutual narrative and a beginning of their separate fates.

After the short ceremony was over, ices, sweetmeats, and cakes were served, and tea, in compliment to the Americans and English. There was conversation in English, French, and German, accompanied by a great deal of gesturing. Finally, the party began to disperse. It had been a rather bustling day, and it was time to order the carriages. The large sprig of orange blossoms which the bride had pinned to her veil was already starting to wilt.

Lafayette, who had long ago rejected his aristocratic "de," and whose behavior was accordingly amiable, kissed the bride and prepared to return to life on the grand scale at La Grange, decorated with paintings of the destruction of the Bastille, and a facsimile of the American Declaration of Independence. He continued to enjoy his role as virtuous patriarch and comfortable symbol of freedom everywhere. Fanny Wright did not return with him. Her recovery complete, she took a seat on the outside of the London diligence, in company with Mrs. Trollope, the course of whose life she was about to change. These two, who were to be the heroines of the story, were from the first strongly attracted to each other, and would serve as competing role models for the women of their acquaintance.

Following their fateful ride from Paris to Harrow, Mrs. Trollope's first letter to Julia told the story of a sudden heightening of that old attraction.

> You know who I traveled with, and will not wonder that even the top of the diligence was delightful. Never was there I am persuaded such a being as Fanny Wright—no never—and I am not the only one who thinks so. Some of my friends declare that if worship may be offered, it must be to her—that she is at once all that women should be—and something more than woman ever was— and I know not what beside—and I for my part applaud and approve all they say. Miss Landon, to whom I had mentioned her being here, has written to ask leave to look at the most interesting woman in Europe.

Mrs. Trollope's fascination for the woman, coupled with her own problems and tentative ideals, had determined her own immediate future. She asked Harriet:

> Will it be possible to let her depart without vowing to follow her? I think not. I feel greatly inclined to say, "where her country is, there shall be my country." The more I see of her, the more I listen to her, the more I feel convinced that *all* her notions are right. She is pointing out to man a short road to that goal which for ages he has been in vain endeavoring to reach. Under her system I believe it possible that man may be happy. . . .

She ended on a note of that old hope of a community of friends: "Do something to amuse and comfort yourself—next year perhaps we shall be amusing each other at Nashoba." Frances Wright had finally gained a worker-companion for her colony.

Frances Trollope was undeterred by the rumors then surfacing about Fanny Wright. She knew that Charles Wilkes, another of those strong men who had been protectors of the Wrights and Garnetts, had written to report his change of attitude toward the Misses Wright. He addressed himself to Julia upon her recent marriage, but his letter had another purpose. Once past the expected congratulations and felicitations, he raised the distressing subject of Frances Wright.

> You have long known my sentiments on their original plan. I certainly thought it in the highest degree honorable to them & that it could neither have been conceived or executed without the most enthusiastic virtue—My impression was that it would never do as much good as they expected, but that it could not fail to make the immediate objects under their care happy & worthy to be so.

But after having been shown a Baltimore paper "purporting to be an account of the proceedings of the trustees at Nashoba," he saw the colony professed other views, in his eyes, disgusting. In the midst of other "ridiculous circumstances," the newspaper stated:

> That Camilla Wright had upon some occasion, delivered to a meeting of the slaves the opinions of the trustees as to what, in their cant, they call the sexual intercourse, which was declared to be THAT THE ONLY PROPER BASIS WAS THE UNRESTRAINED & UNCONSTRAINED CHOICE OF BOTH PARTIES. I cannot dwell upon the subject—in short, it was clear, if the publication was authentic, that there were to be no marriages & to put the matter beyond the least doubt, one of the trustees declared in person & in the presence of Camilla, that HE HAD, THE NIGHT BEFORE BEGUN TO LIVE WITH MADAMA-SELLE JOSEPHINE—who it appears was a woman of color. My first impression was indignation that such a base calumny should be published—but further information made me fear that there was some foundation in truth & I wrote to Camilla begging some explanation & expressing my feelings. She tells me that she has sent you my letter & her answer—I need not therefore dwell upon them. Her answer contained the most distinct avowal that the publication was authentic, that the society was formed on the basis mentioned—that she & her sister disapproved of the marriage tie as irrational & pernicious & a subtle invention of priestcraft for poisoning the purest source of human felicity etc. etc. & in short, that she & her sister had supposed themselves able to make a new modification of society to dispense with marriage & the ties connected with it

& also with those arising from & connected with the love of children, who under their plan were to be separated from the parents & to become the children of the community. Such is the issue of the plans of these excellent young women, for excellent & virtuous I still cannot doubt their being—such is the consequence of their overweening confidence in their own judgments. That such young women should be the dupes & the victims of the wretched sophisms of a madman like Owen—is truly lamentable.

Once again, men blamed men. How could women be held responsible for such views? Still, Wilkes concluded, like Mylne and Sismondi before him, that all relationships with the Wrights must cease.

With such opinions thus openly promulgated & accompanied with opinions on religion & morals equally absurd and mischievous & equally calculated to shock and offend 99 out of 100 in every decent and civilized society, you will, at once, see that any future intercourse between them & any of the ladies of their acquaintance here is quite impossible.

Wilkes continued to act faithfully as the Wrights' financial adviser and banker, but friendship was impossible. He was particularly horrified that Camilla so "glories" in the ideas and "courts publicity." At the last, he carefully reminded both Harriet and Julia how close they had come to following Fanny to America. He returned to the subject now in particular, "if there were any prospects of either Harriet or you being persuaded to accompany Miss Wright on her return & to express how much I should regret your doing so."

But there was no need for worry. Fanny Wright was already making preparations for her return, not with the Garnetts, but with Frances Trollope, the single prospective Nashoba resident gleaned during Fanny's European sojourn. Probably, much of the scandal surrounding the colony was kept from old Mrs. Garnett, who expressed surprise but not shock at Mrs. Trollope's sudden decision. She told Julia, "Will wonders never cease!" Had she seen either Mylne's or Wilkes' letters, she would not have reacted so mildly.

Fanny sent a brief farewell note to Mary Shelley, who had come to see them off. "Dear love, how your figure lives in my mind's eye as I saw you borne away from me till I lost sight of your little back among the shipping." The two women never met again.

Sismondi, kept informed of all Miss Wright's plans, had little doubt about the outcome of this new adventure upon which Frances Trollope had now staked reputation and fate. He wrote:

These unhappy women! What a fate is it that they have defied. What dangers and suffering, and when sickness comes upon them, when in their isolation they are bereft of all the little conveniences that the poorest find here at their disposal, how sadly will they contemplate their future, and how near must discouragement be to reaching them. . . . After all, women should be women; they cannot choose with impunity that destiny of dangers, of undertaking, of independence for which we [men] have been formed. The sooner your friends give up their attempt, the better pleased I shall be, and so will they.

In her war on public opinion, he was sure Fanny would be crushed. "She is giving her life, her talent, her reputation, not to serve but to injure those negroes and men of color for whom she feels so generous a pity. Poor Fanny, how sad, with such power to effect such great things!" Whether she would finally destroy herself was no clearer than whether Frances Trollope would reap success or failure for her strenuous middle-aged effort at changing the course of her life. These two, whose lives would be such compelling exemplars for the rest of their friends, were about to tread upon the arduous path leading to achievement and fame.

The Garnetts had long since returned to their Paris life, to dinners, served on gold and silver plate and rich china, with the de Neuvilles, to soirees, tea parties, and visits. They took German tutoring, entertained Mrs. Jameson, Mary Shelley, and some South Americans who lauded their native Chile, claiming that even its earthquakes gave an agreeable "mouvement" to the earth. Harriet replied characteristically, "I should prefer the monotony of terra firma."

Julia and Mr. Pertz were in the midst of their slow, steady journey east and north to Hanover. Their trip lasted about two weeks, almost an equivalent of a modern honeymoon. They were alone now, as never before or after, traveling over rolling hillsides and past romantic vistas, with fine rocks below and hills rising one above the other, the trees rich with autumnal tints, the morning mists rolling gradually away, replaced by a sun shining over all. Day after day, through Brussels, Liège, Aix, and Cologne, they passed by crystal streams and wooded hills, watching through the coach windows as cows grazed quietly under varied foliage. There were countless stops at inns, and overnights, and the newly married pair ate pumpernickel bread and drank bad lemonade in good spirits. Julia was getting some necessary practice at making herself understood in German. The last town at which they made a stop was pretty Little Hamelin, where Julia charmingly recalled the old legend of the Pied Piper and was proudly shown the very gate through which the children were said to have been decoyed. She looked at a nearby house with a long inscription of which she could distinguish only the word *verloren,* lost. The next day, she herself passed through that gate headed for Hanover and her new life from which she, like those fatally charmed children, would never return.

Everything was progressing nicely. It was as though some master of ceremonies had handed each of them the seats appointed and set the performance going. The story of their individual lives was about to begin.

REFERENCES

PAGE

23 In 1814, George Rapp (1757–1847), leader of a religious group called Harmonists, founded the village of Harmonie in Indiana. In 1825 he sold the town to a social reformer and pioneer in cooperative movements, Robert Owen (1771–1858) who renamed the settlement "New Harmony." William Maclure, a wealthy scientist and "Father of American Geology," taught at New Harmony.

24 "Alas, Alas! . . ." FW/HG & JGP, January or February 1825, GPC.

24 "I could have wept . . ." FW/HG & JGP, 12 April 1825, GPC.

25 "start creating her world. . . ." For published selections from the Nashoba letters, see Cecilia Helena Payne-Gaposchkin, ed., "The Nashoba Plan for Removing the Evil of Slavery: Letters of Frances and Camilla Wright, 1820–1829," *Harvard Library Bulletin* 23 (1975).

25 "the new and glorious career . . ." CW/HG & JGP, 8 June 1825, GPC; and FW/HG & JGP, 12 November 1824, GPC.

26 "I marvel not . . ." CW/HG & JGP, 8 June 1825, GPC.

26 "Their intellectual roots . . ." For the impact of the Enlightenment on women writers see Miriam Leranbaum, " 'Mistresses of Orthodoxy': Education in the Lives and Writings of Late 18th Century English Women Writers," *Proceedings of the American Philosophical Society* 121 (12 August 1977), 281–301.

26 "Their mission . . ." Aime Martin, *Woman's Mission* (1840), pp. 124 ff.

26 "Should all my hopes . . ." CW/HG & JGP, 8 June 1825, GPC.

27 "The heat . . ." CW/HG & JGP, 8 June 1825, GPC.

28 "Without some fixed . . ." FW/HG & JGP, 4 December 1825, GPC.

28 "Geometry had been . . ." FW/HG & JGP, 4 December 1825, GPC.

28f. "I can truly declare . . ." FW/HG & JGP, 4 December 1825, GPC.

30 "I am assured . . ." Charles Wilkes to CW, 10 January 1825, GPC.

30f. "Sarah Pears, for example . . ." Information from "New Harmony: An Adventure in Happiness. Papers of Thomas and Sarah Pears," Thomas Clinton Pears, Jr., ed., *Indiana Historical Society Publications* 11 (1933), 7–96. Cf. also Ross F. Lockridge, *The Old Fauntleroy Home* (1939).

35 "While I admire . . ." CW/HG & JGP, 10 January 1826, GPC. For George and Eliza Flower, see *Dictionary of National Biography.*

35 "Our conversation and friendship . . ." FW/HG & JGP, 11 April 1826, GPC.

36 "Remember dear loves . . ." FW/HG & JGP, 11 April 1826, GPC.

37 "Yet think not . . ." CW/HG & JGP, 20 August 1826, GPC.

38 "They love us dearly . . ." L/JGP, 5 September 1826, GPC.

38 "far more formidable . . ." CW/HG & JGP, 12 November 1826, GPC.

38 "For three months . . ." CW/HG & JGP, 12 November 1826, GPC.

38 "I have yet . . ." CW/HG & JGP, 12 November 1826, GPC.

38 "we shall lose them . . ." CW/HG & JGP, 8 December 1826, GPC.

39 "Slaves released from fear . . ." Robert Dale Owen, *Threading My Way,* pp. 303–4.

39 "would be utter madness . . ." FT/JGP, May 1827, GPC.

39 "It would be especially impossible . . ." S/JGP, 11 February 1827, GPC. Sismondi's letters to Julia, part of the GPC, are a particularly valuable source for studying male attitudes toward achieving and domesticated women in the early nineteenth century.

40 "The only thing . . ." S/JGP, 24 April 1827, GPC.

40 "I had been led . . ." RCM/HG & JGP, 2 June 1827, GPC.

40 "this temptation . . ." S/HG & JGP, Spring 1827, GPC.

40 "he blamed Owen . . ." S/JGP, 11 February, 24 April, and 12 June 1827, GPC.

41 "even for the sake . . . " L/JGP, 14 June 1827, GPC.

41 "this so very cruel silence . . ." L/JGP, 14 June 1827, GPC.

41 "You will readily conceive . . ." CW/HG & JGP, 6 July 1827, GPC.

41 "six-seven days . . ." FW postscript, CW/HG & JGP, 6 July 1827, GPC.

42 "I cannot torment . . ." S/HG, 8 August 1827, GPC.

42 "Camilla Wright informed . . ." Waterman, *Frances Wright,* pp. 114 ff.

43f. "her sister alone . . ." James Mylne to HG & JGP, 12 August 1827, GPC.

44 "If they (the Chinese) . . ." FW/HG & JGP, 17 August 1827, GPC.

45 "As the daughter . . ." FW to Mary Shelley, 22 August 1827, in Florence A. Marshall, *The Life and Letters of Mary Shelley,* pp. 168–71.

45 "Our circle already . . ." FW to Mary Shelley, 22 August 1827, in Marshall, *Shelley.*

46f. "The memory of my mother . . ." Mary Shelley to FW, 12 September 1827, copy in JGP's hand, GPC.

48 "Always to support . . ." FW/HG & JGP, October 1827, GPC.

48 "I do want one . . ." FW to Mary Shelley, 15 September 1827, in Marshall, *Shelley,* pp. 172–4.

48 "A delicate nursling . . ." FW to Mary Shelley, 15 September 1827, in Marshall, *Shelley.*

49 "December 1826 brought me . . ." Georg Heinrich Pertz, Memoir, GPC.

50 "Don't be frightened . . ." FT/JGP, 17 May 1827, GPC.

50 "We had never spoken . . ." Georg Heinrich Pertz, Memoir, GPC. Dr. Pertz's recollection is confused; there is no character by this name in the play.

50 "I *think* he will . . ." JGP/S, 3 September 1827, GPC.

51 "I have no sort of doubt . . ." FW/JGP, 30 August and 26 December 1827, GPC.

52 "Affectionate disposition . . ." MG/JGP, 26 October 1827, GPC.

53 "It seems to me that ..." S/JGP, 13 January 1828, GPC.

53 "Mr. Owen has much ..." JGP/S, 3 September 1827, GPC.

53 "Oh! that you were here ..." JGP/S, 3 September 1827, GPC.

53 "I see by your letter ..." S/JGP, 9 September 1827, GPC.

54 "I cannot bear to think ..." FW/HG, Autumn 1827, GPC.

56 "You know who ..." FT/JGP, 7 October 1827, GPC.

56 "Will it be possible ..." FT/HG & JGP, 7 October 1827, GPC.

57 "You have long known ..." Charles Wilkes to JGP, 15 October 1827, GPC.

57 "That Camilla Wright ..." Charles Wilkes to JGP, 15 October 1827, GPC.

58 "With such opinions ..." Charles Wilkes to JGP, 15 October 1827, GPC.

58 "Will wonders never cease! ..." MG/JGP, 31 October 1827, GPC.

58 "Dear love ..." FW to Mary Shelley, 4 November 1827, in Marshall, *Shelley.*

59 "These unhappy women ..." S/JGP, 1827, GPC.

CHAPTER THREE

The Transition

Venerable are letters, infinitely brave, forlorn, and lost. Life would split asunder without them. . . . These lace our days together and make of life a perfect globe.

VIRGINIA WOOLF, **Jacob's Room**

M y dearest Julia,
Your letters are so valuable to us, that I would not run any risk of their being lost or delayed.

HARRIET GARNETT, **10 Nov. 1830**

NASHOBA WOULD prove an important touchstone for all the women of this circle in the matters of self-definition and occupation. For each of them, it was the pathway into a new life. Frances Wright had been the initiator, conceiving the experiment and working hard for its realization. Her labors in the colony made her into a managerial woman, supervising her male co-workers, female associates, and also the slaves. Perhaps the better to convince everyone of her efficiency, she wore male clothes; she became aggressive and direct, and learned that thought could be on the spot translated into effective action. Nashoba was the key to her life, making her activist, rebel, leader. At once, she abandoned the kind of writing she had done earlier—plays, poems, a travel account—and poured her energy into pamphlets, speeches, articles, and other polemical works which better projected her own insistent voice into a world always somewhat sluggishly out of step with her fervent reformer's zeal. Her colony, testing the ideas of slave emancipation and free love, was also her call to women to carve out a meaningful area of activity for themselves. Alas, it was also the cause of her sister's eventual destruction. For Camilla Wright, more than for anyone else connected with Nashoba, the experiment was a disastrous plunge into a way of life the rough, unsettling freedoms of which, together with her almost abject devotion to her sister, made a fatal combination.

The Garnetts, themselves raised in America, had been sorely tempted to join in the work. Harriet dallied with the idea for over a year, but finally drew back out of deference to her mother's opposition and dread of losing her own "respectability" through association with the increasingly radical experiment.

This timidity and fear of the opinion of others would prove hampering factors throughout her life. Nashoba was but the first moment in a life which would never bear its full potential, and yet would find equally important sources of satisfaction in subsequent relationships with other women, and in the care of her aging mother and valetudinarian sister.

Julia, because of her marriage, was, of course, no longer considering participation in Nashoba. Indeed, just as the others were landing in America, she was beginning that preparation for motherhood which she had often been told was the noblest function of women. She would be quite unready for the way it would involve her total physical being over the next several years, as she bore children and recovered from the various ordeals surrounding her pregnancies. In weekly letters, Julia's mother delivered the advice common to the age, but somewhat new to Julia, whose own life seemed already alarmingly secondary to that of the child she carried within. "Do not overwalk yourself this spring, for I have always heard and believe the truth that it is fatiguing for the constitution of a young married woman and will prevent the accomplishment of your wishes." In these communications from Mrs. Garnett to Julia, a sense of restriction abounds. When Julia protested, her mother scolded: "Confinement is nothing when you consider the object of it and you have in your good husband everything that is kind and consoling." Repeatedly, Mrs. Garnett importuned her daughter to "be content to remain on your sopha," and not to "weed or plant in your little garden."

Mrs. Garnett's choice of image, though referring literally to Julia's small backyard in Hanover, nevertheless resonates symbolically. For Julia, there must be no more cultivation of her own spaces, no more sowing of her own seeds, no more tending of her own plants, in wild, outside territories, where one could look up and dream of escape from the confines of life. Julia must stay indoors, and cultivate that domestic region which was now her allotted portion. Of the women in this circle, only those who seized the Nashoba moment and went to plant in gardens in the new world would escape the narrow domestic role which was even now becoming more rigidly prescribed for women of this class. All the members of this circle, perhaps because they shared backgrounds which provided them with a recollection of potential freedoms, were consciously or unconsciously restless in that domestic sphere which was increasingly their proper place.

In making their various choices about Nashoba—though the colony itself was really irrelevant, lasting not even a year—they located the place where the diverging road made "all the difference." Harriet had settled down in Paris with her mother to the salon life and the single state. Julia was in Hanover, chafing at the monotony of motherhood, writing Sismondi, who consoled her with the accepted wisdom of the age. Despite the "tinge of melancholy that they say pregnancy produces," there was no question but that Julia would find happiness in selfless devotion. "Happiness is to be found in these duties so intimate, so close, that they permit of no hesitation, and the sacrifice of oneself to another, first to one's husband, then to one's children, is made without one's even thinking of it." The other friends were off on a voyage of discovery into the unknown. Soon, the Wrights were in Nashoba, Fanny at the brink of a career as activist, reformer, public lecturer. Mrs. Trollope was heading for Cincinnati, beginning a long and strenuous career as a writer, though no one, least of all herself, could have foreseen such a future in 1827. The fortuitous circumstances that had linked their lives thus far were now unravelling, yet, paradoxically, a new kind of sisterhood was about to start in earnest, as they began to write the letters which would tell their individual stories, bind them together, and provide the materials for a history of women like themselves.

Their separation was the start of a massive correspondence, centering around Julia, and preserved by her for twenty-five years, treasured as a sign of a vanished, sacred reality existing in no other palpable form. Daily, weekly, monthly, disembodied voices spoke to one another from the sitting rooms which were the focal points of their lives. Fate had destroyed the possibility of that daily intimacy which would have made written communication unnecessary, but these letters have preserved a record of shared inner lives.

Several times during the course of this lifelong correspondence, Julia's sister Harriet begged her to destroy some of the letters, but Julia did not. As the wife of a professional historian who had himself pioneered in publishing original documents as the sole basis for writing history, Julia treated her correspondence as a memorial to the worth of women's lives. Her feelings about it were so strong that upon her death, her husband could think of no finer tribute to her memory than to assemble her own letters and set his youngest son to recopying them. Only Dr. Pertz's remarriage within a year interrupted the proposed task of constructing a monograph of his late wife's life which, given the size of this large collection numbering in the thousands, might have been a prototype of that kind of women's history which Virginia Woolf was still calling for 100 years later. Julia's collection, carefully preserved through three generations of her female descendants, now makes possible the reconstruction of this uniquely feminine world during the first half of the last century.

Letters had always been more a female than a male form of expression. Letters could be written in the midst of life, in spite of interruptions and other tasks. Indeed, they were tiny fragments of life, private, daily, formless, seemingly trivial and unimportant. One did not need a classical education to write them. They found their most proper form in the expression of the self, its development and worth, the opening out of perceptions about what exists and is possible to the individual consciousness. Fanny Burney, with her epistolary novel *Evelina,* was the first to give professional direction to letter writing which had hitherto been a purely amateur medium. The lifelong correspondence of this circle, seen in its totality only by Julia, was a mode of literature which recorded its world, "half created, half perceived," like most writing. It had a plot, the unfolding story of their lives; characters aplenty; few heroes and many heroines, of whom the first was Frances Wright and the last Frances Trollope; a point of view, which was strictly female. Its theme emerged gradually from the many pages of crossed and crisscrossed scrawls: the experience of women was potentially richer and more complex than many of them had even thought.

Julia had sensed the significance of these letters, which bore witness to the worth of women's lives. Later, Virginia Woolf would ask, "What is the worth of a woman?" Where was the mark to measure her achievements? "There are no yard measures," Mrs. Woolf continued, "neatly divided into the fractions of an inch that one can lay against the qualities of a good mother or the devotion of a daughter or the fidelity of a sister or the capacity of a housekeeper." Yet Julia's preservation of this collection of letters makes such measurement possible, for it contains a lifetime's experience of a disparate group of women who reveal their goals, successes, failures, struggles for self-realization, and their manifold searches for meaningful occupation. In these old packets of letters, Julia caught and preserved one group of women's shared awareness of the special challenges of their womanhood. Their experiences and views of it are still of value. Their struggles toward selfhood form part of the pedestal upon which rest any number of subsequent female accomplishments.

REFERENCES

PAGE

64 "Weed or plant . . . " HG&MG/JGP, 8 May 1828, GPC.

65 "Letters had always been more a female than a male form of expression . . ." Duncan Crowe, in *The Victorian Woman* (p. 62), describes the middle-class woman's letter-writing as an important means of "passing the time" which accelerated in the Victorian period because of significant changes in the British postal organization. The testimony of many Victorian women also confirms the importance of correspondence in their lives. Cf. Sally Coles Stevenson, *Victoria, Albert, and . . . Mrs. Stevenson,* p. 200. Virginia Woolf in *A Room of One's Own* (p. 65) cited letter-writing as a permissible activity for women, one which could be pursued without calling attention to the self and even while being interrupted. "A woman might write letters while she was sitting by her father's sick-bed. She could write them by the fire whilst the men talked without disturbing them."

66 "neatly divided . . ." Woolf, *A Room,* p. 89.

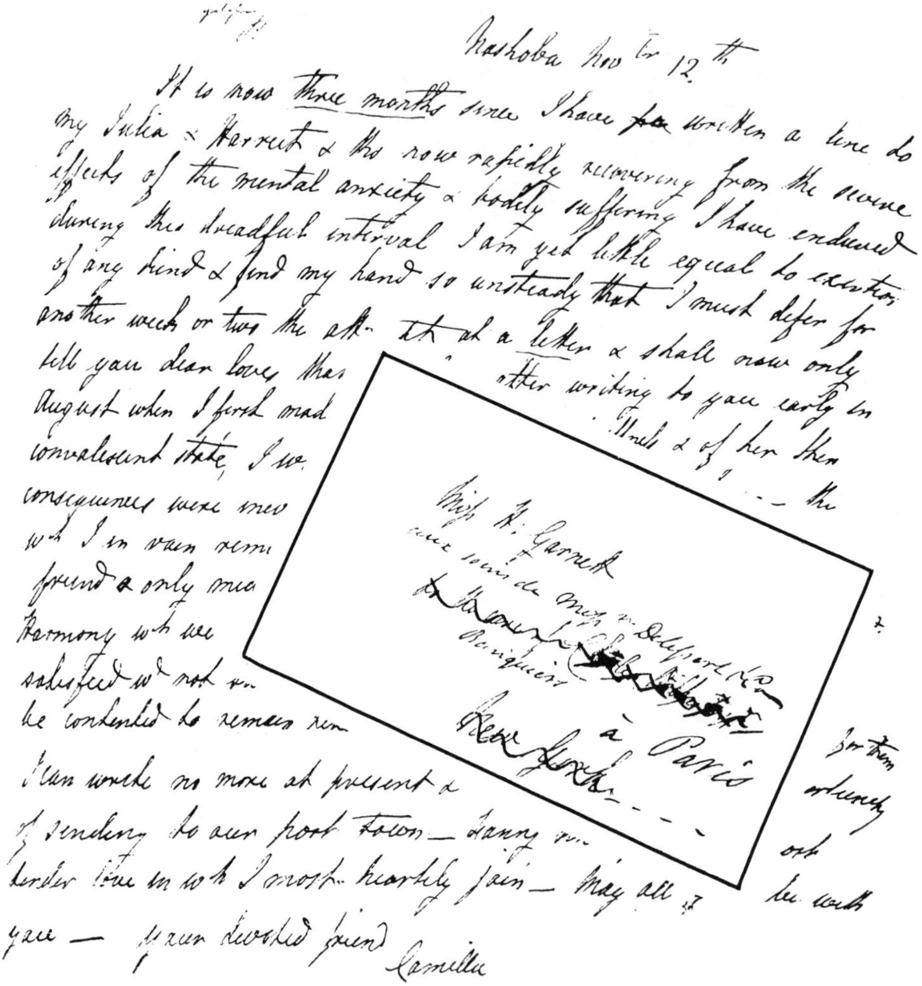

Letter of Camilla Wright to the Garnetts

CHAPTER FOUR

Camilla Wright

*Y*ou know full as well as I do the value of sisters' affections to each other; there is nothing like it in this world.

CHARLOTTE BRONTË

*W*hen I first saw my sister it was as she was lifted out of her crib, at a fortnight old. . . . The passionate fondness I felt for her from that moment has been unlike any thing else I have felt in life.

HARRIET MARTINEAU, **Autobiography**

*M*uch more do I grieve for poor Camilla, the victim of dreams that are not hers.

SISMONDI **to Julia Garnett Pertz, 8 March 1829**

The destruction awaiting Camilla Wright had already seeded itself in the moist Tennessee forest during the long, lonely, sultry summer of Fanny's absence. Cam's life had changed radically between the last day of May, when her sister had been carried on a stretcher to a ship bound for Europe, and this Christmas day 1827, when she awaited that sister, now strong, fully recuperated, and heading up the Mississippi River for Nashoba.

Remarkably, considering her expressed views upon marriage, Camilla had recently wed Richeson Whitby, without asking even the advice of any of her close women friends or that sister upon whom she had ever leaned for guidance. Why? The question still teases, for there are only suppositions and statements after the fact, by way of explanation. As in some modern novel, where the truth lies in the totality of the fragmented points of view, the characters in this story had each a slightly different version of that perplexing event.

Fanny Wright described her sister's unexpected marriage as a love match, arising primarily from emotional attachment and mutual respect. In this version, composed for General Lafayette's benefit, the union occasioned general rejoicing among the whole Nashoba community.

Previous to our arrival, Cam and Whitby, in conformity with her feelings, went thro' the form of marriage in its simplest form as practised in this country—while he renounces in an attested paper to all legal claims on her fortune & person, pronouncing them substantially unjust. He had long been attached to her & the intimate knowledge of his excellence & continued interchange of kindness and affection which their association here had induced ended by inspiring her with similar feelings. This connexion, by making their happiness, increases that of all the family.

Fanny expressed no criticism, either of her sister's choice or of the timing of the wedding which necessarily excluded her or of the decision to marry at all, so at odds with the stated principles of Nashoba. Her rendition, in which the faithful suitor, renouncing all claim on his beloved's fortune, wins her over gradually by dint of long service and faithful devotion, could have come from the pages of a popular Victorian novel.

Mrs. Stone, the Garnetts' eldest sister, one of whose sons had been friendly with Whitby, saw the union as Cam's reluctant concession to respectability. She had heard rumors that Cam had lived with Whitby for five months previous to the marriage and perhaps even suspected a pregnancy. Mrs. Stone told Julia, "Camilla at last went through the marriage ceremony, a small tribute to pay the opinions of the world, even if she thought it erroneous." Mrs. Stone's version was more uncomplicated than those of the Wrights' male mentors.

Lafayette, despite Fanny's assurances, was baffled, and wondered aloud "whether Camilla has married with the new or the old ideas of the conjugal union." Mr. Wilkes saw the matter through banker's eyes, and was encouraged by Whitby's apparent disinterest in Cam's money. He thought that Camilla "had still done better than her sister," but he continued, "I can hardly think she can be happy, altho' she says she is. He has given up all claims to her property, which he resigns wholly to her, which, at least, shows that her fortune was not his object." Sismondi, whose information came from the Garnetts, saw Camilla's situation as a dramatic event in one of his cultural histories. He wondered: "What is poor Camilla doing, ill-married, I fear, & surrounded by beasts and by savage men." Only in their bewilderment were they all in agreement.

Those who knew Whitby even slightly had little good to say of him. Mrs. Trollope, who lived ten days at Nashoba, described him as a "surly brute." She told Lafayette of her pity for Camilla, "with her best friend or companion but a coarse minded, uneducated husband." He had come from a society of Shakers in Kentucky, and, having left behind him that devotion to a life of celibacy which is a mark of the sect, devoted himself instead to order, regularity, and system, as long as those commodities lasted at Owen's settlement. He had proved reliable enough to have been made Commissary, a responsible post. Before long, disgusted with the growing chaos, he left Harmony at about the same time as Camilla did, bringing with him his talent for efficiency and perhaps that resolute grimness which Dickens later noticed in the Shaker community at New Lebanon. Perhaps his time of abstinence from earthly pleasures had endured too long. Together with his disenchantment with New Harmony, it combined to make him a convert to the Nashoba system. That the amiable, fun-loving, and cultured Mrs. Trollope found him unattractive, is not surprising. More enigmatic is Cam's response to him.

During the period of Fanny's absence, Cam had tried to fashion herself on the model of the beloved Fanny, accepting on principle her sister's ideas on all subjects, among which was that sexual relations need involve only the free choice of partners. As she waited alone for her sister's return, the constitutionally dependent Cam felt the need for a companion to lean upon. When she found such a person in Whitby, to deny him sexual favors would have been difficult at best. Surrounded by the wilderness and the slaves, perhaps she found her heart ready to beat in time with accents she had never heard before. Seduction? Rape? The promise of physical safety in return for sexual favors? Whatever the applied force, she plunged into the mysteries of a relationship which ended in the swift union between a delicate and lovely Englishwoman and a rough backwoodsman. If only Hervieu had posed them for a sketch! Perhaps he could have captured the key to the marriage in some facial expression or gesture. All that remains are guarded words.

Cam's own explanation to the Garnetts is exceedingly sparse and formal:

> The tidings of my union with our associate Richeson Whitby will ere this have reached you & no doubt after the perusal of my philippic against matrimony, will not a little have surprized you. I shall only observe that the circumstances which induced me to conform to the legal ceremony of marriage were of a very peculiar nature & such as it were impossible to explain by letter. Should you my loved Harry persevere in your project of joining us in our forest home you shall then if you care to hear it learn all the particulars connected therewith. In the mean time it will I feel assured please you to learn that I am happy in my connection with one who shares all my views and opinions & whose many admirable qualities and devoted attachment have endeared him to my heart.

Even given the nineteenth-century habit of reticence, Cam's letter implies an unwilling entrance to the marital state. "Induced me to conform to the legal ceremony of marriage"—would Cam have spoken of her momentous choice in such stilted phrases, every word of which suggests reluctance, or, at best, acquiescence? Her friend she addresses as "my loved Harry," and her husband as "our associate Richeson Whitby," who possessed only vague and perfunctory "admirable qualities" and "devoted attachment." In this letter to her most intimate friends, Cam's language was no emotional match for the heartfelt rhetoric she had always used for her female friends and Fanny.

The married life of the Whitbys was short and turbulent. United sometime before November 1827, they were immediately struck down by malaria during most of that winter. Mrs. Trollope, who saw them upon her arrival, reported that both Cam and Whitby looked "miserably ill." By March, they had left for New Harmony to recuperate in that healthier climate. Perhaps, too, Whitby thought to separate his new wife from the compelling presence of her sister, with whom he now had to compete for Cam's affections. He soon would learn that Cam's deepest attachment was to Fanny. Cam could never live for long separated from Fanny. As she told Harriet upon her arrival at Harmony, "Nothing else but [reasons of health] could have induced me to leave the dear lamb in her present solitude." By May, having thrown off the effects of fever, Cam was pining to return to Nashoba. As she told Julia, "We have executed our errand and are now returning, longing much to be again in our own dear quiet woods and agreeing that no one who ever lived in an association of suitable friends can ever live out of it."

But in her resolution to return to life at Nashoba despite the rigors of climate and its impending decline, she no longer wished to involve others. She ceased to invite her friends to share her fate, and told the Garnetts: "There was a time, sweet Harriet, when I should have said, come & share a sister's home in Nashoba but that once pleasing vision is ended & I find myself again about to be launched into a world as yet uncertain whither I may turn my steps." Nashoba was in trouble, and it looked as though Fanny would soon be leaving her residence there. The community had been poorly planned and administered. Financially, it had been a disaster. In the first year, the plantation produced $150 worth of corn, $25 worth of fodder, and 3000 pounds of cotton which sold at about $60. Furthermore, its radical ideas had made its members outcasts in early nineteenth-century America. By the end of 1827, the Wrights had conceded the sole solution for slaves would be emigration and transportation abroad, once the free black had learned skills and worked out his price.

Fanny had now taken over editorship of the New Harmony *Gazette,* believing that such activities were more worthwhile than her slave colony, providing, as they did, a means "not only for promulgating and more fully explaining her views to the public but of greatly augmenting the number of subscribers" to the paper. She had also started a career on the lecture circuit, and was enormously pleased with her success. She planned a trip to Cincinnati, to deliver a "course of public lectures." Cam described her sister's steps with her usual pride.

> The prejudice regarding her opinions was there [Cincinnati] as elsewhere so strong that her first lecture was but thinly crowded & scarcely one female form was to be descried. The 2nd the house was crowded, and at the 3rd upwards of 500 individuals were obliged to return without accommodations. . . . The whole town was in a state of excitement: men and women crowded to listen to the heretical doctrines of the "Priestess of Infidelity" as the priests style her, who warned their flocks against the dangers awaiting them, but all in vain. Having delivered four lectures she was publicly requested to repeat them, which she did with renewed success & increased interest. . . .

Cam's lengthy account ended with an outburst of praise: "I wonder at her transcendent talents as a public speaker and almost admitted her eloquence to be irresistible."

The conflict in women between personal goals and the utopian dream had re-emerged, this time in Fanny Wright herself. Nashoba was a losing cause. Its founder's ideal of free love had been the crucial destructive factor. For the ignorant slaves whose economic and intellectual equality she had wanted to establish in the eyes of white society, it was a costly and unnecessary luxury in the raison d'etre of the colony. Scandal and neglect quickly did their work. Soon only a handful of founders was left.

At once, Cam joined with others in persuading Fanny to "devote the six ensuing months to visiting the larger cities of the Union and thereby more effectually trying the temper of the times." Aspiring to a leadership role as mover of men's minds, she was ready to admit that her strenuous communal quest for a new world at Nashoba was over. Henceforth, she would work alone in the broad public area. Henceforth, she would enter the world of men, using the *Gazette* editorship and the lecturer's platform as her arena. The round table of women had failed to materialize and produce the desired results. It was Cam who rationalized Fanny's decision to abandon the experiment in the name of which so much money, time, and human effort had been spent. She wrote:

> All hopes of an association at Nashoba being ended she thought it would be a poor appropriation of her talents to sit down & devote herself to the emancipation of a few slaves, besides its being an employment for which she was altogether & in every respect incompetent. It was therefore her intention to seek an individual who would undertake that charge.

By November 1828, Fanny turned the management of Nashoba over to Whitby. Part of the debris in this first step in the dismantling of Nashoba was Cam herself. Devoted as ever to Fanny, she immediately made plans to follow her sister and leave Whitby behind, despite the fact that she was now carrying his child.

> As I had from the first told him, I again repeated that no circumstances & no tie that I should ever form in life could separate me from Fanny & that wherever she resided there I should be also. With this prospect before him he nevertheless decided to remain here & superintend the property at least for the space of one year from next Xmas, during which period Fanny would have time to make other arrangements if required.

Given such a choice, Whitby had a clear decision. Despite his "devoted attachment" to Cam, their union was over. Fanny, impatient to start her new work in New York, had already left, while Cam remained behind with Whitby temporarily. She explained her future plans to the Garnetts:

> I in the mean time shall remain here till next spring when I shall expect to learn her decision as regards her future destination & my own. As I look to be confined in January, to reconcile Fanny to leaving me alone at such time, I promised her to remove into Memphis to a most commodious little dwelling. . . . I shall have my good friend Mlle Lolotte . . . and from her I shall receive a mother's care and attention.

That a sister's care was not forthcoming troubled Mrs. Trollope in Cincinnati, where she had now established residence. Cam had written Mrs. Trollope of the recent changes, and she in turn relayed her version of events to the Garnetts:

> Poor Camilla is lying in at Memphis—with no friend near her, and I should think with very indifferent medical attendance. I could not but feel a pang for her, when I contrasted the circumstances under which she had become a mother with those of . . . Julia! Poor devoted Camilla! Fanny at least feels triumph and enjoyment . . . but Camilla, with her best friend or companion but a coarse minded, uneducated husband, must be wretched.

Then, there was further news.

> Since writing the above, I have been told that Camilla is to join Fanny at New York, as soon as possible after her confinement—and that her husband is to be

left at Nashoba with the charge of the slaves, and an allowance from his wife of $500 per annum.

Those who knew the sisters well feared the consequences of Cam's decision to "marry" herself to Fanny. Sismondi saw the sisters as inhabitants of different and conflicting worlds. While Fanny, with her ever-increasing motion toward the public life, was now far more in her element ("the prodigious activity of her mind could not long adapt itself to retirement"), Cam's situation was different.

> I grieve for poor Camilla, the victim of dreams that are not hers, lost in the deserts without anything to stimulate her, without anything to move her, without the plaudits of the crowd for her domestic sorrows.

He could not resist reminding the Garnetts how narrowly they had escaped such a fate.

> This surprising woman has been on the point of victimizing others who have escaped her. When I first knew you, you were still hesitating as to whether you should not follow her to the banks of the Mississippi, whether you should not confide your whole fortune to her, and now you would have been abandoned in these flooded plains, alone, or would have married men unworthy of you, while she went from town to town preaching strange doctrines.

And in one respect he was right: the more aggressive the woman, the less her need for the protective arms of sisterhood. As Fanny Wright went on to forge her own destiny, she became less concerned for Cam, or for any of the other women of the circle. And, correspondingly, her friends came less and less to regard her as their "ideal" woman. Mrs. Trollope drew back from Fanny Wright, not only because of her own disappointment at Nashoba, but because of her sympathy for Cam. While women wanted women to achieve, they still looked for them to maintain their "feminine" quality of caring for other human beings.

Indeed, the sole description of the circumstances surrounding the birth of Cam's child comes from the warm-hearted Mrs. Trollope, who continued to lament the lonely situation in which Cam had delivered her infant, "in such a place as Memphis, and without the sustaining presence of her sister. Neither was her husband with her. She has given birth to a boy, after great and prolonged suffering. The weakness consequent upon this, has hitherto . . . prevented her joining Fanny at New York." Mrs. Trollope was anxious about

Cam's future, and despite her own troubles, remained concerned about her old friend. She told the Garnetts:

> I would go at any hour or in any weather to embrace her once more. Her fate touches me deeply. I am told that she is separated from her husband, having settled $500 a year on him. They say she is to live at New York with her sister. . . . I have, since I came here, heard such an almost endless variety of lies about F and C. . . . Though of the separation from Mr. Whitby there is no doubt. Poor, poor Camilla! she deserved another fate. Never did I love her so well as during the ten wretched days we passed together at Nashoba. I saw then, that her eyes were opened—That she foresaw her own misery, and also the constant disappointment of Fanny in all her schemes.
>
> But I cannot describe to you how sweetly she behaved under these most bitter feelings. I am *sure* that she would have been a good wife to the surly brute her husband, if he would have let her—but I felt it was impossible she could long exist as his wife. I own I then thought it very likely that her early death might release her from the direful consequences of her blind compliance with her sister's wishes—but I find she has quite recovered her health—will she ever recover her happiness? What shall prevent Whitby from tormenting her? not his virtue I fear. . . . I tremble for her.

As for Fanny, Mrs. Trollope continued, she had bought a church at New York "for the purpose of preaching in it herself." She would feel contented in her situation, but what of Camilla, that too-willing victim of dreams that were not hers?

Sure enough, once Camilla gathered her strength, she packed up her infant and headed up river to Cincinnati, where she visited Mrs. Trollope for two weeks before continuing east to New York to join her sister. Once again, Camilla stood on the brink of being absorbed into her sister's turbulent life.

While Mrs. Trollope worried about Cam, she hoped the occupation of motherhood would save her and maybe Fanny as well. To the Garnetts, she described Cam's visit as well as her hopes for Cam's future.

> This has indeed been a pleasure to me. She is wonderfully recovered in health and in looks since I parted from her at that miserable Nashoba. She is again the sweet, the elegant Camilla I knew in Europe, and the *extreme pleasure* with which I see her again look as she did then, is perhaps a weakness—but it is a weakness that I am almost sure you would both share. Her child is one of very uncommon beauty, and appears in all respects just what a mother could wish. Dear Camilla! Her fate is not a happy one.—but I think her boy will give interest to her life,

and I fondly hope many future years await her more happy than those that have past. When I look at her beautiful babe, I think that perhaps it may wind round Fanny's heart—make her forget her wild schemes of universal improvement, and give the energy of her ardent mind to the welfare of this precious child.

About Cam's marital arrangements, Mrs. Trollope knew little, only "that she is separated from her husband—and I rejoice at it, because I never thought him in any way worthy of her. Whatever may have been the circumstances that led her to form so unsuitable a marriage, or those which have obliged her to break it, I feel sure, that she has been more sinned against than sinning —and that she still deserves all the fond affection that it is so impossible to withhold from her."

Perhaps Mrs. Trollope already suspected some cooling in the Garnetts' attitude toward the Wrights, and feared lest Camilla, who clearly needed the help of her women friends now more than ever, would be twice victimized by her sister's carelessness about reputation and respectability. Mrs. Trollope emphasized her point. "I trust, dearest Julia and Harriet, that you are not separated from her for ever. I am mistaken if she does not look with affection and regret towards Europe, and the dear beings she has left there." Perhaps Cam had told Mrs. Trollope of her hope to find some refuge with the Garnetts. After all, who was left? Mrs. Trollope was in desperate straits, herself adrift, too poor to help, and she too had been somewhat tarnished by her association with Frances Wright. The Garnetts were the only women who could offer refuge, and in a guarded, but still transparent way, she made an appeal on Camilla's behalf.

> Fanny Wright has made herself too unpleasantly conspicuous in New York, for any person so insignificant as myself to venture to brave public opinion by holding intercourse with her—but I do not believe it possible that any circumstances *can* occur which should prevent my seeking the society of Camilla Wright whenever and wherever I could obtain it.

But neither Harriet nor Julia would be as courageously generous in the matter of public association with the Wrights as the less conventional Frances Trollope. For the immediate future, however, there was no problem. Cam proceeded to New York, where by August she was again living with Fanny, once again ready to devote herself unsparingly to her sister's efforts and ideas.

United with Fanny, Cam lost all doubts. Her life began to wind like a two-stemmed vine around her sister and her infant son. Whatever marriage had meant for her, it was in the past now. Whitby was at Nashoba, and she would never live with him again. It was time to look ahead. As Cam told the Garnetts:

> Now that I am once more united to our loved Fanny & that I find her engaged in pursuits so well calculated to promote the cause of human improvement & so well suited to her taste and talents, I begin to feel as though life were not without its solace, nor its evils unmixed with good—and then I am blessed with a lovely boy, who promises to be all that a mother's heart could wish—he is thought greatly to resemble his aunt whose name he bears, and could you look on his large blue eyes beaming with sweetness & intelligence, his broad forehead, his round and dimpled cheeks, you would think with me, that he is much more her child than mine.

As Cam wondered what Julia's boy looked like, she was drawn to make a remarkable speculation.

> We might perhaps discover some . . . points of resemblance between him & my son, more especially if there be any truth in the opinion that the resemblance is through the imagination of the mother, for I feel assured our thoughts were not unfrequently engrossed by the same image.

While one could not deny the biological paternity of a father, one might deemphasize its importance. Camilla, desirous of completely forgetting Whitby and of bonding herself totally with her sister, seemed determined to make her baby at least in part Fanny's. If women could not impregnate women, they could impress them mentally, imprinting their faces, forms, and spirits on new life as well as men, through "the imagination of the mother." Once again infatuated with her sister, she created a fantasy life in which she and Fanny were parents to her child, whom she called, with great significance, Francis. Thus, having shed her unsuitable husband, she sought to create a family group and situation which would, however remotely, resemble the "simple" domesticity of Julia's life and help Cam regularize her own orbit which had grown too complex and unmanageable for the fundamentally conventional young woman.

Yet, in spite of the aura of scandal which surrounded her sister's activities, Cam had remained loyal to Fanny.

> Think not she is destitute of friends and such as are heart & soul devoted to the cause she advocates, that of the amelioration of the condition of man, to be effected by means applicable only to the rising generation whose habits and opinions may be influenced and controlled by a rational and practical system of education.

Fanny had hoped to direct her efforts towards "establishing a plan of national instruction accessible to all classes of society." Her sister, for one, was convinced:

> Her eloquence as a public speaker surpasses all I have ever before heard in man or woman & if life remains to her she will I feel persuaded be the means of effecting a great moral revolution throughout this country.

Once again, Cam was ready to take up her cross at the side of her sister.

Then, suddenly, something terrible happened. Even as Cam concluded her letter of August 1, her infant fell ill. Saving the letter sheets because room remained to write more and because she was suddenly distracted, Cam turned her energies towards nursing her son, but in two weeks' time, he was dead. As she picked up the old letter to add this dreadful news, Cam was once again alone with her sister.

> Alas! Alas! how shall I paint my bitter sorrow and anguish! My son, my lovely babe, who was playing at my feet when I wrote the above, now sleeps in the cold earth while his wretched & bereaved mother yet lives to bewail her irrecoverable loss. A sudden attack of the cholera infantum, connected with teething, terminated fatally on the 11th day during which time every remedy suggested by my own experience in similar complaints, aided by a skillful physician, proved inadequate to surmount the violence of the disease. Fanny returned from her late visit to Boston in the midst of my distress but while I had still hope to see my precious lamb rescued from the impending danger. Indeed, but for her presence and soothing care and tenderness, I should have been bereft of reason or of life by this stroke, so sudden, so severe. Though now somewhat more composed, there are moments in which grief will have its way & my shattered nerves & frame seem to indicate a speedy termination to my sufferings. Can time efface . . . that last moment in which I wiped the death drops from his beautiful brow, and inhaled the parting breath of the precious being, that for seven months had sucked his nourishment from my breast. Oh never! never can I overcome this loss—Oh could you have seen him—his brilliant eye beaming with sweetness & intelligence beyond what is usual at so early an age—his finely developed forehead, which recalled to some of my friends the busts of Napoleon Buonaparte, you would not marvel at the hopes that I cherished for a being apparently endowed with nature's choicest gifts & placed in circumstances in every way calculated to favor their development.

Fanny added a brief postscript which sharply contrasted with the effusive, even unbalanced outpourings of Camilla, illustrating the differences between the two accounts, one so full of lyric emotion and the other so cool and even condescending towards such emotion. Fanny congratulated Julia upon her baby: "May you be more happy in it than has been our poor Camilla in her little creature of beauty and promise. It is sad to centre the affections too strongly & closely in beings so fragile, yet how to help it!" Yet she had learned the secret, having not, for many years now, centered her affections in fragile humanity, preferring instead the undying idealism of a cause.

By November, Cam's grief over her child's loss had not slackened; she spoke of the event as having "so embittered each hour of my existence, that every avenue of pleasure or satisfaction in life seems closed to me forever." As she admitted, "time has done but little to assuage my grief, or ease my sorrowing heart, nor is it surprizing that my health should have suffered severely in the conflict." Now, in her despair, she turned not to Fanny, but to Julia.

> Often, in my soul's desolation have my thoughts turned to thee sweet Julia, as one who could sympathise with my affliction and pour the balm of comfort into my wounded spirit.

Indeed, but for that strong sense of duty which compelled so many such women to persist in intolerable situations, she would long ago have left.

> I had perhaps sought relief to my bereaved heart, in a change of scene, & a recurrence to ties & affections which however broken and interrupted, yet are ever present in my mind & endeared to my heart by many precious and cherished recollections.

Camilla was ready to leave the sister she had idolized since she was ten. But how to do it? Where to go? Where to find shelter and help? She asked Julia:

> Would it afford you pleasure to see an old friend, for *ten years* have now elapsed since we first met in this city? or is your heart so filled with engrossing objects of interest and tenderness, that the place I once held there, is mine no longer?

Fanny had already left Cam alone in New York. She was attending to the final disposition of the Nashoba slaves in company with M. Phiquepal, who would go with her to Haiti, whence the slaves would find a home. He, "whose experience and familiar acquaintance in early life with the west India Islands renders him a valuable assistant in her present undertaking," was yet more important, for in a short time (1831), Fanny would marry him, acting in opposition to her principles for the sake of the child she was carrying. No

doubt Cam knew of her sister's "attachment" to Phiquepal, and was anticipating the time when she would be once again left alone.

She was now living in Fanny's main residence on the East River, five miles
from New York. She described both the place and her function in it to Julia.

> The house is large and commodious, sufficiently so as to comprise the printing
> office for the Enquirer—as you must imagine the household arrangements of
> such an establishment require an assiduous & careful superintendance, & in as
> far as the state of my mind and health permit I have endeavored to discharge
> the office, but should Fanny be successful in engaging a valuable person with
> whom we are acquainted, & who has lately left her situation in the family of
> Mr. Owen at Harmony, I shall be released from my present responsible situation
> as housekeeper & consequently at liberty to consult my feelings as to my future
> destination.

Her metamorphosis had been long and painful: from devoted sister, friend,
amanuensis, nurse, and companion, Cam had become domestic help. It was
clearly time for her to leave, and she now made a direct request of Julia.

> Give me your *free and candid* opinion as to the possibility of my taking passage
> from hence to Hamburg, should circumstances at some future period incline me
> to do so.

Making no further allusion to specific plans, she asked Julia to direct whatever reply she made to Camilla alone, thus marking visibly the separation
which now existed between the sisters.

Camilla had directed her appeal for help to Julia and not Harriet for two
reasons. First, of the two sisters, Julia had always been the more warmly
compassionate one, especially in her relationships with her female friends. It
was Julia who, despite her marriage, had retained the stronger ties to sisterhood through her letters. Slower than Harriet to condemn, she had ever
remained loyal to persons, even while disapproving of actions. Even more
important, Julia was a married woman, and no doubt Camilla thought, able
with a greater degree of impunity, to offer shelter to one whom the world had
condemned. Harriet, as a single woman, had to be more circumspect, lest her
own chances for "moving in society" be jeopardized. Then, too, old Mrs.
Garnett had long disapproved of Fanny Wright. Even in the old days in
America, when the Wrights had first come and captivated the girls and John
Garnett, Mrs. Garnett had remained aloof, perhaps slightly jealous of the
ardent young stranger who had so easily won the hearts of all her family.

Afterwards, when Fanny began preaching against marriage, Mrs. Garnett knew that her first instincts had been correct, and that association with the Wrights was to be avoided. With Harriet still living with her mother, Camilla showed good judgment in addressing her appeal to Julia. What she did not reckon upon was Harriet's fierce protectiveness of Julia.

In making her decision, Julia consulted Harriet and her mentor Sismondi, writing them both of Cam's hope to settle in Germany. Sismondi's predictable reply arrived first.

> Poor Camilla! What a cruel fate! What a terrible responsibility rests on her poor sister, and makes her still more unhappy. It was because she attached so little meaning to marriage, that she left her exposed to the risk of a marriage unworthy of her and that she did not [give] them the support, the patience that might have saved her, no longer united to the man she had chosen, near her child. The death of that child, which has robbed her of all her strength, is made more tragic by the fact that she spoke of it with such hope at the beginning of the same letter.

Anticipating Henry James' later query ("What are we to do with all these presumptuous girls?"), Sismondi blamed Cam's situation upon her sister's impudence and ambition, upon her deliberate departure from the permitted sphere of womanly activity.

> O women, who can shed so much charm and happiness on life, when you add to your distinguished talents, modesty and submissiveness of spirit, avoid the presumptuousness of wishing to lead and reform the world! The task is beyond your powers, its whole organization is beyond your span. Perhaps it is beyond ours also . . . but however short our view may be, we still see more than you do, and a man would never have committed all the imprudences that FW did, especially a man who stood above his sex, as she stands above her own.

Peripherally, he glanced at the problem of Cam's resettlement, which in his view, was as complex as if she were returning to another planet.

> I have no doubt that the time is coming when the two sisters will be disabused of their illusions at the same time, and then how much more wretched will they not be? For the moment I wish they had some asylum, far from the public with whom they have fallen out, far from the hostilities that they have aroused, and that they consider today to be some sort of triumph. If poor Fanny were to bring her sister back to Paris, perhaps it would still be the country in the world in which she would find herself best situated.

But wishing she would find some "asylum" in Paris was not the same thing as suggesting that Julia provide one in Hanover.

Harriet was torn between two loyalties, both to women she had loved deeply. But while sympathetic, she never hesitated in her instinct to protect Julia. Harboring Cam would clearly jeopardize Julia's "respectability" in stuffy Hanover, where wives did not have even the amount of freedom they had in England. Not trusting Julia to refuse, Harriet volunteered to write the letter which would strike the final blow to Camilla's hopes.

> I will write to poor Cam, as if I had not seen [Julia's letter] and speak of the difficulties of the language—of the cold—of the aristocracy—of your husband's situation—all as objections to *our* living at Hanover. This I think I can do better than you—for her coming to you would not do. Poor Cam, she might better come to Paris or go to Scotland. The Millars could receive her without danger to themselves—you could not. I think I act as you would wish me to & is most prudent for you. . . . You will feel the impossibility of your receiving our poor Cam. Alas, how deeply must we deplore this. My heart bleeds for her. I will make the general write to her uncle to invite her to come to him. She might keep house for him & take care of the good old man and her situation there would be respectable.

Although Harriet was an intelligent and generally sympathetic woman, and in most cases a faithful friend, she was not ready to risk social ostracism, either for herself or for her sister, to protect a friend. Respectability was one of the limits of sisterhood, and the strongest of women's chains, one they repeatedly helped forge themselves.

Before she received the letter which was to end forever her dream of returning to the circle of friends, Cam wrote again to Harriet, opening herself up with new honesty. For the first time she permitted herself to complain of her sister. It is sad to think of her painful confession, written even while Harriet's clumsy rejection was on the way.

> Yes, dear Harriet, to your bosom I will confide the painful truth—the sister— the friend with whom I have suffered much & with whom I have sympathised still more is no longer the sharer of my thoughts & feelings & only ceased to be so from my discovery that *I shared not hers.* And yet strange as it may seem I have never at any period of my life seen her so apparently happy & contented with her situation and prospects than at present—her time fully occupied, her thought engaged by pursuits which are certainly congenial to her tastes—& which seem admirably qualified to exhibit & usefully to employ her extraordinary talents. It is not surprising that all minor objects of interest—which once sufficed to fill her heart should now be lessened if not altogether lost in the midst

of the wide sea whereon she is now embarked—the regret therefore which I may have felt was purely selfish & has already in a great measure yielded to the satisfaction which I experience in seeing her engaged in a cause worthy of her talents & which I consider as all important to the welfare of generations yet unborn—& as the only means that can effectually save this country from running the mad career of all nations that have preceded her.

Even while she was aware that she was no longer important to Fanny, she recognized the fulfillment of her sister in her work. Undeceived, but unwilling to hurl recriminations at the sister who had grown beyond her, Cam reminded Harriet that she herself attached no blame to Fanny for the impending separation of their lives. The dream of a static sisterhood had been theirs, not Fanny's.

And let us recall dearest Harriet that at the time when we saw F surrounded by a circle of admiring & adoring friends *she was not happy*—there was a yearning after something which was wanting to fill her mind and give full exercise to her uncommon powers and energies—this she has now attained & I repeat that she now appears to enjoy greater tranquility of mind, more equal spirits & better health than I have ever known at any period of her life.

Forwarding this letter to Julia, Harriet added a note that Uncle Mylne's house would provide "her safest & best refuge—for I cannot wish her to go to Hanover." If he were unwilling, the Millars might be asked. As she told Julia: "Her situation in New York must be a very painful one & is a very exposed one, as she can have no respectable female friends." When the Millars eventually sent a letter of invitation ("she says her house and her arms are always open to Fanny and Camilla"), Cam declined, having done, one supposes, with the help of female friends forever.

The correspondence of Fanny Wright and her female friends had long since drawn to a close. From the first, she had been wary of the female impulse to ground life upon the "diamond sparks of affection." Instead, she had rooted herself firmly, often ruthlessly, in work and external goals. In the classic balance between love and work, women had ever emphasized the former. As Fanny Wright did not, the women around her increasingly characterized her manner as "masculine." Mrs. Trollope had been the first to note this change in Fanny, when she saw her lecturing in Cincinnati. "Every time I see her I am struck by the increase of that dry, cold, masculine dictatorial manner that has been growing upon her since she commenced her public lectures - Oh, how unlike the Fanny of former days! In Camilla's manner, if there be a change, it is for the better—she is indeed a lovely woman."

Throughout the rest of the summer 1830, the Garnetts heard no more from Cam who surely felt the rebuff deeply. She was not the woman to ask twice for help. The events preceding her eventual return to Europe in the fall with her sister are shrouded in mystery. All at once, the Garnetts and other friends heard that the Wrights had returned. Old Mrs. Garnett told Julia:

> The Miss Wrights are arrived in England. I am sorry to say, this is all we know of them or their plans. It is said [Frances] could not longer remain in New York —so strongly was the public opinion against her.

Both Mr. Wilkes and General Lafayette confirmed the reports. Harriet wrote Julia with thinly veiled concern: "How very strange this seems! I cannot understand what their plans are—nor what to wish as regards myself." Obviously, she was torn, half wanting to hear from them again, half worrying what she would do if she did. Finally, when the expected letter did not materialize, Harriet wrote to Fanny, who was in Paris, to ask for Cam's location. When it came, the reply was disappointing. Harriet told Julia:

> I have received one letter from F.W., but a letter that gave me no pleasure or I should sooner have made known its contents to you; it is so cold, so changed from her former letters that I have not had courage to reply to it; she says Camilla was well and traveling with friends in the south of France—that she shall return to America in the spring but intends returning again to Europe to prosecute studies she can only continue in France.

Harriet was careful to conceal her writings from her mother, and concluded her letter with a warning: "Do not take notice of what I now say in your answer to me."

But inevitably, old Mrs. Garnett found out about the reopening of the correspondence, and for a time, the household was thrown into mild turmoil, confirming Harriet's fears about her mother's reaction to any resumption of relationship with the infamous Wright sisters. In Harriet's next letter to Julia, Mrs. Garnett refused to add her usual postscript, as she explained, preferring to write her own letter; she threatened that should Harriet invite either of the Wrights to Geneva, she would immediately leave the house, thus allying herself with the cry that females be "respectable." She told Julia, in the one private letter she ever wrote her daughter, "I never will resume any intercourse with either sister."

After finding the address through other means, Harriet finally wrote Cam, but all at once there was no longer any need for concern. At the age of thirty-five, Camilla Wright was dead, in a strange country, in the company of casual friends, with neither the beloved sister by her side, nor any of the circle of friends with whom she had corresponded across her brief lifetime. Separated from her husband, her infant son dead, estranged from her nearest relatives, she died absolutely alone. Harriet reported the event to Julia on March 25, 1831:

> We have lost our poor Camilla and bitterly do I lament her death, altho' little happiness in life seemed to await her. . . . I wrote to her about a month ago enclosing my letter to Fanny who had never sent me her address—Alas! when that letter arrived from the South, she had hired an apartment by herself, not with Fanny, who remains with Mr. Phiquepal, and the 4th day after her arrival she expired, probably of inflammation, which she was always subject to. I have heard from the general, who tells me all happiness is over for Fanny, who intended to make France her home. . . . Poor Fanny! would I were near her at this trying moment. I know all you will feel, but I wish I were with you: on this subject you alone can sympathise with me.

Poor Harriet! Afraid to display her emotions even before her mother, she poured them out in her letters to Julia. Several times, Mrs. Garnett referred to Harriet's depression (no doubt in part precipitated by guilt) following Camilla's death. A month later, she was telling Julia: "Harriet is rather out of spirits. The death of poor Camilla is very shocking—and we know Harriet does not possess the temper of looking on the bright side of circumstances."

Two weeks later, Harriet received a "very kind letter from my dear Frances Wright," indicating the intention to make France her home. In the United States, at least from Mrs. Trollope's report, Frances Wright had already passed from the public eye. From Alexandria, Virginia, at the home of Anna Maria Garnett Stone, Mrs. Trollope had written Julia:

> How easily do the wonders of a day pass away! Last year I hardly ever looked at a paper without seeing long and repeated mention of Miss Wright. Her eloquence, and her mischief, her wisdom & her folly—her strange principles, & her no principles—were discussed without ceasing. Now her name appears utterly forgotten. If you mention her, the answer begins with "oh—the woman that made such a fuss at N.Y.? I don't know what's become of her, I expect she's dead" or "That joke is over" & so the subject is dismissed. But there are some of us who have felt her influence too deeply to forget it so easily.

Not the least of these was Camilla Wright. In August 1831, when Mrs. Trollope heard of Cam's death, she wrote Julia: "Alas, our dear Camilla! What a sad history is hers." Now that brief history remained only in her few letters to the Garnetts. There was not even a picture, for the "sweet likeness" done by Harriet long ago had vanished. Now restored to her friends by her early death, she became once again a permissible subject for conversation. Now they could feel for her, think of her, wish that something had been done for her.

Fanny had also unexpectedly been restored to respectability, not by death, but by marriage. She had returned to France with the fifty-two-year-old William Phiquepal d'Arusmont whom, in spite of her views, she married in July 1831, five months after Camilla's death, in a Paris ceremony at which Lafayette was a witness. When Harriet learned the news in October, she happily reported it to Julia.

> I have this day received a letter from Frances Wright which has surprised and pleased me very much; she is *married;* and has been privately married for some time;—her present name is Mme d'Arusmont. . . . Is it not strange? It will give me great pleasure to see her husband.

Somewhat naively, Harriet seems to have expected to resume her old friendship with Fanny as though nothing had happened. And when the Garnetts subsequently removed from Geneva to Paris, one of the first calls Harriet made was on her old friend. Mrs. Garnett could have no further objections. But Harriet's visit was not satisfactory, for she could find no traces of the old Fanny in the woman she now met, living in lodgings near the Jardin des Plantes. She was now a mother, too, and had apparently settled into a domestic regime which startled Harriet by its squalid ordinariness. She described the visit to Julia.

> I have seen F.W., now Mme Phiquepal d'Arusmont, for her husband is Dr. Phiquepal, whose name you must have heard. I found her with a child a twelve month old, a little girl, like her, & naked, for she wears no garment except when she goes out—I mean the child, not Fanny, who seems to dote on her child, & appears herself very happy & much attached to her husband, a good looking but elderly Frenchman. Fanny received me kindly, but coldly; old friendships I think she has forgotten,—old scenes have vanished from her mind; she did not speak of poor Cam, who certainly felt the same thing with her sister. I was agitated at this meeting, but Fanny herself quite composed. She looked well & not older except from the deep furrows of her forehead: the sweet playfulness of her manner is gone; it was her—and yet not her; this I felt as I saw her caressing the naked child, Fanny en robe de chambre, a stove & child's victuals cooking—how different from the elegant boudoir in which we used to find our Fanny writing. I thought of the past—of you &

poor Cam,—& I own I felt very unhappy. I have not had the courage to return, and shall probably seldom see her I have loved so well—too well alas!

"It was her—and yet not her." Fanny had changed. The ideal woman as thinker, intellectual, moral reformer, had betrayed her friends, first by her scandalous behavior and theories, and now, perhaps worst of all, by lapsing into a role as a dowdy housewife. "How different from the elegant boudoir in which we used to find our Fanny writing." The tableau was a picture out of the last century, with Fanny the intellectual center of her circle of friends. It bore little resemblance to the Fanny of Nashoba days, high astride in her saddle and leading a cadre of dedicated female warriors toward the salvation of the world, or to the Fanny cooking cereal for a child amid domestic disarray. Indeed, it was a portrait existing only in the imagination of others, as Harriet herself now dimly realized. Now the heroine of former days had withdrawn from public life and even from her friends. Hereafter, there would be no more letters. As Harriet told Julia, "I have not written to her,—and why should I write,—she will only think it a trouble to answer my letter. She does not think of any of her friends—of those who have been so much attached to her." Three years later, she started lecturing again in America, but her power and importance had waned. There were frequent separations from her husband and daughter, after which bitterness and money troubles combined to end her brief interlude of domestic satisfaction. In 1851, her marriage ended in divorce. A lonely woman, she continued to write and make public appearances. In 1852, after breaking her hip in a fall on the ice, she died in a hospital in Cincinnati, the city of Mrs. Trollope's bazaar, a month after the death of her old friend Julia Garnett Pertz.

To the end of his life, Lafayette kept Fanny's portrait in his room. Evenings, when he looked at it, he was brought back in memory to former times. As he told Harriet, "Her portrait in my room incessantly retraces to me the days of her, Camilla's, Julia's, and your happy presence at La Grange." It was his final picture of the sisterhood of women, assembled in the rarefied and protective atmosphere of his elegant French estate. Fanny's attempts to transfer that vision into the rugged American wilds had proved disastrous. Her own analysis of her Nashoba failure might stand as an epitaph for all her unsuccessful attempts to energize her women friends around the ideals of work and active sisterhood. "In principle we were right, but [in] . . . practice in the existing generation, we were wrong."

REFERENCES

PAGE

70 "Previous to our arrival . . ." FW/L, 15 April 1828, GPC.

70 "Camilla at last . . ." AMS/JGP, 30 May 1828, GPC.

70 "whether Camilla has married . . ." L/JGP, 3 June 1828, GPC.

70 "had still done better . . ." Charles Wilkes to JGP, 30 September 1828, GPC.

70 "What is poor Camilla doing . . ." S/JGP, 3 May 1829, GPC.

71 "The tidings of my union . . ." CW/JGP, 26 April 1828, GPC.

72 "We have executed . . ." CW/JGP, 26 April 1828, GPC.

72 "There was a time . . ." CW/HG & JGP, 20 November 1828, GPC.

73 "The prejudice regarding her opinions . . ." CW/HG & JGP, 20 November 1828, GPC.

73 "All hopes . . ." CW/HG & JGP, 20 November 1828, GPC.

74 "As I had from the first . . ." CW/HG & JGP, 20 November 1828, GPC.

74 "I in the mean time . . ." CW/HG & JGP, 20 November 1828, GPC.

74 "Poor Camilla is lying . . ." FT/JGP, 1 February 1829, GPC.

75 "I grieve for poor Camilla . . ." S/JGP, 8 March 1829, GPC.

75 "This surprising woman . . ." S/JGP, 3 November 1829, GPC.

76 "I would go at any hour . . ." FT/JGP, 27 April 1829, GPC.

76 "This has indeed been . . ." FT/JGP, 20 May 1829, GPC.

77 "Fanny Wright has made herself . . ." FT/JGP, 20 May 1829, GPC.

78 "Now that I am . . ." CW/HG & JGP, 1 August 1829, GPC.

78 "We might perhaps discover . . ." CW/HG & JGP, 19 August 1829, GPC.

80 "Often, in my soul's desolation . . ." CW/JGP, November 1829, GPC.

80 "I had perhaps sought relief . . ." CW/JGP, November 1829, GPC.

80 "Would it afford you pleasure . . ." CW/JGP, November 1829, GPC.

82 "Poor Camilla! . . ." S/JGP, 8 November 1829, GPC.

82 "O women . . ." S/JGP, 8 November 1829, GPC.

83 "I will write . . ." HG/JGP, 12 January 1830, GPC.

83 "Yes, dear Harriet . . ." CW/HG, February 1830, GPC.

84 "and let us recall . . ." CW/HG, February 1830, GPC.

84 "Her situation in New York . . ." HG/JGP, 27 March 1830, GPC.

84 "Every time I see her . . ." FT/JGP, 12 March 1830, GPC.

85 "The Miss Wrights . . ." MG/JGP, 3 September 1830, GPC.

85 "How very strange . . ." HG/JGP, 12 October 1830, GPC.

85 "I have received . . ." HG/JGP, 27 February 1831, GPC.

85 "I never will resume . . ." MG/JGP, 5 February 1831, GPC.

86 "We have lost . . ." HG/JGP, 25 March 1831, GPC.

86 "Harriet is rather out . . ." MG/JGP, 15 April 1831, GPC.

86 "How easily do the wonders . . ." FT/JGP, 18 April 1831, GPC.

87 "I have this day . . ." HG/JGP, 2 October 1831, GPC.

87 "I have seen F.W...." HG/JGP, 26 November 1831, GPC.
88 "I have not written ..." HG/JGP, 28 May 1832, GPC.
88 "In principle we were ..." FW/HG & JGP, February 1828, GPC.

Miniature of Mrs. Mary Garnett

Two Ladies from the Garnett Circle

CHAPTER FIVE

Harriet and Fanny Garnett

It is the single women, belonging to those supernumerary ranks, which political economists tell us, are yearly increasing, who most need thinking about.

MRS. CRAIK, *A Woman's Thoughts about Women* (1864)

There exists a genuine need to hear from the multitudes of mute, inglorious females of whom no biography was ever written, who never did or said or thought a thing that would distinguish them from the mass of women of the day. Of course, the great problem is lack of sources. Biographies are written because a few individuals left material behind them.

PATRICIA BRANCA, **Silent Sisterhood: Middle-class Women in the Victorian Home**

HARRIET AND Fanny Garnett's story resumes after Frances Wright departed with Mrs. Trollope for Nashoba and Julia left with Dr. Pertz for Hanover. Apparently content with her Parisian salon society, Harriet continued her deep interest in the lives of her sister and her friends, and began that correspondence with them which would have such primary importance in her life. She wrote her deepest thoughts to Julia, whom she often cautioned about the privacy of their letters: "You know how sacred I consider a letter, and I always write as I should speak to you quite alone." Together with her sister Fanny, she commenced the study of German, a command of which would keep her close to Julia, who now must master the tongue as well. She tried to transplant herself in imagination, and revelled in Lord Byron's beautiful descriptions of the Rhine, which she quoted at length to Julia.

> *Adieu to thee fair Rhine! How long delighted*
> *The stranger fain would linger on his way!*
> *Adieu to thee again! a vain adieu!*
> *There can be no farewell to scenes like thine.*

Begging Julia to "read all he says . . . you who have so lately seen the beauties he describes," Harriet projected herself into the landscapes through which her sister had so recently passed.

She contemplated a move to Hanover or, more daringly, to Nashoba, of which Frances Wright, in great spirits "from her success in carrying out so many disciples," sent glowing reports, still urging Harriet to join the colony the following autumn (1828). For the moment, Harriet hung suspended between alternatives, between her relationship with her sister, always strong and important, and her friendship with Fanny Wright, almost like infatuated love. Now, her sister and women friends were all gone, having achieved on the one hand a conventional, and on the other, an unorthodox goal. Only Harriet had remained in the old life, marked by the daily calls and evening soirees which were the activities of the women of her class in those days. Evenings, she was pleased to hear Julia "universally missed and regretted." Party after party "went off well: we had cards and conversation, tea, english plum cake, sirops & orgeat, the refreshments in the little drawing room." Mornings, they went off to "confirm their acquaintance" with notables like Mrs. Jameson, and even Byron's mistress, the Countess Guiccioli, about whom Harriet remarked, "She is handsome and interesting, as fair as a lily, but not melancholy enough for Byron's mistress." Harriet was still enjoying herself, and despite Julia's new entreaties that the family move to Hanover, refused. "I like Paris far better than I ever did: to those who have not children and husbands to amuse them, it is the only place to live in."

Early that winter, the first unpleasant rumors about Nashoba had reached the Garnetts. Although Harriet was sure that "slander and ill nature" had taken the field against her friend, she felt the dangers of joining Fanny now. Mrs. Trollope's reputation had already been ruined. "The step once taken," Harriet wrote her sister, "there is no return—at least for a woman. The gates of the most rigid convent are not so insurmountable a barrier betwixt the world and the nun they enclose as public scorn makes against a woman who has joined such a community as Nashoba." Yet, as Harriet frankly confessed, "were it not for you, dear Julia, for a family to whom I think myself of use —I too should have joined Nashoba from the love I bear to my Fanny. Without approving, God knows, of its principles." Harriet worshipped Fanny Wright, but she feared scandal, unlike Frances Trollope, the vicar's daughter and mother of five, who had scoffed at the power of "a few dear me's," and whose even greater familial responsibilities had been seriously jeopardized by her action. In Harriet's ultimate decision not to go, family pressures, especially a sense of duty to her mother, combined with her fear of scandal, had played the greatest part.

But Harriet was not eager to abandon her present way of life; she was bewitched by the restless conviviality of Parisian society. Every night in the week was taken up by some soiree or engagement. Monday was the Garnetts' own night for entertaining, and their "little rooms" were usually filled to overflowing with old friends and new visitors. Prosper Mérimée and Stendhal continued to be regulars. Mérimée liked to affect "the flegne Britannique," with studiously quiet voice and manner, more English than French, as he said calmly and gently the most startlingly caustic things. Stendhal seemed attracted to Harriet, but their relationship was an uneasy one. Whenever Harriet mentioned Beyle to Julia, she bristled. He is "disagreeable—to me at least," "rather fatter than formerly," "cross and disagreeable as he generally is," and she found his flirtations and stories of "piercing Spanish eyes" annoying. She did not like to hear him bragging about his female conquests, and was delighted when Mérimée would catch him in "an idle boast." "I shall not be sorry to have him punished for his rudeness—you know I owe him an old grudge," she told Julia. He called Harriet, "ma chère enemie" in a phrase that aptly described their stance toward each other. Repeatedly, their encounters, as reported by Harriet, were charged with antagonistic feeling. Only once was there a hint of something more. On a warm June night, "after Mamma and Fanny had gone to bed, Mr. Beyle walked in and sat a little while with me—he expressed himself much pleased with our apartment—inquired after you—said that I looked so much like you that if he remained *il deviendrait amoureux de moi* from the resemblance. I told him that he could not please me more than by telling me I looked like you." Even in her letter, Harriet avoided translating the phrase about love.

These encounters were part of a life Harriet was not yet ready to relinquish. She clearly stood at the center of the dynamics. As Mrs. Garnett told Julia: "You know Harriet's love of little meetings. . . . her acquaintance is enlarging daily." For her, the company of these intelligent friends and literary people seemed important enough to shape a life around. Harriet advised the newly married Julia to lose no time in making "intimate friends at Hanover—for friends are a great addition to the happiness even of the happiest *menage.*" For her part, old Mrs. Garnett sighed: "I wish I could see with her eyes the charms of this city, certain it is that she will *not* leave it." Julia had been suggesting, and Mrs. Garnett inclining towards a German residence. "I wish Harriet liked Paris society and soirees as little as I do. I begin to be too old to like them and I think I should like better than anything to be near you." By 1828, even stronger importunities were coming hard and fast from Fanny Wright: "Cam and I say every day—Our life would just suit dear Harriet. How often I shall wish you with me this summer which I expect to pass quite alone." Then, in February 1828, Harriet's decision to remain in Paris became a necessity.

Madame Hyde de Neuville, an old friend from American days and wife of the cabinet minister, fell down an open cellar at the Garnett house, breaking her thigh "in a dreadful manner." At once, all plans to visit Julia were canceled, and Harriet threw herself into the care of Madame Hyde during her long and painful recuperation. Harriet spent long hours each day in Mme. Hyde's room, receiving her friend's "incessant" company, happy to be "of real use to Mme. Hyde," who felt "the necessity of talking irksome" during these difficult days. Harriet seized upon the old lady's incapacitation as an excuse to delay or refuse invitations to make her home elsewhere. Mrs. Garnett marveled at her daughter's zeal. "Harriet never fails to be with her from twelve til six doing the honors of a crowded little bedroom, for she thinks it necessary to admit all who call to see her." Harriet delighted to watch "all the ultras of Paris" passing before her eyes.

Harriet still hoped to build her life around the French salon tradition, even now in its most brilliant period. Beginning almost as a benevolent institution, a refuge for homeless literary men, the salon had evolved into a vehicle for women who sought influence and power. Mary Clarke's taste for society had developed during her long association with Madame Récamier. Society quickly became her absorbing interest—indeed, her vocation. Despite a lack of rank or fortune, she had made her high-perched, shabby rooms, without chandeliers or large suppers, a space in which she enjoyed an unrivaled position. Simply by dint of personality, intellect, and *esprit,* she had surrounded herself on Friday evenings and Wednesday afternoons, with the most remarkable personalities of her time. Mary Clarke had once remarked that social occasions were works of art in their way, and looked upon her guests as responsible fellow-artists. She took notes each evening of the way her guests had behaved: "M.X.—took no trouble to make himself agreeable. Madame Y.—was grumpy, sha'nt ask her in a hurry again. M.Z.—went away too soon; very rude of him. M.A.—was delightful, and so on." Harriet was torn between the salon life and the Nashoba experiment. Both were manifestations of the spirit of community, the one elegant, intellectually demanding, and rigidly enclosed, the other rough, physically taxing, and opening out to the redemption of others.

But by the spring of 1828, Nashoba's fate was decided. Reports from the colony were truly dreadful, and the demise of the experiment seemed certain. Harriet agonized over the destiny of her friend. "Poor Fanny. . . . I cannot bear to think of it—. It is the state of her own mind I most fear—to what can she now turn her attention?" Not really concerned with the collapse of the colony (of which she had little sympathetic understanding), Harriet feared most for the mental state of her friend, should her source of occupation disappear. Still, though Harriet thought Fanny Wright could never return to polite society, she had taken up editing and public lecturing, indifferent to her social ostracism.

Even Mrs. Trollope, after leaving Nashoba, had made the best of things, as she was wont to do, and had bravely told Harriet: "I can truly say, that I had much rather have seen all I have, and all I still hope to do, of America, notwithstanding all contretemps, than to have remained at Harrow." Her plans for her Cincinnati Bazaar were already under way. Thus, both Harriet's friends were achieving some success outside the narrow domain permitted to women in the society which had so far occupied and satisfied her. Their efforts moved Harriet to contemplate the direction of her own life. Contrast with her sister's lot was obvious, too, for Julia was expecting her first child. Even the pathetic Cam had married and was pregnant, a condition of which Harriet remarked, "This will be some amusement to her," in spite of the ruin of her life. It must have seemed to Harriet that she alone lacked private or personal goals.

Gradually, her idea of concentrating on the salon life changed; her letters began to contain complaints about "dull" evenings and dinners ("I am quite tired of hearing of balls") and were full of critical accounts of beautiful but mindless women. After one long afternoon of tea drinking with friends of Mary Shelley, Harriet left in disgust what she described as a dull "flirting party." In December she met an American lady, Mrs. Butler, whom she depicted as "childish, silly and gay.... Happy to talk nonsense and be admired for her beauty.... She is dressed with all the elegance Harbaut and Mlle Victorine can give. As I look at her faultless features, I cannot help thinking that sense or feeling would have changed their regularity and would have made them more pleasing, if less perfect." Harriet came away "feeling kindly towards her, as to a lively, happy child."

In her search for personal usefulness, Harriet realized the significance of the loss of her female friends, and sought to reconstitute the circle which had given such strength and support to their earlier various endeavors. Since her ideal woman, Frances Wright, had disappointed her, she sought to replace her from among the women of her present acquaintance.

At first, she thought Mary Shelley's friend Mrs. Douglas "beautiful and clever and amiable," but when the lady turned out to be just another Parisian coquette, she noted: "It is painful to change our opinion of those we have liked." Later, she attached herself to a Mlle de Klustine, a twenty-year-old girl whom Harriet found "a prodigy of learning and talent—and full of vivacity and good humor." But the new friend soon departed, bestowing on a young Frenchman who had won her heart, her fortune, her time, and her conversation. Harriet longed for her friends in America and for her sister, to whom in a telling aside, she confessed: "I feel life a dreary void, now that I am absent from you."

Studying German and reading became her main activities. In the spring of 1829 she found the "circulating library in the rue Caumartin . . . a great amusement. . . . For 4 francs a month we get all new and old books." She read the works of her friends Mérimée, Sismondi, and Stendhal, and looked over numbers of the *Revue de Paris*, lent her by Mérimée. Lady Morgan's tales she found amusing, and she liked *Vivian Grey*. From Lafayette, she received a bundle of Robert Dale Owen's *Free Enquirers*, which she read with deep interest, surprised to find them "moderate in their expressions. . . . The writings of people secure of their success." Association with the learned and vivacious Mary Clarke further broadened Harriet's horizons. Mary talked not of nonsense, but with raptures "of German literature, especially *Wilhelm Meister*, and read with pleasure Niebuhr." Harriet was intensifying her cultural interests in the casual and haphazard way of most middle-class women of her generation.

Then, in the summer of 1831, Harriet began thinking seriously about centering her life around some intellectual occupation which might also be financially rewarding. An old friend had sent the Garnetts a copy of her book, "Memoirs of a Gentlewoman of the Last Century," which seemed "interesting . . . but not . . . a book that would be generally amusing." Still, she mused, "I dare say writing and publishing it entertained her very much." And Mérimée had published a new book, *La Chronique de Charles Neuf*, a historical novel which "seems to excite great attention." Even more important, "he has been well paid for it." Her letters often mentioned Mérimée's popularity and financial success: "The next day 600 copies sold!" Harriet saw that intellectual activity could provide two of the most important goals for which women were striving—occupation and economic independence.

Even Harriet's strange, introverted sister Fanny was busy at work, drying wild flowers, "which occupation she . . . does . . . very neatly." The problem of occupation was severe for the early nineteenth-century woman. Confined to the home, dressed by servants and served by cooks, the intelligent woman, especially one without husband or family, had to create her own occupations. And so, while Fanny dried her flowers, Harriet began to write, at first telling no one about her activity. At the same time, the family contemplated a move from Paris, primarily for financial reasons. They enquired about Edinburgh, but finally decided on Geneva, where the Sismondis lived. This move was only one of many across Harriet's lifetime. Her increasing restlessness, expressed in her letters, also found outward manifestation in these frequent changes of abode.

Before leaving Paris in June 1830, Harriet learned of the failed projects of her friends. Frances Wright had given up Nashoba and was embarking with her thirty blacks for Haiti, where she planned to free them. Her five years of work for slave emancipation were over. Mrs. Trollope's subsequent business venture, too avant garde for nineteenth-century Cincinnati, had involved her once more in financial ruin. And while the example of her friends was not promising, it was Harriet's turn to try her hand at occupation. First, however, she must renounce the debilitating social round.

Just after Julia gave birth to a second son, the Garnetts announced their last soiree, and moved to Geneva. Harriet confessed: "I do not leave Paris without regret, even tho' I am pleased to go to Geneva—everyone here tells us we shall repent and return to our friends here—but I doubt this." But the move was at first a disappointment. Geneva, although agreeable, was "a little dull perhaps—I feel the change, I own, from Paris—we have as yet so few acquaintances." The Sismondis had already warned them that Genevans were inhospitable.

But behind the scenes, Harriet's new occupation began. In June 1831, she had finished a short novel, *The Jersey Laurel,* which she described to Julia:

> And now I must tell you a secret—I have written a little tale and read it to the Sismondis, who encourage me to send it to London and have it printed. What think you of this my dear? The story is an American one, and they say very pretty; and so says Fanny. Mamma will give me no encouragement, but should it succeed I will try another. I do not intend to be known this time, so *be secret* dear Julia. I have a copy to make, and as you may suppose, am much engaged. It will amuse me at any rate and if I succeed, tant mieux!

Such unwarranted activity needed some justification. She told Julia, "I have not, as you have, sweet children to amuse me;—I must make other occupations." To make her work acceptable, she must refer to it as "amusement," undertaken to while away the idle hours, certainly not as serious, money-making activity. Her sister Fanny explained to Julia: "Harriet amuses herself by writing stories. She has begun another one, and she told me that she had told you she had finished the first. I think it pretty, but the *great* advantage is that it is an occupation—something to do."

That August, Harriet sent her manuscript to a London publisher, calling herself "Maria Smith" and professedly "very anxious to preserve a strict incognito." Prosper Mérimée liked the tale and engaged to write a preface, which compared Harriet's style to Dr. Johnson's. Harriet sent a copy to Julia, calling her book "the penseés of my *child*" which, she anxiously added, was not nearly so interesting as Julia's accounts of her children.

Harriet's novel was laid in America, in New Jersey. Its heroine married a young man whose birth was shrouded in mystery. Having inherited a large estate with 100 slaves, he decides to visit the South, where he learns, as did

Frances Wright, the terrible truth about slavery and the unnatural relations it creates between whites and blacks. Revolted, he decides, like Harriet's old friend, to take his slaves back to Haiti where they can live free lives. As the plot thickens, he finds himself to be the son of an exploited slave girl. When his delicate wife learns the truth, she shrinks from his embraces. Harriet rendered his despair in florid style: "Must he see her cold averted eye avoiding his? Must he feel her hand tremble, not with love, but horror at his touch? . . . He would not drag on so miserable an existence, condemned by her he loved." So saying, he commits a bloody suicide. While the story was melodramatic and the style unexceptional, the handling of the subject matter indicates that Harriet might well have developed into a popular writer, had she needed to persevere. *The Jersey Laurel* was no better or worse than much of the popular fiction of the time, yet Harriet never succeeded in placing it with a publisher. In part, her failure stemmed from the unconventional length of the novel, far under the usual three volumes. The subject matter, miscegenation, might alone have sold it, had Harriet consented to flesh out the narrative to the usual length. Basically, hers was a failure of inexperience, aggravated by a lack of persistence and adaptability.

Still, after the tale had gone out, Harriet continued to write. She could not talk frankly to her mother or Fanny about her new occupation, but she could tell Julia how important it was becoming to her. She confessed that writing was not mere "amusement," but rather a genuine activity, "very fatiguing to body and mind." She worked away at a second novel, which she hoped to make longer than the first and hence more acceptable. She told Julia, "I only want money—not fame. I will try and get some." Like many women writers of the period, Harriet lived on the edge of genteel poverty, albeit surrounded by the ubiquitous servants. Her family could use extra money, and writing could provide some.

But all did not go well. The great John Murray himself read Harriet's MS and "approved of it, but said that without a known *name,* he prints nothing at his own expense." A year later, there was still no news of Harriet's "poor progeny." She began to grow restless, and to long for Parisian life once again. By October 1831, she had arranged for the family to rent their Genevan lodgings, and to manage a six months' "visit" to Paris. She told Julia, "I am glad to return to *old Paris,* our home I believe eventually—no other place quite satisfies our selfish minds. You are happy to have objects that render all places indifferent to you." She protested: "You will say *this is Harriet's whim,"* but claimed that her mother's nervousness and low spirits had prompted her to suggest the trip, which "has quite wound her up again."

There was another powerful magnet in Paris. Frances Wright had returned from America and was living there. Immediately upon their return, Harriet visited her old friend, but was depressed by her reception which, although kind, was cold: "Old friendships I think she has forgotten." But Harriet did not regret her return to the city "which for us unites advantages no other place can offer: *mouvement,* independence, and resources of every kind." Now her life had a double focus: social activity and writing. She told Julia, "I have so little time! I am copying all day my story, then visits, walking and talking —I have scarcely time to look into a book." While she awaited news from publishers, she attended some courses at the college, near their Parisian lodgings. Mrs. Garnett dropped her opposition to her daughter's ambitions when she saw that Harriet was "much happier for constant occupation."

Meanwhile, in 1832, Mrs. Trollope's travel book on her experiences, *Domestic Manners of the Americans,* had appeared, and was highly praised. In desperation Harriet sent copies of her own tale to friends in America. Charles Wilkes pronounced the tale "unexceptionable in morals" and promised to try to publish it in Philadelphia, but his efforts failed, and Harriet told Julia: "Hitherto I have had nothing but disappointment. Never were children brought into the world with such difficulty." A note of sad discouragement entered her letters. In one, she stopped abruptly, claiming that her eyes and head were weary with writing, "and until I can publish and gain something by publishing, I am little disposed to write a third." Paris itself had become a dreary and anxious city. Cholera was everywhere; it was "truly the city of the plague." Harriet watched from her windows "the great black cart filled with dead bodies, the dying carried in the blue tick beds to the hospitals—the general consternation and horror." The three women passed their evenings nervously, and "never went to bed without every preparation for illness and trembled at the idea of a pain in the stomach." The city's mood was at one with her own.

Indeed, the fall and winter of 1832 had been a low point for all the sisters. Harriet was depressed by her failure to place her novel. Fanny had hurt her thumb, and the injury made it impossible for her to do needle work, that ripping and turning of old gowns which she so dearly loved. Harriet worried about her sister's mental state. "She has been unable to do anything and therefore this trouble has taken great possession of her mind. . . . If it were possible to *amuse* Fanny, our greatest evil would be over. . . . Do not allow *nervousness* to destroy *your* happiness. I see so much of this disease that I think it is one to struggle with most vigorously." She advised the once again pregnant Julia to be content with her "dear boys . . . and think of the little April girl who I trust will complete your happiness."

Julia, too, was beginning to fret about her life. At thirty-nine, she had two infants and a third baby was on the way. Still somewhat alone in Hanover, and clumsy with her German, she longed for the company of her mother and sisters. She needed more than a life as wife and mother and was beginning her own search for personal occupation.

Meanwhile, Mrs. Garnett was annoyed that Harriet continued to visit the infamous Fanny Wright d'Arusmont. She and her daughter Fanny positively refused to let the erstwhile "priestess of infidelity" visit their house, in spite of Harriet's begging. Frustrated, Harriet told Julia:

> I am but *one* and must yield—but I do so very reluctantly and am much hurt and vexed. Why have feelings been given to me? They are only a source of pain to me. I wish I could be satisfied to eat, drink, and sleep, & neither think nor feel. I believe there is no attachment in this world that gives unalloyed happiness to women except that of a mother,—for a parent alone can *make* the happiness of others; but I must not express to you my melancholy view of life; thank heaven you cannot in this respect sympathise with me!

Harriet was feeling keenly the restrictions of her single life. She was almost forty, and yet she could not invite her old friend to her home. She had tried to make professional occupation for herself and failed. At least her sister, so it seemed to Harriet, could find meaning in her children's lives.

> I envy you the hopes for the future that children give you; what have I to look forward to to close a dull life and leave none behind to recollect and love me; each day that proves to me that my youth is passing is only marked to you by the growth and improvement of your children: when I reflect how much happier your fate is, I check the regret I feel at your being so distant from me.

Declining a visit to some old friends, she remarked, "Life is scarcely, I think, worth the tedium of a journey."

But Harriet pulled herself out of the doldrums once again with a new occupation: translation. By the fall of 1832, both she and Fanny were back at their German, and Harriet was striking a new tone in her letters to Julia.

> If you knew how busy I was you would scarcely expect me to write oftener or longer—and yet I feel I ought to do so. I am now putting in English verse a Swedish poem (translated in French prose by Frye), and this occupies my time and attention. Richard Church is to do one half and I the other. I have just finished the 4th canto—Frithiof and Ingeborg is the name. . . . Unless you had attempted a thing of the kind, you know not how very engrossing it is. I am ever seeking for rhymes, and planning metre: and in the mean time busy and amused. If we succeed, my partner (who is very clever) would take the trouble of publication.

By Christmas time, she had finished translating twelve cantos of the poem.

> It does amuse me very much: we shall send it to London & I do hope for some profit,—but alas; I have been so often disappointed. To see it in print would be some pleasure,—to receive pence a greater.

She had indeed been busy. She had also completed a translation of *Der Taucher* by Schiller, and a partial one of *Undine,* in English verse. "So you see," she told her sister, understating what must have been a rigorous routine, "I am not idle." She found "writing verses . . . far more amusing than learning German," and told Julia to "write of your children, as I do of mine." Her identification with her work, its connection with her deepest self, was complete. While the work went on, Harriet awaited news of her translation. As a woman, she could do little to advance it herself, but Major Frye planned to go to London, where he promised to "push the work on." Harriet's optimism was high. "I hope soon to see what the public say."

Mrs. Garnett understood little of the forces that impelled Harriet to write. Her daughter's constant occupation with translating and writing was often inexplicable to her. But gradually she hoped that Harriet would succeed, simply because the family needed money. Harriet was by now so busy with her work that she began to leave letters unanswered. She explained her preoccupation to Julia: "Poetry is so amusing—so engrossing—that I cannot help it,—& I will persevere, in spite of all the numerous difficulties I meet with."

Fanny worked along with her sister on the German, no doubt to distract herself from the miseries of the thumb ailment which mysteriously persisted. The doctors now thought the affliction to resemble ringworm, and advised her to rub the nail with sulphur ointment. While she suffered no pain, she was constantly annoyed by incapacity. Harriet and her mother soon learned not to refer to the ailment, for Fanny was "a little nervous on the subject," and had covered the finger with a thumb stall, which made it "rather useless." Harriet, on the other hand, was "very very busy—and therefore happy." Indeed, her translated poetic saga *Frithiof,* after a refusal by Murray, had found a publisher and was scheduled for a January print at the authors' expense. Bolstered by even this small success, Harriet threw herself into a regular writing schedule.

> I write and study German from 9 till 2, then walk and pay visits; we dine at 5, —and drink tea at 6. After tea, if we do not go out, I study again till 9, and at 10, we go to bed. Thus passes my life.

It was a routine not unlike the one later adopted by her friend Frances Trollope. It should have produced results.

Frithiof's appearance and favorable review might "pave the way for other translations." As she made room for the necessary round of social duties, Harriet seemed productive and satisfied. Yet Sismondi, looking over his brief and infrequent letters from Harriet and Fanny, detected instead unhappiness and increasing withdrawal. It seemed to him that she had failed to distinguish herself both privately and professionally. He told Julia:

> Poor Harriet, she really has not a fate that can satisfy her; endowed with a tender heart and a distinguished mind, she has not complete satisfaction either for the one or the other. She would have needed to love, to be married, to have children, and she has not even affections of the second degree. Her dear sister is settled far from her; the friend of her preference (F.W.) has shown herself so unworthy of her that their old ties have been loosened; she feels uprooted and far from all those that she was used to love in her childhood. It is the same with her mind; she feels in her self the hope to place herself in the front rank, but she is transplanted far from her native tongue, far from that sympathy that a common origin confers, and neither her imagination nor her eloquence are able to make the effect that they deserve to do upon the French. Hers is an incomplete fate. . . .

Harriet had not achieved the fullness of love as a wife and mother, nor had she enjoyed the intimacy she desired with her sister or her friends. Intellectually, too, her growth had been stunted through lack of the stimulation and sympathy available to a writer working within a community. In the context of Sismondi's analysis, the achievement of other women writers looms even larger, working as they so often did, without the kind of support male writers took for granted.

As 1835 opened, Harriet's problems were intensified by straitened finances, shared by others of her circle. Mrs. Trollope, in spite of her literary successes, had not completely re-established her debt-ridden family, and was living in Belgium after eviction from her Harrow home. It was her dark hour. She had just lost her son Henry, and in her grief, wrote little to the Garnetts. Harriet's financial situation was at best precarious. The Garnetts' whole income did not exceed £260 a year, even with what they still received from America. "Such," her mother told Julia, "have been the sad changes in our life. Your sisters really take their change of circumstances very well. We could live only in Paris, poor as we are, with respectability, as no one here enquires how you live or what you spend." Her view of Harriet's work had changed, and she now regarded her daughter's translations as "meritorious," an attempt to make "a little independence." Still, Harriet lacked the important ingredient: *patronage*, "not an easy thing to find, you well know." Maria Garnett rejoiced that Julia was "exempt from our pecuniary life, having a husband to secure [her] a comfortable income."

Before long, Harriet was engrossed with the troubles of actual publication.

> I have been so much occupied by the printing of *Frithiof*, that I have come in so completely knocked up from the printing office (which is in the rue Montmartre) that I have been unable even to write to you. I hope the worst is now over, but we have fallen into the hands of bad printers & I have had a great deal of anxiety and trouble. Neither Major Frye nor Mr. Church have lent me the least assistance, & but for Mr. MacGregor's kindness, I should never have got through it. Major Frye and I share the expense of publication.

She had planned to send her poem to Miss Hay, her governess of earliest years, but the news had just arrived of Miss Hay's death. She who had followed the Garnetts to America, and who had so hopefully opened the first school for young ladies in New Brunswick, had died poor and alone. At first, Harriet mourned her passing, and then, recalling the thankless and lonely life of such women, checked herself: "But all her cares and anxieties are at a close, and our regrets for this valued friend are selfish, for what enjoyment or comfort had she in life?" Her comment reveals her own depressed mental state at this time.

In the end, instead of earning money, Harriet had to finance the publication of her poem singlehandedly, deserted by her male co-translator and agent. Her hopes had not been grandiose, merely to pay the expense of printing and publishing. Mrs. Trollope, at least, had begun to reap the rewards of success. Again engaged by her booksellers to write an account of Paris "at a very *high price*," she had only just sold a novel *"very highly* to Bentley." And while she had pronounced Harriet's poem "beautiful" and said that "it must make its way," it seemed to its author "a friendless little offspring at present." Mrs. Garnett asked Julia to help: "Write to any one you can for it. Harriet is so modest that she will not even mention it." Discouraged, Harriet vowed never again to publish for herself. In hopes of some American sales, she sent three hundred copies of *Frithiof* to New York.

Harriet's view of her work had been changing. From a project undertaken merely to "amuse," it had become a more serious occupation, and had ultimately come to represent financial independence. She felt her dependent state and wanted to earn some money of her own. She told Julia: "I trust I shall one day *maintain* [myself] and this is the first object of my life: If I cannot do so, I truly feel that life is of no value in my eyes." In the end, *Frithiof* became a great expense, a situation which "mortified and vexed" Harriet more than she could say. She communicated her melancholy to her family. Fanny's thumb ailment worsened correspondingly, tormenting her unmercifully. The baffled family packed her off for Ostend with a friend. Now the physicians were saying that the whole complaint had arisen solely from "a debilitated constitution and nervous complaints." Then as now, nervous complaints commonly afflicted women, and were sometimes cloaked under the single term Neurasthenia. Harriet had again lost heart. Julia was beseeching the sisters to pay her a visit, and Harriet refused.

> I do not wish you to love us less, but to consider a little more our situation is different from yours, and that each individual in life must have different objects. Mine may all end in disappointment, I confess,—and then I may, perhaps, create another pursuit, or be contented to have none, doze on till the last sleep overtakes me, and yields me quiet at last. I sometimes wish that day were come.

By the summer, favorable reviews of *Frithiof* began appearing. Encouraged, Harriet again began writing, this time a poem dedicated to Chateaubriand. Frances Trollope promised to insert it in her Paris book, trying to give her friend a boost in the only way she could. Despite physical separation, she and Harriet gave each other encouragement until the end of their lives. News from America was optimistic, too. George Wilkes had ordered a dozen copies of *Frithiof,* as did other old friends, and Harriet began to hope again. The giant's song from the saga was scheduled for insertion in *Fraser's* Magazine. As Harriet saw it, "Every trifling step forward is an advantage, or may be one hereafter."

But by summer 1836, a year later, Harriet still had earned no money from her venture, and was again ready to concede defeat. Mrs. Trollope, passing through Paris en route to Italy, narrowly missed seeing Harriet, and took the opportunity to give her some important advice, via Julia. In Mrs. Trollope's view, occupation was a necessity for women, and she was disturbed that Julia's mother and Fanny seemed "rather [to] wish her to abandon every attempt, than that she should be subject to future disappointment. This is a doctrine which I greatly disapprove. I should do so in every case, but most particularly in that of Harriet, where success itself would in my judgment be of less importance than the blessings of *occupation*. It is the want of this, dearest Julie, which produces the *tristesse* of which they all complain, without being conscious of its cause, or aware how completely the remedy is in their power." Mrs. Trollope had no doubt about Harriet's powers. "She has *genius*" —but, the more experienced author noted, Harriet lacked "firmness of character—and such a degree of condescension to the popular taste, as would enable her without pain to write in conformity to its demands." She had talked with Bentley, her publisher, regarding Harriet, and he, too, called Harriet "a woman of *very* superior powers." Still, translation was a dead end, and such works, "be they ever so excellent, from an unknown hand, cannot be published with any hope of success." She was sure that Bentley would be ready to take some of Harriet's original work *"of the usual size"* at half and half profits. Mrs. Trollope regretted Harriet's stubborness in allowing her promising work to languish. "Few *beginning* authors have so much encouragement even as this—but I hardly *dare,* unless in the course of conversation, to repeat all this again to Harriet." Mrs. Trollope knew how difficult the struggle was, but implored Harriet to make yet one more effort.

> She is *vexed* (and who can wonder that she is so?) but she must rouse her courage anew, and the success she deserves is still before her. The best feature in the business is, that first struggle once past, the rest is easy—nothing more being required than just so much application to your pen as may suffice to produce the *quantity* you desire to *sell.* This is not very sublime, but it is very true.

Deaf to her friend's advice, Harriet remained doggedly entrenched in translation. On a visit to the Lafayettes, she reviewed an English version of the General's memoirs which she found "ill done," and offered to do another herself; the family gratefully accepted. Unsure whether they planned to pay her, Harriet worked hard, because "it must be an advantage to me hereafter."

Sometimes she even contemplated another removal to the new world, in search of that fortune which seemed to be constantly eluding her.

> We are hearing such accounts of the rapid fortunes made in the state of Michigan in America, that if mamma were some years younger, I should endeavour to persuade her to go there, certain that in 5 or 6 years we should have made a fortune. . . . How cheaply would future competence be purchased by a few years of privation & hardship—and some enjoyment also, for the country is a delightful one, & fertile beyond belief, with game of every description, sugar from one's own maple trees, & fish from one's own river & fine land selling at 1 dollar & a quarter an acre! & people offering you a hundred percent for your money! . . . Nothing ever equalled the present prosperity of America, & I hear that the moral improvement of the people keeps pace with their increasing and almost incredible prosperity. It is delightful to think that such a country exists for the many who cannot live in Europe—and we are amongst those who cannot increase their fortune. But it is impossible for us, situated as we are, to return to America.

Instead, Harriet worked on the translation of Lafayette's memoirs, and by April 1837, the family had drawn up a financial arrangement. She was to work with Mr. Church, and received 500 francs for her share of each volume, the first of which was already complete. When she had been paid, although the Garnetts had precious little to spare, Harriet, reveling in her new sense of power, used part of the earnings to buy Julia an expensive Geneva watch. Exultant, she wrote:

> I cannot tell you how delighted I feel to have a little money I may call my own, & our removal having been an expensive one, the money comes in very opportunely; but I am delighted also to have the power of sending you a watch, which you will wind up & value for my sake.

By autumn, she expected another 500 francs for another volume. Having protected herself from criticism and her family from comment by her incognito ("no one knows I have translated it"), she was exhilarated by a new sense of accomplishment, made manifest in her ability to indulge her sister with a handsome gift.

Indeed, many women in her circle seemed freer, more able to find occupation, and even, sometimes, to earn a living. The Garnetts' friend Marianne Skerrett had found a good position in the royal household which, "besides handsome apartments and a very elegant table, gives her considerable, about £200 per annum." Mrs. Trollope was in London, moving "among clever literary people, which is the circle [Harriet] loves and is formed to shine in." Mary Clarke was enjoying her incessant soirees, in Mrs. Trollope's view, "a singular original . . . with all her wild vagaries; she has talent." Women were creating their own individual styles. Late in 1837, still another event put women in the forefront, and the chauvinistic Sismondi had a passing comment for "that strange organization of society" which had given the government of millions of men in England "to a young girl of eighteen, and later to the lover that she will deign to take." Victoria was on the throne, and a new age seemed about to begin.

While Harriet occupied herself with translation, Fanny, on the other hand, sank further into a series of psychosomatic complaints. As Mrs. Garnett explained to Julia, "She is a little nervous and feels everything very much." By August 1839, the family contemplated a removal to Nice, hoping (as they so often did when they moved) that change of scene would improve Fanny's nerves and spirits. Harriet told Julia: "To see her half the day in tears is more than mother and I can bear." Her mother, too, required "a great deal of soothing and humoring,—and so does Fanny, who must not be contradicted."

As soon as they proposed the Nice trip, Fanny's headaches disappeared. Julia was aghast at her family's plans, but Harriet was adamant:

> I really believe a change of plan would kill her. I could not live with her dissatisfied on this head. She would cry night and day and be in a continual state of nervous irritability which would be dreadful.

She added guardedly: "You do not know what the consequences of opposition to her wishes might be. I am writing in fear. Pray burn this. Believe I act for the best and do not be displeased with me." Alarmed, Julia stirred herself to pay a lightning visit to her family, with whom she passed "a stormy fortnight," sharing their pain and anxiety over Fanny's mental and physical state. But her trip was not in vain. Julia persuaded her sisters to settle in Boulogne, which also had sea air, but which was not so far as Nice.

A few days after Julia had returned to Hanover, Madame d'Arusmont came to see Harriet and was saddened at having missed Julia. One month later, Mrs. Trollope passed through the city. How nearly did these five women come to meeting again! Their circle, so close in 1827, was twelve years later widely dispersed. Camilla was dead. Fanny Wright d'Arusmont was married and had a child. Julia was the mother of three boys in Hanover, a settled German matron. Harriet and Fanny were in Paris. Mrs. Trollope had moved to London and was living near Anthony and Tom. Never again were the old friends to be within such a short distance of one another.

In March 1840, when Anthony Trollope passed the day with the Garnetts on his way to Paris to join his mother for a month, Harriet made a last reference to her abortive career as a writer. Those efforts were now part of a dead past. New tasks lay ahead.

> I have not even a perfect copy of the *Jersey Laurel,* the cat having torn it. You are very good to like it, but it is from affection that you are pleased with it. I shall never write anything again, & have not even time to read anything. Talking, talking, talking, from morn to night meets my often wearied ear. Fanny is certainly better.

Although the last terse sentence seemed to have little to do with what went before, it was an announcement of Harriet's new orientation. Having struggled so long with private goals and failed, she would take up the care of her elderly mother and valetudinarian sister with a new sense of vocation. In this period, the letters are full of references to Fanny's mental and physical state and to Harriet's creation of diverting occupations for her sister.

Fanny had become a kind of semi-invalid, subject to nervous complaints, totally dependent on her family, never venturing forth from home. At first, the removal to Boulogne had made her "fretful and violent," but Harriet soon succeeded in making Fanny "calm and good humoured" in their quiet and secluded life. Sometimes headaches confined her to bed all day. But on her good days she bathed, pressed flowers, or collected shells. Fanny was kept "very busy sowing sweet peas & mignonette in pots for transplanting later; she has lost very few plants by frost this winter, & gardening is quite her passion & a very great & constant occupation at all seasons; I never saw her in better health and spirits." With the instincts of the therapist, Harriet noted Fanny's occupation and her corresponding improvement. "The garden occupies her almost constantly, & makes her happy. She succeeds very well in her flowers, & now understands their management." Fanny had found a profession of sorts at last. "Fanny . . . lives in the garden & is so fond of her flowers that she requires no other society, & always finds some occupation in watering, planting, or transplanting or weeding." Four years later, her interest continued strong: "Fanny nurses pots of cuttings & young seedlings with maternal love, & really understands the culture of flowers extremely well." When the Garnetts moved again, to Brighton, Fanny took up another hobby —collecting sea weeds—"her present delight." She was, noted Harriet, "much amused with sea weed, which she dries extremely well, & has really a pretty collection of them."

Substituting a career as nurse for that of writer, Harriet freely offered the sacrifice for which she had long been made ready by the prevailing consciousness of her age. When Julia invited her to visit for several months to help her with German translations, Harriet chided her: "Think of Mama's age, & the care she necessarily requires, & you will not wonder at my leaving her behind out of the question. . . . Her nerves are very weak,—a trifling thing keeps her awake all night—& the least imprudence in diet affects her health & eyes." Harriet was pleased that Julia had recently found something to do in addition to her domestic functions: "I am glad you have so interesting an occupation as translating your husband's book, which I am sure you will do very well, 'tho' I too should like to assist in the work, if it were possible for me to go to you—but alas! it cannot be,—for I am tied to home, & must make up my mind not to desert my post." Harriet professed herself totally "reconciled to the life we lead."

Other occupations interested her sporadically. Since the spring of 1843, she had been painting, but, as she told Julia, "It is not an easy art, & very slow in painting & drying." In the next year, she returned with renewed vigor to her translating. This time she worked on German tales, and Mr. Pertz persuaded John Murray to promise to look at Harriet's work. She proceeded "assiduously" with Fredericka Bremer's stories, Eckermann's *Gespräche mit Goethe,* Lessing, Grimm's fairy tales, and Voss Homer. And, although she heard nothing from Murray, she resolved, "I will go on striving at translations & not feel discouraged. I have at least improved my own German."

While nursing and translating had afforded occupation, neither of them brought economic independence. Then, in August 1845, Harriet received that financial margin of relief she had herself been so strenuously trying to provide. It came unexpectedly and dramatically in the form of a legacy from an old woman friend, Madame de Pontheiu, who lived alone, and who had always enjoyed her visits from the Garnett women. Now she had left them a tidy sum which meant a measure of security. Harriet calculated the yearly profits: "At the least rate of interest it will be £120 a year between us, & this will add essentially to our means of giving comforts to our old mother."

But Harriet was never totally happy with life as a quiet recluse. Upon another occasion she complained to Julia: "Mother & I lead the dullest lives you can imagine. I do dislike this place more than I can describe—not a single amusement or advantage does it offer, except a pretty country, but that alone is not enough for happiness. . . . I have here neither society nor friends. . . . I feel very much depressed at present & very much alone."

Harriet was approaching a culminating point in her life. Her correspondence with Julia was nearly twenty years old. In all those years, she had inhabited an essentially female world, and, as if she had worn enchanted eyeglasses blocking from her vision everything but the fates of women, she had filled her letters to Julia with information about the destinies of her female friends. Neither her faithful nursing nor her sporadic attempts to make her name as a novelist and translator were to be her real occupation. Harriet's most passionate concern had ever been the fates of women—her own, her mother's, her sisters', her friends'—but increasingly, her interest extended beyond her immediate circle. Her epistles to Julia had contained the life stories of literally hundreds of women. Harriet had made her life's work the continuing chronicle of the existences of women like herself. She had told the stories of the "mute, inglorious females" who had never spoken for themselves.

The men of Harriet's acquaintance had been by comparison shadowy, insubstantial figures; of even the most famous among them, she took comparatively little notice. Indeed, Harriet sometimes did not enjoy Mary Clarke's soirees because her "set" was somewhat "limited as to ladies." On those occasions when the Garnetts found themselves "the only ladies and 4 or 5 men," she was clearly annoyed, consoling herself with the knowledge that, in any case, "Miss Clarke is always amusing." For Harriet, women's company was always more interesting, even more "brilliant" than that of men. Taken as a whole, her letters to Julia provide a kaleidoscopic view of that essentially female world inhabited by the upper-middle-class woman between 1820 and 1850; in the end, the correspondence broadened the horizons both of those who wrote and those who read.

Although the letters are amply punctuated by the love and ritual characteristic of such feminine correspondences, their most significant aspect is not this vocabulary, but rather the amount and quality of sharp reportage about women's lives. Once the conventional greetings were over, the women passed before their shared vision the comings and goings, the triumphs and failures of the large circle of their female friends. These little nuggets of biography are as revealing of Harriet herself as they are of the women whose lives she briefly rendered.

Harriet's letters gave substance to an ongoing female community which raised women's personal aspirations and encouraged their varying attempts at creativity and self-realization. In definite, if shadowy, outlines, the correspondence prophesies the passing of the old ideas and gives fair promise of something new. And while Harriet herself was already trapped in an ineluctable past, she was an apt pupil of the as yet shapeless future. Gradually, through this knowledgeable, epistolary sisterhood Harriet discovered a subversive truth which, while it was too dangerous for articulation in general terms, stood out clearly in the bright specifics of the little histories she recorded in the letters. Like most earth-shaking ideas, it was both obvious and simple. It was this: Marriage, far from being the "natural destiny" of the female sex, was instead a dangerous mold into which women poured themselves at great cost. Perhaps in the end, the single state was best. This dawning realization provided a counterforce to all the popular wisdom of the age and gave some women the strength to set out on their own, even though they were considered, in George Gissing's subsequent telling phrase, "the odd women."

On the close, often cross-lined pages of her sheets, Harriet had watched an endless alphabet of persons, from Mrs. Aitken, Louise Angelucci, Miss Bache, and Miss Bright of Bristol, to Mrs. Webb, Elizabeth Weston, and Mrs. Wilson. How fared it with these friends? Some were admired by men and bore their children; others were quickly widowed; some remained forever unattached and virginal. In this epistolary compendium, the meaning and worth of their lives might be measured. These vignettes from real life provided both readers and writers with an education which, like most good ones, shaped their collective consciousness forever.

Judging at least from this correspondence, Harriet was primarily curious about the subsequent fates of her married friends. Given the Victorian habit of reticence, the details of marriage had always lain hidden behind a veil of silence. Sexual adjustments were beyond the pale of discussion, of course, but women also had no access to printed information about the psychological and social adjustments they might have to make in marriage. The novels of the early nineteenth century had been mines of knowledge for young single women on how to avoid seduction and achieve marriage. A young girl could learn about everything from hairstyles to how to behave at parties from Miss Burney's *Evelina* or Miss Edgeworth's popular tales. But information on the marital state was harder to get. The manuals, the sermons, the popular printed wisdom of the day was generally, if vaguely, unanimous: marriage was woman's fate and her only source of lasting happiness. It was necessary to know no more. Even the friendly novelist, who had been so much more forthcoming on the subject of courtship, closed the curtain after the heroes and heroines made their appointed matches. But real women knew the most interesting part of the story was just beginning: what followed the fateful choice? The stories of women's lives which Harriet pursued and passed on were clues to a puzzle she was gradually figuring out. Since every woman had individual information on marriage from her own experience, the only way for women to come to a general consciousness of the marital state was through sharing those isolated experiences with a broad circle of correspondents.

The Garnett letters, offering a wealth of such shared information, were full of discouraging discoveries. Marriage was a state of life fraught with dangers. Its outstanding characteristic, contrary to popular ideas, was the insecurity of the women who committed themselves to its state. Instead of providing liberation from parental control, usefulness, or occupation, it brought only greater vulnerability, both psychic and economic. Harriet's dawning insight into the realities of marriage as recorded in this large correspondence, was part of the general female response, as the passing years produced increased possibilities for self-fulfillment outside of marriage.

The whole concept of self-fulfillment was at odds with the ideals of self-effacement and duty which were the touchstones of traditional marriage. In 1831, Mrs. John Sandford, in her *Woman in Her Social and Domestic Character*, printed some advice to the young wife, indicating how pervasive such ideas had become.

> Domestic comfort is the chief source of her influence.... Nothing conduces more to improve the character of men than domestic peace. A woman may make a man's home delightful, and may thus increase his motives for virtuous exertion. She may refine and tranquillise his mind.... Her smile may be the happy influence to gladden his heart, and disperse the clouds that gather on his brow. And she will be loved in proportion as she makes those around her happy,—

as she studies their tastes, and sympathises in their feelings. In social relations, adaptation is therefore the true secret of her influence.

Given the perils of marriage, the new multiplicity of roles possible for women, and an ever more insistent search for self-fulfillment, perhaps a woman could remain single and, even within the confines of Victorian society, live a purposeful and interesting life. Certainly Harriet had concluded that to be the "trembling handmaid" in the "conjugal Bond" was an unattractive prospect, and that surely the single state was best.

This revelation came gradually, as Harriet considered the evidence of the lives of her friends, as she recorded them in her letters to Julia. Certainly, many of the unions of her friends, while promising high happiness, had changed women's lives for the worse. Women's fates were inextricably bound up with those of their husbands. Milton had spoken in exalted terms of the relation between the sexes: "He for God only, she for God in him." But sickness, financial distress, oppression, or death were poor substitutes for intimations of the divine.

Of course, Harriet knew Mrs. Trollope's dramatic story. Her husband's physical and mental decline, then total bankruptcy. His subsequent intolerable temper, her shielding of the children. Her desperate struggles as breadwinner. Her nursing of terminally ill children. Her eventual successes, while sweet, had been hard won. The letters abound in such terrible stories, but lack Mrs. Trollope's final triumphs. One was the case of "poor Mrs. Barclay," whose husband went suddenly mad, and after a lengthy illness, which left the family ruined, ordered a fine carriage and went about telling his acquaintance that "he was now rolling in wealth." Harriet told Julia, "He talked in the wildest manner imaginable. His poor wife looked pale & grave and touched her head and said 'his mind is quite gone.' " The story intensified in her next letter. "Poor Barclay is confined in a madhouse & his wife as you may imagine is in great distress. We have seen a great deal of her lately." Eventually Harriet tried to help, writing Barclay's brothers, begging them to come forward and help her friend. Finally, a brother-in-law appeared, and the father settled £500 a year upon the family and so, as Harriet reported, "they are no longer in any pecuniary distress." Her last look at them found the husband and wife "living in great comfort at Montmartre." Still, the helplessness of such unfortunate women stood in clear relief. While Harriet could visit Mrs. Barclay, console her, commiserate with her, and solicit help from all sources, there was little else to do but follow the story. For most of her other distressed friends, there were no such satisfactory resolutions.

The physical and mental ailments of their spouses was only one kind of pitfall faced by women who committed their fates to men. In this dangerous economic period, countless men were financially ruined, leaving their wives and families destitute. Women who could not wield a pen, as had Mrs. Trollope, could do little more than follow their husbands to whatever temporary haven of obscurity and relief they might find. Mr. Bolling was ruined in July of 1828 and "absconded." Harriet reported, "His poor wife joins him in England, and is soon to be confined. What a wretched marriage." Mrs. Cruger was always "vexed about money, her husband sends her no remittance." Whenever this lady appears in the letters, the subject is the same: "Mrs. Cruger at Cooper's place, but much out of spirits. The old story: no remittances." Mrs. Hunter's husband, after twenty years of hard work in the Mauritius, "was supposed to have realized *a very large* property" but "lost it all thro *Free Trade.*" At fifty-three, he had to begin the world again, but as another friend reported, "Of course it will be years before they can hope to be independent. He has taken his wife and children all back to the Mauritius —a sad disappointment. . . . She thought she had returned to live comfortably in England for the rest of her life." This pious Christian correspondent was more prepared to accept such reverses than was Harriet: "Such are the trials we are exposed to, whilst pilgrims here on earth."

Other women were literally worn to death by the rigors attending their husbands' financial distresses. Harriet's old friend Miss Stephenson now lay dying as the penniless Mrs. Jeffrey. Indignantly, she told Julia of these desperate troubles:

> She is in a deep decline & has two little girls of 5 and 3 years. I think the exertion she has made & neglect of herself has brought on her death, for her sole object has been to save every sixpence she could for her children, & she has led a very hard rough life, and she was too delicate to bear it. Her husband was in the Coast Guard, and they lived in a very small, uncomfortable house, with one ignorant country girl as a maid of all work; so she was obliged to do a great deal herself. Poor thing, I am very sorry for her. . . . Her illness has occupied & grieved us very much, for she was a kind-hearted affectionate creature & we have seen a great deal of her.

When she died a month later, Harriet told Julia, "It is a relief to me to know her sufferings are over, so painful and hopeless was her state." One after another, the financial shipwrecks surface in the Garnett correspondence. Mrs. Phillipon's husband "has been unfortunate in business." "Poor Mrs. Taylor! I thought them so rich & they seemed so happy! I am truly sorry for them." Mrs. Taylor herself, a pious woman, accepted her trials without protest. She told Julia, "I shall at last get hardened to trials, and look on this life merely as a pilgrimage to a better—or at least I hope to learn to bear them patiently."

But bearing one's troubles too patiently could lead, and often did, to some intolerable varieties of male tyranny.

One of the most dramatic and enigmatic concerned one "poor Mrs. Smith," who "walked about with her husband until she told us her leg was completely raw. She then set out to travel three nights and two days to Bordeaux, & this with her wooden leg is a dreadful confinement. Her leg swells dreadfully when she is fatigued, & her nerves have been much shaken by all she has endured. She appears as fond as ever of Miles, & he seems attentive to her, but how could he allow her to go through so much fatigue?" It was a question women could not answer. Given women's philosophical orientation, so sensitive to the needs of others, how could men be so different? Perhaps one should find an answer before marrying. An even stranger story came from an article on distinguished German women, which Harriet read and found remarkable enough to recommend strongly to her sister. It contained an account of the life of Charlotte Steiglitz, "whom you must surely have seen, for she went to Hanover, to visit her relations there, who killed herself from conjugal love to rouse her husband from morbid depression of spirits." While most women were not so violent or final, were not these married women of Harriet's acquaintance all such willing victims of sorts?

Domineering husbands were a natural outgrowth of the Victorian patriarchy. At least two of Harriet's circle of friends struggled with the problems of tyrannical spouses. How many more suffered in silence is unknown. Clara Ranke's solution was an abject and saintly acceptance of her lot, and her stance alternatively troubled and enraged Julia Pertz. Mrs. Fauche fought back by leaving her tyrannical husband and devoting herself to the care of her children. While Harriet praised the self-sacrificing Mrs. Fauche, who denied "herself everything to educate her children well & a more devoted mother I never saw," she recognized the difficulty of such a life. "Mrs. Fauche is very proud of her son, but looks ill herself. . . . She has a very anxious & fatiguing life, & I fear her health will sink under the exertion she makes." Three years later it was not Mrs. Fauche but the much admired son who was sinking into an early death. As Mrs. Fauche wrote, "I have spent more than I could afford in justice to the girls & I have sacrificed my own ease for years to give an education which would have rendered him an ornament to Woolwich Academy, but since I came to reside in Paris . . . he has been ill & during the last six months he has been slowly but surely dying. I need not tell you how I feel!" A year later, after her son had died, new troubles arrived, this time surrounding her eldest daughter Mary's impending "advantageous marriage."

But despite the good intentions and assistance of Harriet, Julia, and Mrs. Trollope, the Fauche story came to an unhappy conclusion at last, even though Mary's marriage, so much in jeopardy, eventually took place. In 1849, four years after Mary Fauche's friends had rallied to expedite her union, Harriet had one more name to add to her catalogue of women whose marriages had gone bad. She told Julia:

> I do pity Mrs. Fauche & Mary. Fauche was an angel compared to Schuster, who is as mean and contemptible a creature as ever breathed & a most wretched husband. Mary is very fond of her little girl, & only too happy to escape from him. But he may always give her trouble. Poor thing, hers is a hard fate, for she was a child of 16 when she married this man. He has gentle manners, & Mrs. Fauche believed him to be all that was excellent. I suppose he married hoping she would maintain him & his wife.

The daughter's fate had run in parallel lines to her mother's. And so, it must have seemed, did the destinies of so many women who bound themselves forever to men in marriage.

Even if the health and personal character of husbands were good, there were, of course, the ever-present dangers attending the bearing, rearing, and education of children. The letters contain countless references to women ill or dying following childbirth. Harriet recorded their stories sadly and swiftly. Captain Wilson's wife died in childbed. "A violent storm at sea occasioned the birth of her child. Her husband was taking her to the place he had obtained with an immense salary." "Mrs. Capper & her infant are both dead at Lisbon." Mary Glover suffered terribly from the illness following the birth of her child. Harriet asked Julia, "Cannot you feel for her? . . . It is truly a pity."

After children were safely brought into the world, women faced other problems. In the nineteenth century, children's illnesses were severe and often deadly. Mrs. Trollope lost four of her six surviving children to tuberculosis. Mary Shelley reared only one of hers, and the horrors attending the early deaths of her other infants provided her with powerful metaphors of violent and horrible births which emerged in *Frankenstein*. Frances Wright bore two girls and lost one. The percentages were not good. Not surprisingly, women watched with almost neurotic caution over their children. Like those unnatural madonnas of early Christian art, they spent lengthy hours focused only upon their infants. They expended much of their time and energy upon the physical and mental development of their children, whose early education and care fell largely in their hands. When Harriet described the devotion of one young widow to her children, the rhetoric was revealing: "She had the misery of being a widow very young, left the world and confined herself entirely to the education of her children." Like a nun's devotion in some cloistered convent, a woman's to her children often became as exacting and final a commitment as any religious vow.

Women's fates were bound up with those of their children. Bianca Mileri, as Harriet reported, was "devoted to the education of two little boys, and she lost her eldest boy." Poor Mrs. Outram, who succeeded in rearing her excellent son to manhood, was shocked to learn of his sudden death in India in 1830. Harriet reported her very great depression: "He was her favorite child —very handsome and very clever. We must go & see her as she had no friends here, poor woman." Devotion to others, sacrifice for them, ultimately loss. Such seemed the triple crown of the married woman.

Finally, when husbands died, good or bad, they often left their wives and families in dire straits. Repeatedly, stories of distressed widows cross Harriet's pages. Mrs. Carter, a "good little woman who lost her husband in the East Indies" and who was left with two little boys to support, lived in pensions and slept in the dining parlors of kind friends. When young Deninson died, he left his wife, a Scotch girl, to bear him a fine son. Her lying-in coincided with his funeral, and Harriet told Julia: "Her situation is a dreadful one." "Poor Eliza Henry lost her husband suddenly in an apoplectic fit—he has left her with five children of her own, six unmarried of his, and $30,000 only to provide for all. . . ." Harriet's analysis followed: "What a melancholy situation for her." Madame Regnarine's husband protected his honor by fighting a duel, but lost, leaving his wife to wear weeds and live "in great distress at St. Germain where the family still reside."

A particularly affecting case concerned Mme. Salazar,

> a poor woman in great affliction . . . the widow of the Columbian minister to the U.S. Her husband came here last summer to see Europe, bringing with him his wife & 4 children. She was confined a month since, and immediately after, her husband fell ill & died. She was strongly attached to him. . . . She is left in very reduced circumstances from being a minister's wife & with 5 young spoilt children—herself a weak-minded helpless South American. We go often to sit with her as she cannot bear to be left alone. I never saw a greater picture of distress and helplessness.

"Distress and helplessness"—those were the key words describing Harriet's female acquaintances who had married, and "poor" the recurring adjective which modified the noun of their encumbered womanhood.

The story of the Hickeys, cousins of the Garnetts, illustrates how the death of the male head of the household could set off reverberations from which women could not free themselves even after the passing of a generation. Events began in the usual way. "Just as Mr. Hickey was to leave India and return home to his wife & children, he was seized with the cholera and died in a few hours. His wife was very much attached to him, and is, as you may suppose, overwhelmed with grief. . . . She is left with 10 children. . . ." Seven years later, after struggling with her enormous burdens, Mrs. Hickey herself died, "leaving 5 girls." What happened to the remaining five children is unknown; perhaps they were men, who were able to strike out on their own. In any event, Harriet was "very sorry to receive this intelligence; the poor girls must be very unhappy, for she was a most affectionate mother & they were much attached to her. I pity them from my heart." Fortunately, Mrs. Hickey had a married sister from India who soon promised to take the elder girls with her to India upon her return. Once again, "the old-girl network" was ready to help. By March 1851, Harriet reported the successful marriage of one of the Hickey girls "to a man of £3000 a year & a very respectable & excellent man, 20 years older than herself, but handsome & agreeable." There seemed no alternative but marriage for dependent women. Harriet seemed to approve: "This is a great thing for the two who are here & going out next summer. I have no doubt they will marry well also in India. . . ." Yet she applied the usual adjective when she contemplated their futures. "Poor things! They begin early to act & struggle for themselves. . . ." When summer came and they were ready to embark, she wrote again, "Poor girls! . . . What a voyage for two young things. . . . We have seen the girls almost every day for a year & are of course interested for them." One wonders with Harriet about their futures. Clearly, they sought for themselves no greater good than marriage to a man with so many hundreds a year. What did they gain for their bargains? Madness? Ill health? Death in childbed? Genteel poverty? Happiness?

But surely Harriet knew of some successful marriages? She seemed satisfied with her sister's union with Dr. Pertz, but then, she saw very little of it. Still, her comments on good relationships frequently contained mention of the woman's separate occupation, and, in some cases, even separate living arrangements. The earliest such story appeared in the summer following Julia's marriage, when Harriet reported: "Heloise is happily married. . . . Not a rich but a respectable man of fifty. She continues her school & wrote in happy spirits." As the years passed, Harriet remained curious about the ways in which married women arranged the context of their lives. When the Garnetts went to Geneva, they observed Louis Simond and his wife who, Harriet found, was "kind and good natured—rather pretty—looks in perfect health and is better than she has been since her marriage & is able to walk." The rest of Harriet's letter explained the reasons behind the conjugal blossoming of Mrs. Simond. "She breakfasts and I should think sits a great deal in her room pursuing her own occupations. Simond makes no fuss with her or his child. . . ." This freedom to go one's own way, to pursue one's own occupations, was a rare treasure. Seldom possible for single women, it was most unusual for a married lady. Mrs. Simond's position was worthy of notice.

Mrs. Trollope introduced the Garnetts to the famous writer Mrs. Marsh. At Brighton, the Garnetts had tea with her several times. In describing the authoress to Julia, Harriet mentioned Mrs. Marsh's independence within her marriage. "Her husband is a banker and business detains him chiefly in London; but when he has a holiday he comes to her. She has a son and 6 daughters, the eldest 20 years old, & is a fond and devoted mother, and enjoys society very much. . . ." When her friend Sophia Weston married in 1851, Harriet praised the arrangements. "She has 700 pounds a year and he has even more, and has settled all he can dispose of upon her. So, if she survives him, she will be a rich widow, and she is to be uncontrolled mistress of her own fortune and leave it to whom she pleases and spend it as she likes and live wherever she pleases, and so she has managed her affairs well." To manage one's affairs well enough to do what one pleased—that was the highest felicity. Of emotional satisfaction or love, Harriet said little. But in the letters, women rarely found lasting happiness in marriage, and seemed worse off than spinsters.

While in the multi-colored web of the letters, marriage was woven in darker tints, the correspondence reveals a growing optimism about women's potential for creativity. Harriet and her friends eagerly circulated stories hailing the appearance of some female genius. Indeed, two of the lengthiest brief lives in the letters concern so-called "women of genius" who stood out from among their sex because they had donned "brain-armour" and thus belonged to what Mrs. Craik later called "the neutral realm of pure intellect." Genius was amazonian, not the natural state of woman. Genius thrust one before the public, not only mentally, but sometimes physically, as had Frances Wright's skill in public lecturing. Another dangerous aspect of such talent in women was its potential egotism. As Mrs. Craik noted in her discussion of allowable female professions in 1864, " 'Each for himself' seems implanted in masculine nature, for its own preservation; but when it comes to *'each for herself,'* " well, such a result would only be regrettable. Yet why should only women's gifts be hidden under bushels? Clearly, superior intellectual promise in women was something to be applauded and nurtured.

Twice Harriet watched over the apparent budding of such genius in women; twice she was bitterly disappointed in its outcome. The first bright intellectual star to rise on Harriet's horizon was a Mlle. de Klustine, with whom the Garnetts became acquainted in Geneva in the 1830s.

> Last night we met . . . a Russian lady—Mme de Klustine, whose daughter, a girl
> of 20, is a prodigy of learning and talent—& full of vivacity and good humor.

—she is very much admired here and passes the summer close to us. . . . She is very gracious and engaging in manner, as tall as F.W., with the finest black eyes I have ever seen—full of intelligence and sweetness.

Having lost her old friend and genius on the rocks of failed respectability, Harriet eagerly welcomed this new, more purified version of intellectual accomplishment in women. A week later, she wrote Julia at length about her new acquaintance "(I may say friend) . . . from whose society I derive such pleasure!"

She speaks and writes perfectly well English, French, German, Italian, & of course, the Russian language. She understands chemistry, mathematics & botany, draws, paints, plays on the piano & dances & embroiders very well. Her knowledge of general literature & history is very extensive, & her conversation animated and amusing. She has a deep feeling & just knowledge of the fine arts. The learned men here call her *un miracle.* Sismondi & Bonstetten & Candole dote upon her—last year she wrote a long letter to Candole, on the state of Russian literature, which he published & very clever it is. But all this is only wonderful. Her chief attraction lies in her kindness, her simplicity . . . the sweetness of her manners, which is truly bewitching. She has traveled a great deal and been much in the first society in Paris & Italy and has a large fortune which she is going to bestow on the young Frenchman who has won her heart —the Comte de Courcourt—& happy man he is—& seems sensible for his great happiness. . . . I wish you knew Anastasie, for there is a charm in all she says and does which one must see to understand, but all who know her think & speak of her as I do. She is or appears very fond of me & I love her truly.

The new friend planned to make Geneva her summer residence, but, as Harriet noted to Julia with guarded disappointment, "her plans will now depend upon another. She has hitherto lived with a gentle kind widowed mother who has given her every advantage of education & truly adores her daughter." What a lord and master might do with her intellectual potential was uncertain. Quickly, Harriet betrayed antagonism towards the future husband. Anastasie it was impossible "not to love . . . uniting as she does so much talent, to sweetness of manner & disposition," but "her intended I do not like." Harriet regretted the match, for "she is superior to him in every respect." She told Julia, "I have some fears." Moreover, "as he is usually sitting with her . . . I have less pleasure in going to see her than before her engagement." After her marriage, and during her second winter in Geneva, Harriet's friend was in "the prospect of having a child" and was duly "suffering from her situation." Then, all at once, she vanished from the letters

altogether. There were a few last gasps of interest. "Suffering." "Very delicate." And finally, "perhaps we may never see her again." So ended the clever
"miracle" who had become Mme. de Courcourt.

Ten years later, another accomplished female entered the letters, a child
prodigy of thirteen who, Harriet reported, had written so much that it "would
fill from the floor to the height of a table." Once again, her letter fluttered
with the old excitement.

> She is in perfect health of mind & body. Her father is a clergyman of the name
> of Willis, living near Bow-wood. . . . And neither he nor the mother are persons
> of distinguished abilities; but they are judicious in wishing to keep her back
> instead of urging her to learn, & in not wishing her to be known at her early
> age, or publishing her works.

Miss Willis was also an acquaintance of Julia's friend Julia Smith, whose letter
about the young lady Harriet recopied for her sister's benefit.

> She reads Latin and Greek with perfect facility; she not only reads but speaks
> fluently & has written tales of her own composition in French, German, Italian
> & Spanish. All the moral writers & poets of these countries she has read. She
> plays superbly and composes admirably. Horsely heard her the other day & the
> next day presented her with all his works. She is a superior arithmetician &
> mathematician. The first professors have given her the most difficult problems
> & she has solved them with singular facility; they purposely gave her faulty
> equations and she detected them directly. She most excels in poetry and prom-
> ises to be the first poet after Shakespeare & Milton we have ever had; this,
> Milman, Southey & Wordsworth say of her. This last corresponds regularly
> with her. He was written to last year to compose a national anthem, he declined,
> & said he knew of no one who could do justice to the theme but a little girl of
> 12 years old. Her fancy is boundless, her ear for rhyme is faultless, her purity
> of thoughtful piety & feeling so angelic that Anne & her sisters forbad my
> reading any more of her poetry aloud, so vehemently were we all affected by
> its sweetness. The grandeur & loftiness of her thoughts are inconceivable. The
> Bible she knows by heart & tho' steeped in adulation, is as humble, unobtrusive,
> simple & unspoiled as an angel. The queen has had her three times to pass the
> evening with her in private. She has never alluded to these interviews to any
> living soul. Lord Lansdown, Crocker, Milman, Wordsworth, the Bishop of
> Salisbury, & many other distinguished men have visited her, but she never
> thinks more of them after the interviews. I feel embarrassed in her presence; she
> gives me the idea of being a spirit.

At present, the young girl's primary fame stemmed from a short poem she had written at the age of eight, which the august Wordsworth himself had noticed. Enthusiastically, Harriet transcribed it for Julia.

On a sound heard in the air on a perfectly cloudless day
in the summer of 1836

Whence art thou, thou mysterious sound,
With thy low deep murmur gathering round.
Slow rolling o'er the fair summer skies,
As their vault in its cloudless beauty lies.

Thou dost not come on the breeze's wing;
No breath doth the rose's perfume bring.
Thou dost not ride on the thunder cloud,
The heavens no gloomy vapours shroud;
Thou dost not spring from the tempest's ire.

No deadly flames of forked fire
Herald thee thro' the firmament.

Whence art thou then & wherefore sent?
Would I were skilled in mystic lore;
Would I thro' starlit paths could soar;
Oh! were I not chained to this parent earth,
Sound, I would know thy wondrous birth!

Say, in some bright revolving star,
Are countless millions waging war?
Are thou the sound of their armies flying?
Art thou the groan of their millions dying?
Or, still more dread, is thy sound, oh say?
That of worlds like our own that pass away?

And so it went on, for about six more lines which have been irretrievably marred with the many foldings and re-crossings of the letters. Here was clear evidence that women could be geniuses and poets too; Harriet and her circle waited eagerly for the appearance of that female Shakespeare who would herald the new coming of woman to the hitherto exclusively male sphere of poetry.

In 1844, when the young genius had reached sixteen, there was more, this time from another single woman, Julia Smith, who also was watching over the progress of "the little poetess whose lines 'on a sound heard in the air' etc., you and I admired together in the beginning of our acquaintance." The girl was also an acquaintance of the Nightingale family.

> She had been at Embley where the Nightingales live. Florence Nightingale tells me she is as simple & childlike as can be & that there is no doubt she really wrote the verses you know. Her father takes a great deal of pains with her & with all of them and is quite discreet in encouraging no display, more so than the mother, but the child's own truth of character is the best safeguard against all such mischief. She is very musical and composed long ago very prettily. Now she is no longer a child; perhaps she may be sixteen. I shall try and hear of her if it is consistent with the not making her a 'lion.'

It is not surprising that Florence Nightingale interested herself in the young poet. For women who hoped to succeed, every evidence of female brilliance promised the further emergence of the new woman. But alas, the blossoming of Miss Willis was not to be. When the girl reached nineteen, Julia Smith reported to the Garnetts once more:

> I have always meant to tell you that the little sister who wrote certain lines, 'on a sound heard in the air one calm summer's day' is grown into almost a woman without doing anything extraordinary & is now going to be married, so of course she never will. She has indeed written some beautiful poetry, but has not made a pursuit of that or of any distinct subject, I understand; she has the irregular, uncomfortable habits, without so much as one hoped of the glories & the joys of genius.

She is now "going to be married, so of course she never will." The situation was so obvious as to be unarguable. Marriage and the consequent lack of steady occupation in her craft were twin cankers at the heart of the rose which had failed to bloom into the first female genius.

But despite such disappointments, the correspondence offered hope that women could earn some degree of success through writing. Mrs. Jameson, Miss Mitford, and Mrs. Trollope were supporting their families on their earnings from writing fiction and drama. Harriet Martineau, "the daughter of a merchant at Norwich who failed," had used her pen to influence the course of pending legislation. To write her *Illustrations of Political Economy,* focusing on the poor laws and other economic problems, she had been entrusted with government documents. Her stipulation at the outset indicated her sense of importance: "She must be left entirely to herself." More and more, the middle-class woman was coming into her own.

Writing was not the only path to independence. Emily Ronalds, in Surrey, who had long ago made financial contributions to Nashoba, now "has formed and conducted in her neighborhood an excellent infant school, and taken her stand in favor of human improvement and liberal principles in opposition to old friends and relatives." Mrs. Fletcher, whom Harriet met in 1830, had come for a Paris visit, after which she and her two daughters had departed for a small country town near York, "taking charge of an old aunt who is now in her dotage and does not even know them & this life they have led for two years and will do so while her aunt lives." Harriet was astonished that Mrs. Fletcher, "who shines in society and loves, cheerfully submits to this sacrifice." When she remonstrated with her new friend upon this dreary life, Mrs. Fletcher claimed to have found that it had done her good. "It has taught me to depend on my own resources." How important an achievement it was to survive, depending simply on oneself, and asking for nothing! Harriet was impressed: "Such a woman I should like to see every day."

Even Julia Smith, despite her age, was part of the change. She was pleased to see people like "Lady Byron and my friend Emily Taylor" who were "really undeniably useful." She told Julia Pertz: "I have just returned from spending five days with Emily Taylor at Ealing, where she is superintending a labour school established by Lady Byron. A very pleasant sight it is, one only wishes that instead of one there were a thousand such." She felt herself part of a new world. "Surely it is a fine privilege to live in these times for those who can interpret them in some measure rightly; the old routine is broken up and mankind *must* think & feel and search out new ways. We may hope that the world is better prepared to do so than it was half a century ago. . . ."

Her niece Hilary Bonham-Carter was surely in the forefront of the movement toward the new woman. Just the other day (June 1848), she had attended a lecture by the radical American, Ralph Waldo Emerson, on Natural Aristocracy, "to which the Duchess of Sutherland, her son-in-law the Duke of Argyll & others were attentively listening."

> It may be partly fashion that makes these people run after benevolent plans and rugged truths, but it is a better fashion, at any rate, than claret & champagne & Mechlin lace pocket-handkerchiefs. I believe the time *will* come when Aristocracy, all but Natural, will disappear.

Were people ready for the most "rugged truth" of all? That women were the equals of men? That the kind of aristocracy which made women lower than their male masters must also, in time, pass away? At any rate, Hilary had made a good start; avoiding the marriage market as had her cousin Florence Nightingale, she had gone off to spend the winter in Paris with Mr. and Mrs.

Mohl (Mary Clarke), as Julia Smith reported, "to make a great stride in her drawing there. She has a great love for it, & has made considerable progress, but her life is so occupied with business and social claims, that she finds scarce any time to follow up drawing at home, & so I am glad she is going to have a period free from all home cares, & in the society of two persons she so much loves and admires. . . ." Even twenty years after Hilary had set off for Paris to try winning a career as an artist, Mrs. Craik, in some words on "Female Professions" (*A Woman's Thoughts About Women,* 1864) was calling art the most difficult, perhaps the most "impossible" profession for women.

> There are many reasons for this; in the course of education necessary for a painter, in the not unnatural repugnance that is felt to women's drawing from 'the life,' attending anatomical dissections, and so on—all which studies are indispensable to one who would plumb the depths and scale the heights of the most arduous of the liberal arts. Whether any woman will ever do this, remains yet to be proved. Meantime, many lower and yet honourable positions are open to female handlers of the brush.

A year later, Hilary was still "working hard at her drawing in and out of the Louvre. She is very happy and will stay a long while, for it is a privilege she has long wished for and is really . . . quite fit to profit by."

Julia Smith was one of the "advanced" women who feared the tyranny of family when it came to women's seeking personal goals. She told Julia Pertz about Hilary: "She is a good creature—but so good that when she is at home (like another dear friend of mine) she can hardly ever get an hour for any quiet occupation of her own, she is wanted by so many." The parenthetical reference was all Miss Smith would trust herself with when she thought of Julia's declining health. A month before Mrs. Pertz's death, Julia Smith expressed happiness "to see all the young women of my acquaintance getting hold of some occupation or at least feeling the want of it. Few sit down contented now, with the life that was considered to do very well in my young days, made up of *a little* music & *a little* drawing and a good deal of visiting. I remember looking round upon the *little* world I lived in & making my *little* reflections, but alas, they did not prevent my falling into the snare." Occupation before marriage: such a radical reversal of the proper order of things showed a new spirit was abroad.

In Germany, too, there were stirrings among Harriet's and Julia's friends. Julia Smith had met Julia's Berlin and Hanover acquaintances, and made friends with the most interesting of them. When she returned to England, she was always asking for news about one or another of them.

I hope you will soon tell me something of [Louischen Piper]. She is a spirited little creature & sure to be doing something. I fancy her rather too spirited & independent for the German taste in young ladies, & I should not wonder if she were to remain unmarried. She will be better able than most to make her own happiness; she is so ready to love, & so willing to help, & besides, she has so much intellectual resources, so I am not going to pity her whatever happens.

"Able to make her own happiness"—that was the key. And toward the end of this long correspondence, it is precisely that gift that Harriet most admires in her women friends. Her cousin Lucy Gilbert had "a restless spirit," and moved freely among her feminine acquaintances, always paying her way, never remaining long enough to outstay her welcome. "Lucy Gilbert is gone to pass two months with my sisters at Brighton," Julia Pertz told a bedridden friend. "What a gay wandering life she leads." Even the Garnetts' older sister Anna Maria Stone, who had stayed behind in America so long ago, was now on her own. After many years of silence, Anna Maria wrote her sisters in 1849 upon learning of her mother's death. She herself had lived through great troubles, the death of her husband and many of her children and family, but she looked forward to the future as an independent woman. "I am once more at 65 years of age earning my bread by teaching music. My sons would prevent it if they could, but they have all large families and I will not let them." There was unconcealed pride in her statement. Anna Maria at sixty-five, could "earn her bread" with the skills of her own hands. Was this not what a whole generation of women had been slowly moving towards?

In all these brief lives, three themes predominate, threading through like some master leitmotif insisting upon its own importance, always longing, in true Wagnerian style, for the unattainable. To be economically independent and self-sustaining; to find worthwhile, self-satisfying occupation; to find some final fulfillment for the heart's deep yearnings for companionship. In their relationships as wives and mothers, there had been so much suffering, struggle, and loss. Those bonds with husbands, parents, and children were marred by the upheavals of an increasingly difficult and changing world. And to seek deep bonds with other women seemed to violate the popular wisdom about "shrieking sisterhoods." Yet from within the solitary confinement of their domestic sphere, women were gradually realizing that the Holy Grail of female happiness lay not in marriage, but in a unique combination of independence, occupation, and bonding. Without these three, even a married woman's life was incomplete.

Recently, Nina Auerbach has identified some prevailing nineteenth-century literary attitudes toward the possibility of self-sufficient circles of women. In Jane Austen, although women were always sitting together, they were merely waiting for men to enter the room and make life begin. A contrasting picture is Louisa May Alcott's *Little Women*, a female world so full that the male friend longs to enter it. Such a picture provides at least an alternative to the marriage market, but none of the March girls succeeded in bringing the completeness of that youthful female setting into their fictional adult lives. Perhaps real sisterhoods could exist only in an inward space, made visible on the pages of letters. Harriet saw how harshly women had fared and also how they had drawn strength from those relationships with women which nothing in their culture had ever recommended to them.

The friends who stood at the center of this new realization were the Bayleys, three sisters who lived together in the prettily named Orient Cottage at Hastings. Harriet had known them since her youth. Indeed, the Bayleys' presence at Hastings was partly responsible for the Garnetts' subsequent removal there, where Harriet, her mother, and sister Fanny entered that small community of women rich in that triple plenitude of independence, occupation, and a satisfying emotional life. The sisters were Eliza, Anne, and Sarah, the latter of whom, after having been a spinster for all of her fifty-nine years, had of late received a marriage proposal from the sixty-year-old Mr. Kenyon, described by Harriet as "very amiable, clever & agreeable, & most liberal on every subject. I do not know whether Sarah will write her intentions respecting him; I think she would be foolish not to marry him. . . . How surprised Eliza and Anne will be." Yet, by the fall following her move, after Harriet had more fully participated in the activities of her friends, she adopted a new attitude toward the "temptation" of marriage, in a voice bearing the inflections of the self-sufficient female community: "We read, walk & talk, and work a great deal, but have no general society. . . . Anne & I walk every day. Sarah I think will not marry. . . ." For Harriet, this bonding with other women was proving a satisfying experience.

The thirst for work, so persistent in these leisured nineteenth-century women, Harriet and her friends quenched in a variety of ways. First, there was the ubiquitous needlework. "Eliza and Anne work beautifully in worsteds, with Berlin patterns & wools; it is amusing but very expensive, & I content myself with useful work, & am busy making flannel petticoats, given me by Eliza and making up bobinet and muslin for the custom house." Then there was the constant task of ministering to the poor, who in those years needed parish assistance. Harriet admired the social usefulness of the Bayleys. They were, she said, "much occupied with attending to the poor, to whom they are very bountiful." When a poor young cousin of Mr. Kenyon's "who is at Hastings dying of a consumption" needed visitors, Anne went to see her every day, endeavoring "to render her last days as little irksome as possible. It is impossible to be kinder or more benevolent than these two sisters." In contrast to their brothers, one of whom was trustee of the Garnetts' properties, they were "superior in character & generous feelings."

But surely, needlework and good deeds could coexist with marriage. Harriet's next letter to Julia makes clear the important factor in Sarah Bayley's decision to remain single.

> I do not think there is any chance of a marriage; Mr. Kenyon I think is cooling, & she does not wish to marry; at 59, her age, it would be rather late I think, & *her habits make independence necessary.* She has every comfort, & the power of traveling & visiting whenever she likes; Orient Cottage is very pretty & well furnished with books & prints; the situation (to which she would go) is a dreary one, a mile from Hastings, & in winter she would not see her sisters of an evening, & not always of a morning. I never saw her look better or in better spirits.

Why marry? With comfort, freedom and occupation, there seemed little incentive. Moreover, that daily "seeing" of her sisters and friends for the purpose of community would be shattered.

And as the Bayley sisters worked designs into their needlework, Harriet fashioned her pictures of that world in her letters to Julia, painting little tableaus in which the dominant feeling was self-contained happiness and cheerful usefulness.

> It is surprising how much good she & Eliza do; they keep books to lend the poor & children, and devote a great part of their time & income to acts of charity. They are most excellent persons. . . .

> I passed my time very quietly there, walking with Anne, reading aloud occasionally, and working. We had no company, & they lead the quietest life possible, but with every comfort and luxury.

These several accounts mark Harriet's dawning discovery of a truth she had known all along: without the traditional focuses of marriage and society, women could find satisfying lives in self-sufficient female communities. She had come full circle, to the old ideas that had inspired them in the Nashoba days. Now the time was riper and the ladies more ready. Their recognition of the joys of the independent female life contributed to the developing feminine consciousness of the century.

The Bayleys and Garnetts at Hastings formed a small utopian colony, an Eden without Adam, a real-life Cranford. Their collective life seems attractive and productive. Soon, Mr. Kenyon was banished to become a friend, not a lover. Sarah Bayley, who still saw him on her vacations, had won the best of both worlds. A year later she was traveling on a vacation to Devonshire "with Mr. Kenyon and Mrs. Reid; the former continues devoted to her with the warmest and truest platonic love, and this feeling adds much to her happiness." During these times Harriet stayed with the sisters, watching them function "with great cheerfulness and patience, devoted to each other, and doing all they can for others also."

From their secure financial position, the Bayleys were unfailingly kind to their women friends. The world they shaped, they generously shared with others. Twice before, the Garnetts had found themselves the recipients of legacies from women, once from their old governess, Sophia Hay (which they, with reciprocal generosity quickly refused, letting it go instead to Miss Hay's more needy sister), and then from Madame de Pontheiu, an old friend and relative of the Wilkes, given a title by the Emperor of Austria, and a woman of means. Mme. de Pontheiu often entertained and gave gifts to the Garnetts. When she died, she made a bequest of £2000 to both Harriet and Fanny. It had made all the difference in their lives. So, too, the Bayleys shared the bountifulness of their lives with their women friends.

> [Eliza & Anne] send us everything that they fancy we can like, oranges, honey, arrowroot biscuits, oysters, wine & brandy, 2 tongues, bacon, a pack of cards, knitting materials & worsted to amuse Mamma . . . & the warm affection with which these presents are bestowed, render them invaluable. When they ask us to dine, which they do repeatedly, they say, "if the evening prove bad, there shall always be beds & fires ready for you," & it is in vain we would refuse these acts of hospitable kindness,—their answer is, what can make us as happy as to contribute to the comfort or enjoy the society of those we love? Never were kinder & more generous spirits formed, & their minds are so highly cultivated, their opinions so excellent, that even if I loved them less, their society would still be delightful from their talents & acquirements. They have a beautiful house, an excellent library, and live in great comfort and even luxury.

In their sisterhood, food, hospitality, presence, and work were truly shared.

To Harriet, the Bayleys lived a complete life, while remaining single. Mrs. Dinah Mulock Craik, self-appointed advisor to the single woman in the 1860s, formulated her theory of the unmarried woman's life on the unhappy principle that married women alone had "realized in greater or less degree the natural destiny of our sex." Single women must fashion a second-hand life, as if in default. In a curious essay on Anglican sisterhoods, Mrs. Craik asked the great question: "Those women who do not marry, what are they to do with their lives?" Her answer was that the great bulk of unmarried women "are a very helpless race, either hampered with duties, or seeking feebly for duties that do not come; miserably overworked, or disgracefully idle; piteously dependent on male relations, or else angrily vituperating the opposite sex for their denied rights or perhaps not undeserved wrongs." Considering the blankness of such lives, Mrs. Craik preferred religious sisterhoods.

Of course, she admitted, there were "exceptional" cases, her description of which calls to mind the community of the Bayleys and the Garnetts.

> I know no position more happy, more useful (and therefore happy), than that of a single woman who, having inherited or earned sufficient money and position, has courage to assume the status and responsibilities of a married woman. She has, except the husband, all the advantages of the matronly position, and almost none of its drawbacks. So much lies in her power to do unhindered, especially the power of doing good. She can be a friend to the friendless and a mother to the orphan; she can fill her house with happy guests, after the true Christian type—the guests that cannot repay her for her kindness. Being free to dispose of her time and her labor, she can be a good neighbor, a good citizen —whether or not she ever attains the doubtful privilege of female suffrage. Her worldly goods, her time, and her affections are exclusively her own to bestow wisely and well. Solitary, to a certain extent, her life must always be; but it need never be a morbid, selfish, or dreary life.

This passage reveals the unspoken assumption that for women, marriage was primarily an economic proposition. A woman who could achieve matronly status without becoming the matron was better off than the married woman with all her concomitant drawbacks. The single woman was "free to dispose of her time and her labor" as she saw fit. In marriage, these commodities were the property of the family. In the female community, they might be shared with the broader world outside.

Mrs. Ellis, too, that great advisor to all states of nineteenth-century women, in her *Women of England,* once glanced at the possibility of self-sustaining female groups, but discarded them as impracticable and visionary. She posited their existence:

> Let us imagine a little community of young women, among whom, to do an act of disinterested kindness should be an object of the highest ambition, and where to do any act of pure selfishness tending, however remotely, to the injury of another, should be regarded as the deepest disgrace; where they should be accustomed to consider their time not as their own, but lent them solely for the purpose of benefiting their fellow-creatures; and where those who were known to exercise the greatest charity and forbearance, should be looked upon as the

most exalted individuals in the whole community. Would these girls be weary? Would they be discontented, listless, and inanimate? The experiment remains to be tried.

But the Hastings community was real. The Bayleys' cottage abounded with treasures which were both real and also spiritually emblematic of something greater. There were good food, cheerfulness, and useful occupation. Their world was both physically and psychically rich. Their community hung poised with the fullness of life: physical comforts (food and fires), intellectual attainments (conversation, reading, and music), fun and usefulness to others (acts of kindness). What more could be desired? It might be heresy to say so, but surely this life was preferable to the possible domination of Mr. Kenyon. It was clear to Harriet, as it was later to Mrs. Craik, that women knew better than men, if not how to earn, then how to use money.

[Men] can earn it, lavish it, hoard it, waste it; but to deal with it wisely, as a means to an end, and also as a sacred trust, to be made the best of for others as well as themselves, is an education difficult of acquirement by the masculine mind; so difficult that one is led to doubt whether they were meant to acquire it at all, and whether in the just distribution of duties between the sexes it was not intended that the man should earn, the woman keep—he accumulate, and she expend.

Certainly, Harriet's sketches of life at the Bayleys' home suggest plenitude and content. These women, who knew how to make themselves and others happy, did not worry about failing to fulfill "the natural destiny" of their sex.

Once, on Eliza Bayley's birthday (1848), Harriet sent her a small gift and enclosed a poem, entitled, "To Eliza, with a china cup ornamented with flowers. On her birthday."

Let lovers fondly pluck the rose,
All heedless of its thorn,—
We, dearest Lizzie, offer thee,
On this thy natal morn,

A gift less bright, less fair, I own:
No perfum'd wreath we braid,
But friendship's truest emblem bring,
In flowers that never fade.

The contrasts between relationships with men and feminine friendship, while unconscious, were not less clear. Lovers might give roses, but roses have thorns. Friends give lasting gifts that do not pain or injure. In Harriet's rendering, the flowers on the china cup stand for the permanence and peacefulness of female friendships.

When the circle was finally broken by the death of Eliza, old Anne Bayley, crippled by an inveterate rheumatism, languid and suffering, still surrounded herself with female companions. One was "a young person who suits her in every respect, and she plays duets on the piano with her." In holiday time, she added Louisa Edwards and "the two Shakles to pass the Xmas holidays with her, & she had, I am sure, plenty of plum pudding and turkey for them & herself." While Dickens' characteristically acquisitive male lived alone with his treasures, needing the prodding of three spirits to awaken him to the double pleasures of benevolence and community, real women knew better. It is hard to feel sorry for old Miss Bayley.

The circle was further eroded by the death of old Mrs. Garnett in November 1848. Julia told a friend: "It is (as my sister wrote me) like the loss of an only child to a parent. . . . My poor sisters are in deep affliction—they have no other object of their love and care—my mother was to them what an only child is to a tender parent—with her life has ended their occupation—and they feel it deeply—their healths have suffered and are still suffering from the effects of grief—they will not be comforted—they weep and lament, and I am too far to nurse and comfort them. . . ." Harriet spent the days thinking of her mother and writing about her to Julia. Even her dreams were of her mother. She told Julia: "I never shall enjoy real happiness again—one thought will ever pursue me. I have not passed, I am sure, 3 nights since without dreaming of poor mamma, and always that she is ill but that I have great hopes of her recovery." Three months after Maria's death, Harriet tried to sum up her mother's qualities, as she studied a likeness of her mother.

> I have a beautiful miniature of her at 18 when she was a celebrated beauty and much admired for her extreme elegance and good manners & the last she ever retained & was strikingly ladylike in manners, appearance, ideas, & feelings—and the most generous of human beings. She would have deprived herself of any thing to give to others, & the clearness of her perception and insight into character was surprising even to the last. In her youth, education was not much attended to, but she was remarkably clever, & by many of her observations I should wish to be guided for the remainder of my life. What a blank she has left in my life!

A week later, she still could not shake her depression.

> I am ever disposed to write and speak of my heavy loss; I do not think the pang of losing a husband or a child can be so bitterly felt as the loss of a beloved

parent when you have the habit of living constantly with that parent. Your whole existence seems changed. Poor dear Mamma! I never showed her enough how well I loved her. I hope she can see into my heart now. . . . But I have an aching in my throat from agitation and must write no more.

Harriet regarded her loss as more painful than that of a partner in marriage. In August 1850, when the sisters visited Julia for the last time in Berlin, Julia was "shocked to see the ravages that 5 years and affliction had made" in Harriet's appearance.

Later, Harriet found other preoccupations. She became "zealous about unfermented bread and brown flour," and even disseminated little pamphlets "recommendatory of them, both for cheapness and for wholeness." Issues of health and diet became an increasingly important interest in her life. She accumulated recipes for preparations of Indian Corn, and prescribed hop tea for the maladies of her friends. She bought an electric galvanizing machine, which she tried hard to persuade the now ailing Julia to use. An early health-food faddist, she bought flour, bran, sharps and pollards, and mixed them according to individual needs, "excellent and very wholesome, and obviating the necessity of taking medicine," she claimed. She advised Julia constantly on the subject of her health. "Essence of dandelion, bought at a good chemist, one teaspoonful mixed in a wine glass of water three times a day" was excellent, along with raw egg and water. She treasured a book of home remedies, and told Julia, "I eat no cakes, no bread but three days old brown bread, mutton, roast or boiled. I drink only two cups of weak tea, no vegetables or pastry. . . . The dandelion is an invaluable medicine."

These new, pseudo-scientific interests prompted Harriet to read the popular *Vestiges of Natural History*, and she was struck, along with her contemporaries, by "the gradual development & improvement of all things and beings —from the rude polypus, the first creation, to the present wonderful structures of vegetables, animals, and man. But the ideas the work gives rise to are bewildering, and the author supposes that man possesses powers not yet developed—that another and superior race must spring from ours." Perhaps the communal spirit she had discovered in her later life was one manifestation of that yet-to-be-developed "superior race." But while most Victorians, along with their Poet Laureate, were waiting for the new, higher type of man, Harriet's dreams were of the emergence of women.

By 1851, Harriet and Fanny, in another of their many moves, settled at Brighton, a few hours away from the event of the year, the Great Exhibition. Still, despite Harriet's admission that the whole was "a noble conception beautifully worked out," she would not "exchange the hills & trees & rocks & birds for the gorgeous Crystal Palace." She told Julia, "It is the fancy of the day to send every one to the Crystal Palace. In Wales I hear servants have left good places because they were not allowed to go, & everyone in Brighton, I believe, sends up their servants. Our cook goes tomorrow & the maid has been & eat ices at the Crystal Palace in the midst of 70,000 persons—the poorest calling for ices and lemonade." Had she been able to persuade one of Julia's boys to visit them, she would perhaps have gone to visit "what every one but ourselves goes to see!"

That autumn, Julia Smith visited Harriet and Fanny and reported the sisters looking "exceedingly well and happy."

> Their house & all its appurtenances looked beautiful. Sister Fanny, what a good creature she is, seemed quite occupied with her bit of garden and green house and told me many anecdotes of her plants, shells, and stones. If I had been clever I could have made a very pretty sketch for the *Household Words* of Sister Fanny's occupations & nobody would have known who 'twas or if they had, they could not have been displeased. Sister Harriet was reading the newspaper as usual, I suppose. Her interests seemed more in the human line. . . . But as to persuading them to come and see the Exhibition, it was impossible. No, they said, they would stay and take care of Brighton.

Julia Smith, sensitive to the significance of the ordinary, saw in Harriet's living arrangements the basis for a story about a community of women. There were only two now, to be sure, but they were still happy, occupied, and interested enough in the world to read newspapers, but not to leave the bastion of sisterhood for the perils of the Exhibition, where individual, not communal effort, was applauded.

Female friendship was a valuable commodity which even more independent and aggressive women might one day find lacking in their lives. Jessie Allen Sismondi, now long widowed, had maintained her connections to the Garnetts. On her seventy-fifth birthday, she received a lovingly embroidered collar and cuffs from Harriet and Fanny Garnett. Madame Sismondi took the occasion to contrast the old and new woman in a letter to Harriet, describing a dinner party to which she had invited her nieces and great-nieces. "Charming as they are," she wrote,

> I could not help doubting whether either generation would at 75 have such a tender gift from younger friends. Not mine the merit but the loving generation of the givers, and which heavenly quality is I fear wearing out—not in them but in the fashion of the world after them. . . . I doubt if there is such another pair of hearts as yours and Fanny's.

Even as some women were pushing forward to new degrees of achievement, others were holding on to more static modes of self-sufficiency which had been no less strenuously won.

Harriet and Fanny maintained their bonds with their friends and each other until they died in their eighties at Brighton where, as Julia Smith had put it, they continued to live in close company with "their living and half living cares," with the birds, which came to occupy a pretty little back room on the staircase of their house, and in the secluded garden, so lovingly bedecked with shells, corallines, and seaweeds.

References

Page

93 "You know how sacred . . ." HG/JGP, November 1848, GPC.
94 "went off well . . ." and "She is handsome . . ." HG/JGP, 31 October 1827 and 21 September 1831, GPC. Byron's affair with the Countess Guiccioli lasted 1819-23.
94 "I like Paris . . ." HG/JGP, 17 February 1832, GPC.
94 "The step once taken . . ." HG/JGP, Fall of 1827, GPC.
95 For HG/JGP on Mérimée, see letters of 15 February and 17 June 1828 and 8 December 1829, GPC.
95 "You know Harriet's love . . ." MG/JCP, 31 January 1828, GPC.
96 "Harriet never fails . . ." MG/JGP, 28 April 1828, GPC.
96 "M.X.—took no trouble . . ." See Kathleen O'Meara, *Madame Mohl,* pp. 43, 107, 114-15, and 240-41.
96 "Poor Fanny . . ." HG/JGP, 12 May 1828, GPC.
97 "I can truly say . . . " FT/HG & JGP, 7 December 1828, GPC.
97 "This will be . . ." HG/JGP, 2 November 1828, GPC.
97 "I am quite tired . . ." HG/JGP, 5 March 1828, GPC.
97 "childish, silly and gay . . ." HG/JGP, 4 December 1829, GPC.
98 "circulating library . . ." HG/JGP, 17 March 1829, GPC.
98 "moderate in their expressions . . ." HG/JGP, 23 November 1829, GPC.
98 "Memoirs of a gentlewoman . . ." HG/JGP, 10 March 1829, GPC.
99 "And now I must tell . . ." HG/JGP, 29 June 1831, GPC.
99 "Harriet amuses herself . . ." FG/JGP, 9 July 1831, GPC.
99 "Harriet's novel . . ." *The Jersey Laurel,* MS, p. 46 for quotation, GPC. Harriet's problems regarding the length of the novel were the same as those encountered by Charlotte Brontë with her first novel, *The Professor,* which was published only after her death.
101 "which for us unites . . ." HG/JGP, 15 December 1831, GPC.

101 "I have so little time . . ." HG/JGP, 17 February 1832, GPC.
101 "much happier . . ." MG/JGP, 12 January 1832, GPC.
101 "Hitherto I have had . . ." HG/JGP, 13 June 1832, GPC.
101 "and until I can publish . . ." HG/JGP, 29 June 1832, GPC.
101 "never went to bed . . ." HG/JGP, 6 April 1832, GPC.
102 "I am but *one* . . ." HG/JGP, 24 June 1833, GPC.
102 "If you knew . . ." HG/JGP, 9 November 1833, GPC.
103 "It does amuse me . . ." HG/JGP, 23 December 1833, GPC.
103 "Poetry is so amusing . . ." HG/JGP, 7 May 1834, GPC.
103 "I write and study . . ." HG/JGP, 26 December 1834, GPC.
104 "Poor Harriet . . ." S/JGP, 8 December 1834, GPC.
105 "I have been so much . . ." HG/JGP, 7 February 1835, GPC.
105 "I trust I shall . . ." HG/JGP, 18 June 1835, GPC.
106 "I do not wish . . ." HG/JGP, 18 June 1835, GPC.
106 "Every trifling step . . ." HG/JGP, 19 October 1835, GPC.
106f. "rather [to] wish her to abandon . . ." FT/JGP, 2 August 1836, GPC.
107 "She is *vexed* . . ." FT/JGP, 2 August 1836, GPC.
107 "We are hearing . . ." HG/JGP, 14 January 1837, GPC.
108 "I cannot tell you . . ." HG/JGP, 17 April 1837, GPC.
109 "I really believe . . ." HG/JGP, 1 August 1839, GPC.
109 "I have not even . . ." HG/JGP, 8 March 1840, GPC.
110 "very busy sowing . . ." HG/JGP, 17 January 1841, GPC.
110 "Fanny nurses pots . . ." HG/JGP, 19 October 1845, GPC.
110 "I am glad you have . . ." HG/JGP, 2 May 1841, GPC.
111 "mute, inglorious females . . ." Patricia Branca, *Silent Sisterhood*, p. 11.
111 "the only ladies . . ." HG/JGP, December 1827 and January 1828, GPC.
113 "Domestic comfort is . . ." Mrs. John Sandford, *Woman in her Social and Domestic Character*, Chapter One.
114 "He talked . . ." HG/JGP, 12 December 1827, GPC.
114 "they are no longer . . ." HG/JGP, 27 January 1828, GPC.
114 "living in great comfort . . ." HG/JGP, 22 April 1828, GPC.
115 "His poor wife . . ." HG/JGP, 15 July 1828, GPC.
115 "Mrs. Cruger . . ." HG/JGP, 29 July and 5 August 1828, GPC.
115 "Such are the trials . . ." Mrs. Emily Taylor to JGP, 17 January 1850, GPC.
115 "She is in . . ." HG/JGP, 22 January 1852, GPC.
115 "has been unfortunate . . ." HG/JGP, 1 July 1828, GPC.
115 "Poor Mrs. Taylor . . ." HG/JGP, 29 June 1831, GPC.
115 "I shall at last . . ." Mrs. Emily Taylor to JGP, 24 April 1844, GPC.
116 "poor Mrs. Smith . . ." HG/JGP, 19 October 1835, GPC.
116 "Charlotte Steiglitz . . ." HG/JGP, 11 June 1845, GPC.
116 "Mrs. Fauche . . ." HG/JGP, 2 May and 26 June 1841, GPC.
116 "I have spent . . ." Mrs. Fauche to JGP, 16 October 1844, GPC.
117 "I do pity . . ." HG/JGP, 12 August 1849, GPC.
117 "A violent storm . . ." HG/JGP, 13 November 1827, GPC.

117 "Mrs. Capper ..." and "Cannot you feel ..." HG/JGP, January and 12 August 1828, GPC.

117 "She had the misery ..." HG/JGP, 1 September 1842, GPC. For the high infant mortality rates, see Lawrence Stone, *The Family, Sex, & Marriage in England, 1500–1800, passim.*

118 "Bianca Mileri ..." HG/JGP, 13 January 1835, GPC.

118 "a good little woman ..." HG/JGP, 27 November 1827, GPC.

118 "Her situation ..." HG/JGP, 15 July 1828, GPC.

118 "Poor Eliza Henry ..." HG/JGP, 9 December 1829, GPC.

118 "Madame Regnarine's husband ..." HG/JGP, August–October 1828, GPC.

118 "Mme Salazar ..." HG/JGP, 4 March 1830, GPC.

118 "Just as Mr. Hickey ..." HG/JGP, 23 January 1842, GPC.

119 "very sorry to receive ..." HG/JGP, 17 November 1849, GPC.

119 "the Hickey girls ..." HG/JGP, 14 March and 23 November 1851 and 7 August 1852, GPC.

119 "Heloise is happily married ..." HG/JGP, 1 July 1828, GPC.

119 "She breakfasts ..." HG/JGP, 29 June 1830, GPC.

120 "Mrs. Marsh's independence ..." HG/JGP, 8 March 1840, GPC.

120 "She has 700 pounds ..." HG/JGP, 1 November 1851, GPC.

120 "allowable female professions ..." Mrs. Craik, *A Woman's Thoughts About Women,* p. 37. See her chapter on "Self-Dependence": "We must help ourselves. In this curious phase of social history, when marriage is apparently ceasing to become the common lot, and a happy marriage the most uncommon of all, we must educate our maidens into ... the duty of self-dependence."

120 "Last night we met ..." HG/JGP, 13 August 1830, GPC.

121 "She speaks and writes ..." HG/JGP, 3 September 1830, GPC.

121 "not to love ..." HG/JGP, 10 November 1830, GPC.

121 "the prospect of having ..." HG/JGP, 27 February 1831, GPC.

122 "She is in perfect health ..." HG/JGP, 18 September 1841, GPC.

122 "She reads Latin & Greek ..." HG/JGP, 18 September 1841, GPC.

124 "She had been at Embley ..." JS/JGP, September 1847, GPC.

124 "I have always meant ..." JS/JGP, September 1847, GPC.

124 "she must be left ..." HG/JGP, 1 February 1833, GPC.

125 "Emily Ronalds ..." HG/JGP, 20 March 1828, GPC.

125 "Mrs. Fletcher ..." HG/JGP, 28 March and 11 April 1830, GPC.

125 "Emily Taylor at Ealing ..." JS/JGP, 30 September 1844, GPC.

125 "Surely it is a fine privilege ..." JS/JGP, 4 April 1848, GPC.

125 "It may be partly fashion ..." JS/JGP, 19 June 1848, GPC.

126 "to make a great stride ..." JS/JGP, late 1849, GPC.

126 "There are many reasons ..." Mrs. Craik, *A Woman's Thoughts,* pp. 50–51.

126 "working hard at her drawing ..." JS/JGP, 6 February 1850, GPC.

126 "She is a good creature ..." JS/JGP, 6 February 1850, GPC.

126 "to see all the young women ..." JS/JGP, 4 August 1852, GPC.

127 "I hope you will soon ..." JS/JGP, 30 May 1845, GPC.

127 "Lucy Gilbert . . ." JGP to Clara Ranke, January 1852, GPC.

127 "I am once more . . ." AMS/JGP, 8 February 1849, GPC.

127 "Recently, Nina Auerbach . . ." Nina Auerbach, *Communities of Women, passim.*

128 "very amiable, clever & agreeable . . ." HG/JGP, 20 August 1840, GPC.

128 "We read, walk & talk . . ." HG/JGP, 20 October 1840, GPC.

128 "Eliza and Anne work beautifully . . ." HG/JGP, 22 October 1840, GPC.

128 "much occupied with attending . . ." HG/JGP, 20 February 1841, GPC.

129 "I do not think . . ." HG/JGP, 29 November 1840, GPC.

129 "The Bayleys and Garnetts at Hastings . . ." HG/JGP, 5 August and 18 September 1841, GPC.

130 "[Eliza & Anne] send us . . ." HG/JGP, 10 March 1844, GPC.

131 "I know no position . . ." Mrs. Craik, *A Woman's Thoughts,* pp. 143–44.

131 "Let us imagine . . ." Mrs. Sarah Ellis, *Women of England,* p. 56.

132 "[Men] can earn it, lavish it . . ." Mrs. Craik, *About Money and Other Things,* pp. 4–5.

133 "a young person who suits . . ." HG/JGP, 12 January 1850, GPC.

133 "It is (as my sister wrote me) . . ." JGP/JS, 18 November 1848, GPC.

135 "Their house & all . . ." JS/JGP, 24 September 1851, GPC.

135 "I could not help . . ." Jessie Allen Sismondi to HG, 15 September 1852, GPC.

Julia Garnett Pertz's Berlin Drawing-room with Her Three Sons

Julia Garnett Pertz

Julia Garnett Pertz

*cA*s we are a doomed race, chained to a sinking ship . . . as the whole thing is a bad joke, let us, at any rate, do our part; mitigate the sufferings of our fellow-prisoners; decorate the dungeon with flowers and air-cushions; be as decent as we possibly can. Those ruffians, the Gods, shan't have it all their own way.

VIRGINIA WOOLF, **Mrs. Dalloway**

*W*e live, or ought to do so, more for others. Is it not so . . . and is this not the most sweet and satisfactory sort of happiness?

JULIA GARNETT PERTZ, 1843

JULIA GARNETT PERTZ'S domestic life intensified dramatically on November 10, 1828, a year after her friends had sailed for Nashoba, when she delivered a pair of twins. The girl, Mary, was named for her mother, and the boy, Charles, after Baron vom Stein, whose biography her husband was writing and who had founded the project which Pertz subsequently headed as editor of the *Monumenta Germanica.* It is difficult to imagine the physical sufferings of childbirth and its aftermath in those days. Despite abundant nursing care and servant help, medical knowledge was still in a primitive state, and, of course, there were no anaesthetics. Julia's delivery had been a long and difficult one. Afterwards, whenever she complained of discomfort, she was leeched; soon she became excessively weak. With this mode of treatment, it is not strange that one ailment followed upon another. Although she had hoped to get around again in her accustomed way, a swelling of the groin (phlebitis?) made it virtually impossible for her to walk. Once again she had to retreat to the inevitable sofa. She told a friend, "Truly I have suffered so much, both before and since my confinement, that some want of confidence in the future is at least excusable."

Once again temporarily immobilized, Julia had intensified recourse to letters; in particular, she poured out her frustrations and loneliness to Sismondi. Older than she, a historian like her husband, he had also married an English wife. She felt confident that he would understand her confusion of feelings,

142

emotions she did not like to discuss with Pertz. Obviously, a distance separated them. She could not talk over her intimate inner thoughts with the husband she felt so far above her. She respected him, and he was considerate of her. But he was busy with weighty matters of history. All at once, they seemed to be living in two totally different worlds. She had thought to find in her marriage the companionship she had once shared with her sisters and friends. Instead, living in Germany, far from everyone she had known, she found herself mired in domestic responsibilities, her only diversion the care of her infants, and infrequent formal gatherings which gave her little personal pleasure. No doubt the cultural and language barriers made Julia's problems more severe; still, most nineteenth-century couples probably did not enjoy the extensive, shared inner life which Julia had thought to find in her marriage.

Certainly, Julia received little comfort from Sismondi, whose responses to her letters read like a manual whose dominant theme was resignation: she must accept her altered circumstances; transplanting was the appointed portion of women; to leave country, family, and friends was merely a heightening of the ideal marital state. He wished his own wife had enjoyed an isolation as unremitting as Julia's: "I might sometimes regret that my wife has so many opportunities of speaking English here [Geneva] that her spirit has more difficulty in making itself French or Genevan." Clearly, women's identities were correctly dissolved in the responsibilities of marriage. "This isolation prepares you better for the future, and identifies you more with the family and the country of your husband." Moreover, in Sismondi's analysis, Julia's temperament was perfectly suited to her new homeland, where he noted a more congenial and pliant spirit in the women, "so tender and so full of enthusiasm, and much charm. . . . It is far more in harmony with you than with most Englishwomen." Sismondi's responses crystallized into a clear message: after marriage, woman must remake herself anew in the image of service to man.

But even as Julia tried to immerse herself in these new tasks, as her gradually returning health permitted, she faced a new trial. Like so many of her contemporaries, she knew the grief of losing a child. In May 1829, little Mary, since birth dangerously delicate, died. Again Julia turned to Sismondi for consolation. Again his message was clear: women with domestic responsibilities must not indulge themselves in the selfishness of grief. Returning to his theme of renunciation, he reminded Julia that a woman's ultimate duties lay outside the self. "It is for you," he wrote, "to spread happiness on every side by your smiles on your husband, your mother, your sisters." It was particularly necessary that Mr. Pertz find his wife tranquil and happy. "Seek out calm ideas, reject sad thoughts from a sense of duty, never permit yourself to weep, avoid so far as it depends on you any sort of emotion." His closing words encapsulated Julia in the century's own favorite image: "I am happy to know you are in a garden, profiting by the fresh air to give strength to you and your child, and welcoming your husband there in the perfumed air, when he comes wearied from his study." By the fall, Julia was sufficiently recovered from the double traumas of birth and death to welcome her mother and sisters on their first visit to Hanover. For his part, Sismondi was sure that Julia's domestic happiness was now complete: "Husband, son, sisters, and mother" —obviously, she had everything a woman could want.

By 1832, Julia and Pertz had added a second boy to the family, and she was expecting a third child. But instead of feeling the charms in what her old friend Madame de Neuville called a "sweet and uneventful life passed in the midst of a family so dear," Julia was becoming increasingly restive. In letters of the period, Harriet and Mrs. Garnett frequently refer to Julia's "nervousness" and profess themselves baffled by her condition. "How is it possible . . . with everything to make you happy that you can allow yourself to be nervous. Keep your spirits good and enjoy your good husband and children. . . . Make Mr. Pertz happy by seeing you so." Once, Harriet added a private word of warning, using their sister Fanny as an example. "Mama is much affected by her *fretting*. Say nothing of this in your answer, but do not allow *nervousness* to destroy *your* happiness. I see so much of this disease that I think it is one to struggle with most vigorously!" Unwitting partners in the century's conspiracy to keep women passive and domestic, the Garnetts joined Sismondi in insisting upon Julia's blissful state. "Who has so much to enjoy as you have? I know no one who has so many blessings. . . . Do not allow yourself to be nervous."

Sismondi's most convincing example, which he repeatedly used to prove his point about the dangers of wilfulness and unpermissible activity in women, was always Frances Wright. Before Nashoba, she had always served as an ideal to the women of her circle. Instinctively, Sismondi saw the need to point out her decline and fall to a woman whose problems in adjusting to the limitations of her new life perhaps stemmed from regrets over the old "road not taken." Repeatedly, in letters of this period, Sismondi contrasted Julia's quiet domestic life with the unfulfilled wanderings of her old friend, whose eloquence had in the end failed to convince Julia:

> When I first knew you, you were still hesitating as to whether you should not follow her to the banks of the Mississippi, whether you should not confide your whole fortune to her, and now you would have been abandoned in these flooded plains, alone, or would have married men unworthy of you, while she went from town to town preaching strange doctrines.

Later, after Julia had borne another child and Fanny Wright had left her forest experiment and married, Sismondi triumphantly returned to the old story, which seemed more than ever to illustrate the correctness of his views on the proper role of women:

> It contributes to our happiness to be under a certain constraint of circumstances, to see the Impossible mark out limits for us. One submits much more readily to the fate that one has received than to that one has chosen for oneself. I see proof of it too in that friend whose name it pains you to speak, of whom you think only with regret. She wished to take in her hands both her own destiny and that of her friends, that of a whole race. She denied all that was established; she doubted everything, she thought that she could overthrow everything in the laws of morality, politics, and religion, and in fact she has only overthrown her own lot, she has only shaken the basis of her own reason: with talents and virtues of a superior grade, she drew down on herself the curses of others' misery for herself; and it is since she retreated into the groove from which she wished to extract humanity, since she became a wife and mother like any other, that she has found happiness again.

But despite his continued and skillful lecturing, Julia still longed after more than the life of wife and mother.

In her restlessness and groping, Julia had reached out to the "wisest" old friend she knew, and he had been strong in insisting that hers was the best of all possible worlds. Her mother and sisters had joined him in applauding the pleasures of her domestic life. Her status as Professor Pertz's wife had made further intercourse with the Wrights impossible. Feeling trapped despite her happy marital state, Julia grasped for some semblance of her lost circle of friends and that past world which had been more personally satisfying than the present all her friends and family had pronounced perfect. Until her marriage, she had lived in a free, loving, and primarily female world. Indeed, had she not sworn vows of eternal friendship with the Wrights and Mrs. Trollope? Yet over the years, the circle had dissolved into the separate paths of their adult lives.

The first defections had come when she herself had turned away in fear from Frances Wright's Nashoba. That break had been irremediable. Then, in late 1829, when Camilla Wright, separated from her husband, her child dead, neglected by her sister, sought friendly refuge with Julia, the Garnetts had discreetly advised against further association with a woman whose reputation had been badly sullied. Julia wanted to reach out to her old friend who had so pathetically asked, "Is your heart so filled with engrossing objects of interest and tenderness, that the place I once held there is mine no longer?"

Ironically, at that very moment, Julia wanted just such companionship. But the snobbishness of old Mrs. Garnett, and the proprieties of Professor Pertz had finally held the day and broken forever Julia's connection with the Wrights. It was with deep regret and pain that Julia heard, within a year, of the early death of Camilla, alone and friendless in France, her famous sister away on the lecture circuit, curiously cold to Cam's more urgent needs, and the Garnetts too much worried about social stigmas to give assistance, even had they been asked. In her loneliness, Julia even tried to invite her old governess to a residence in Hanover, but Sophia Hay, frail and living on a small income, refused.

Next, Julia thought that if her mother and sisters were to move near her, she might with them be able to re-create that free female world of her youth in which she remembered true companionship, a sharing of common thoughts, and a sense of mutual endeavor. But the Garnett women reacted sharply. Arguing Mrs. Garnett's inability to adjust to new ways, Harriet asked Julia not to mention the subject again: "Do not express your disappointment at not seeing us; you know not how much pain your regret gives us." She closed the door upon further discussion. "We feel this disappointment quite as keenly as you can do, but do not I entreat write upon this painful subject, it gives me such pain to read your expressions of regret, when I wish nothing so ardently as your happiness, that I earnestly beg you not to say all I know you feel." No doubt they felt, as the distraught Julia did not, the inappropriateness of their intruding upon Julia's commitment to her husband and family. Aware of Mr. Pertz's formality and conservatism, deeply respectful of his scholar's accomplishments and status, they knew the old world was over, even if Julia did not.

Perhaps for married women, such bastions of sisterhood and female independence were impossible. Sismondi, in accounting for the Garnett's final refusal to change their residence in accordance with Julia's wishes, is able to concede the need for continual social intercourse only to the elderly and single ladies of the Garnett circle. A wife, like Julia, could have no needs beyond those of "the heart":

> Well do I understand your ardent wish that your mother and sisters had chosen the same country. . . . I can quite imagine that their courage failed them. Poor Mrs. Garnett, who does not speak French yet, would never have learned German; she would have felt completely isolated at an age when habits are more important than affections, when one has more need of chatting and the small interests of daily gossip than of the niceties of wit. The burden would have fallen ever more heavily on your two sisters. There would have been nothing in the climate or in nature to compensate what society did not give; already at

their age it is hard to study German, and perhaps they would never have managed it, when they were not pricked on as you were by conjugal and maternal love. . . . Yes, dear Julia, you did well, very well, to take a husband who gives to your heart all that that heart needed so greatly, who gives you a country, too, who leaves you in no hesitation and no doubt in fulfilling and choosing your fate.

Thus bereft of support from those closest to her, Julia, for the time being, gave up the battle to shape a world of her own choosing, and tried to enter her domestic role more tranquilly. Apparently, marriage was a border which could not easily be re-crossed. But the idea of a female community running parallel to her married state, she never totally abandoned. Years later, when her children had grown, she again sought out associations with women and formed deep, if sometimes temporary, female friendships. In the end, she would realize that an equally real community of women had existed all along in the letters she shared with a circle of friends.

In a sense, Julia's long dream of bearing a girl to replace the daughter she had lost was a kind of attempt to compensate for all the female friendships which had thus far eluded her grasp. As her third pregnancy advanced, she expressed this persistent wish to her sister, who felt Julia's insistence on a matter beyond her control somewhat alarming. Harriet cautioned: "Do not expect a little girl. If she comes, so much the better . . . take other circumstances as they come." When Julia eventually delivered a third boy, her disappointment was keen. Harriet consoled her sister by noting that boys, in most cases, "are more valued by parents than girls, and they are, in all countries, far, far happier." Still, this third child was to be Julia's favorite, the most satisfying of all her children.

Harriet, close as she was to Julia, found her sister's unhappy feelings of helplessness hard to comprehend. After all, as a dependent single woman, she herself might be pitiable, but not Julia, who possessed a potential source of power, did she but recognize it. Motherhood gave a woman a future. Harriet, on the other hand, looked forward to a "dull life" and "none behind to recollect and love me." Finding in her sister's position the dynamics she as yet lacked in her own, Harriet began to read the current authorities on child rearing, regularly relaying advice to her sister. She assiduously studied Miss Edgeworth's *Practical Education* and sent it as a gift to Julia. She read the "progressive" education theorists of the day, like Mme. Neckar, who stressed the importance of childhood in the formation of character. Harriet warned: "It is alarming to see how soon the passions and characters of children are formed, and every parent should be aware of the circumstances, and pass over no act of childhood lightly." To Harriet, motherhood offered the potential of creation beyond the womb, of shaping matter, the very thing she had sought so long and unsuccessfully in her writing:

> If I had a child, I would study seriously books of the kind (as Mme. Neckar's), and I am anxious that your children should have every advantage that the best early education can give them. Everything with children depends upon the mother—so say all wise men—& I have a great idea of the high responsibility of a mother's situation.

And old Mrs. Garnett, too, assured Julia that "children never forget to whom they owe their first impressions."

All Julia's acquaintances seemed agreed that she should settle down and find her identity and occupation as a mother. Even the unconventional Mary de Neuville, who years earlier had so romantically run off with the dashing Grasset, finally pronounced it a fact "that a mother's love is the strongest passion a woman feels." Mrs. Garnett and Harriet, weekly the social companions of Mérimée and Stendhal, assured Julia she missed nothing in the exchange of her old life for that of German wife and mother. Wrote Mrs. Garnett, "and so goes on most evenings and generally in the old way, saying the next morning how very dull it was. How much more interesting dear Julia is your life, with your husband and your little host of sons." That Julia was trying hard to believe so, seems certain; and that she was abetted in this effort by the women of her family is clear.

Then, at forty-one, Julia again found herself pregnant. That her condition distressed her is obvious from her family's many remonstrances in the letters of this period. "I am sorry you will have more to suffer from your situation, but we must think of the pleasure that follows the pain and not murmur." Her mother saw Julia's duty clearly: "You must keep up your spirits for your good husband's sake. You have been a troublesome little wife in spite of being a good one. . . ." The unmarried Harriet was even more decided about Julia's impending happiness: "Oh, do not for a moment fancy you are not peculiarly blessed." Then, probably with a sense of relief, Julia miscarried. Whether she thereafter made herself aware of contraceptive practices or simply withheld herself accordingly and on schedule is not known. At any rate, there are no records of any further pregnancies.

The next six years passed quietly as Julia interested herself in the duties attendant to rearing her three boys. Only once did a sign appear that the old problems had not been solved, but merely put aside. In September 1839, Julia abruptly left her family to journey alone to Paris for a brief and highly emotional reunion with her mother and sisters, who had written of a planned removal to far-away Nice, where the valetudinarian Fanny could cure her assortment of ailments with "sea-bathing." Tearfully, Julia begged them to choose a closer spot, and with the evidence of her real distress before them, the family conceded, choosing instead Boulogne. Always, Julia wanted them at least manageably near, although on the issue of a Hanover residence she had long given up hope. That she left her children and convinced the busy and preoccupied Pertz of the need for her trip bespeaks the intensity of her concern that the family remain at least within visiting distance.

Then, all at once, the boys' childhood was over and they were all away at school. Once more Julia was alone, facing the long days and evenings at home while Dr. Pertz, still at work on the *Monumenta Germanica,* traveled and assembled materials. She was ready for something new. Then, in 1840, a note of excitement sparked in Julia's letters, as a new, inspiring woman flashed across her horizon. In a lengthy, often breathless letter, Julia eagerly described *"Mrs. Fry the great philanthropist"* and the "good she has done . . . the *effect* her presence has produced on criminals." Mrs. Fry provided a contrast with Frances Wright, the heroine of Julia's youth. The Quaker lady, while a radical in matters of prison reform, was eminently respectable in her domestic life. But even while she was herself the mother of ten children, Mrs. Fry was sounding the call to goals beyond those of the family and the domestic hearth. She was traveling through Germany to visit the prisons and alleviate "some of the suffering of the unhappy prisoners." Clearly, Julia felt inspired by this woman who was doing something constructive with her life. The underlinings of her letter speak eloquently of the impact upon the restless Julia. Now that she was estranged from Frances Wright, her need for an ideal woman to admire still remained unsatisfied. Her own enforced passivity made her respect the activist's role, even as she would ever remain too conservative actually to grasp it.

Throughout her letter about Mrs. Fry, Julia's focus wavers between praise for the woman's mildness, modesty, and "affectionate heart," and her daring in actually being able to "do good to her fellow creatures":

> Her appearance is just what one could suppose from the effect she has produced. *Grave* without austerity—and *mild,* with great decision in her manner and expressions. It is impossible not to admire her, and to see much of her without loving her would, I should think, be difficult. She has evidently a very affectionate heart; and preaches only what she thoroughly and *strongly* believes. She looks so placid too, so composed, so quiet, a happiness so *deeply felt,* and of being *enabled* to do good still to her fellow creatures. She is so modest too. So *unaffectedly* modest. She has so much excellent sense—and knowledge of human nature, so much kindness of heart—I should think *capability* of being, that I could almost find it in my heart to turn *Friend. . . .*

Her object is to call the attention of humane people to the state of the prisons & prisoners—to free them (if possible) from their chains and dark and damp dungeons, & to give them consolation and hopes of a happier life hereafter. She has given her request to the government, and I hope much good from her visit. I attended her through two prisons, saw the wretched inhabitants, some, that *in order to make them confess,* had been *chained in a dark cell under ground for four months,* and no one allowed to speak the truth, which at least could procure them some alleviations—but I will not dwell on what I *saw.* I *hope* that something much indeed will be done—the Queen has seen Mrs. Fry—has *promised to patronise* the exertions that are made. A society is forming, headed by a very superior man (a clergyman), and ladies are to visit and comfort as much as they can the female prisoners—& when they are let out of prison keep an eye on them and find them *honest employment.* At least this is what ladies have done and are doing in England under Mrs. Fry's guidance—but a Mrs. Fry is wanting. She could alone I believe carry such a point in the face of prejudice, indolence, and hard-heartedness. I am to be on the *committee,* but I shall try hard to escape the *visiting* which pains me more than I like to acknowledge.

Elizabeth Fry came from one of those large, motherless families so common in the early nineteenth century. At seventeen, she underwent an intense religious conversion to strict Quakerism. Perhaps such "conversions" were an ingenious way of giving supreme sanction to the idea that a woman might do something with her life beyond marriage and bearing children. Elizabeth Gurney, at any rate, vowed not to marry. She turned down three proposals from the persistent Joseph Fry until finally, in discussing the central issues of marriage, they came to an agreement. "Could a married woman have any other vocation beside the duties of her home?" Joseph Fry said yes, if she were *his* wife, and so Elizabeth accepted him. She bore her husband eleven children, meanwhile finding time to minister to the village poor, herself vaccinating them against smallpox, the art of which she had learned from a country doctor. She also exercised the Quaker ministry, waiting the while for the grace and opportunity of occupation, which came, unexpectedly, when she visited Newgate Prison in 1813 and was astounded by the savage conditions in the women's ward. Her life's work had greeted her at last. She set about establishing as matters of fundamental principle the prison-women's rights to decent clothing, training in sewing, reading, and writing, education for their children, and the opportunity to hear the Scriptures read. Her achievements were truly astounding. She worked, too, with the outgoing convict ships, visiting every transport which sailed from England with female convicts between the years 1818 and 1841, seeing to it that the women were transported under decent, humane conditions. In her later years, she visited the major continental prisons, bringing her message and her mission to Hanover in April 1840, where she met George and Julia Pertz.

Surely Julia must have wondered how the mother of so large a family could do so much. Part of the answer lay in sheer physical stamina and an unusually tolerant husband, but most of all with the CALL, the inner conviction. Mrs. Fry's journals clearly reveal her many heart-searchings as to the correctness of leaving her family to preach or work on foreign prison reform. But her answer always rang clear: she had heard the call to work, and to fail to answer, was to deny an authority higher than any individual. Indeed, as she once wrote: "May my being led out of my own family by what appears to me duties, never be permitted to hinder my doing my duty fully towards it, or so occupy my attention as to make me in any degree forget or neglect home duties." But the solution was always at hand: "I believe it matters not where we are, or what we are about, so long as we keep our eye fixed on doing the Great Master's work." Surely few women ever searched the question of motivation as relentlessly and continuously as did Elizabeth Fry. If she saw philanthropy as a respectable extension for a woman's life, perhaps Julia, too, could incline towards such service. But she did not have Mrs. Fry's energy and health nor her understanding husband nor her sense of religious mission, and she was soon to face a life-crisis which would bear her away from her hard-earned sense of home in Hanover and from the work with the prison committee which she had, however timidly, begun.

In the early 1840s, Pertz's relationship with the tyrannical King of Hanover grew strained, and along with a group of "liberal professors," he found it necessary to leave the city. Naturally, her husband's profession came first; self-abnegation had ever been Julia's portion. In the upheaval, she drew strength from the woman friend and cousin she had never met, but with whose husband she had so often corresponded, Jessie Allen Sismondi. Jessie, too, was preparing to leave her beloved Chenes for Tuscany, fleeing from the revolution with whose tendencies Sismondi was not in harmony. She, too, feared the "fearful distance" from her "loved country, and . . . its people," and told Julia, "I feel sometimes overcome with terror at the change." Her letter closed with the clear expression of that which Julia had made into a way of life: "Oh, why cannot one annihilate self, and be happy only through others." Jessie quoted to Julia the story of Miss Sedgwick, American author and friend of Mary Russell Mitford, upon whom "misfortunes have fallen thick and fast." Jessie noted, "She bears all with such pious fortitude as to be a beautiful lesson to me at this moment, for any murmuring anticipations." Women themselves were the great teachers of the message to suffer and be still. From one another, they had learned resignation; to follow the available models of bold endeavor required a courage not many could muster.

After their removal from Hanover to Berlin, Julia found her life altered significantly, as the Pertzes entered the most illustrious intellectual society of the city almost at once. The Hanoverian dismissals had made Pertz something of a celebrity. He was offered the post of head librarian of the Royal Library by Frederick Wilhelm IV of Prussia, an inveterate romanticist who wanted to rebuild medieval traditions and had taken up the cause of the *Monumenta Germanica*. He saw Pertz as a great scholar and key figure in the romantic revival which he had made the focus of his regime, outwardly epitomized by his dramatic completion of Cologne Cathedral. In Berlin, new friends were eager to meet Pertz: the Grimms and Bettina, Frau von Arnim. In this first flurry of activity, Julia found little time for herself. "I have written by snatches . . . always interrupted by comers in or goers out. No minister's time is more in demand. What with unpacking old furniture and buying new, what with directions to upholsterers, bell-hangers, carpenters, receiving and paying visits; learning the different manner of living, prices, current money, etc. etc. No, you still can form no idea of the business of my life." This increased social activity left Julia with heightened domestic responsibility, which she clearly found burdensome: "My time is so limited. I have so much to do. Every moment the bell rings, somebody enters—a visitor or a tradesman. You have no idea of all we have had to do. . . ." But the steady stream of socializing did not lessen as time went on, but rather increased. Pertz found himself lionized as the great man and surrounded by a whirl of activity, the likes of which he had never seen. With intensity, he threw himself into this new life, which Julia vividly described to her sisters: "He is driving, driving, driving —there seems no end to visits, and some of them are so exciting and interesting. He returns home heated and dusted, but pleased and animated. . . . All seem pleased to have gained his society." To an old Hanover friend, she wrote: "Dr. Pertz has paid more visits than I have, or hope ever shall pay. He is *driving hard* at it again today—driving for 4 or 5 hours, hard work truly, but it must be done." Gradually, her tone altered, and annoyance crept in. She saw her husband now "only by *chance*—& then he scarcely has time to answer the important questions I have to ask. Visits, visits, visits, . . . nothing can be so different as my way of life here, from that I led there . . . at Hanover."

As she reflected upon the life she had left, especially in the latter period when the children had gone away to school, she regretted the move which had upset the increased freedom and opportunity for development she had finally gained. She wrote, "I enjoyed domestic happiness, independence there. . . ." Indeed, she had just begun to emerge into an activity she regarded as useful with her work on the prison committee. It had almost been like the old days, when she had dreamt of social reform at Nashoba. Now she faced the task of playing the busy hostess in a town the social life of which rivaled that of Paris. But she was not interested in finding self-fulfillment through wielding influence or power in high society. She told a friend about her dislike of Berlin's frequent and large evening parties. "I love the society of a friend, of a few intelligent people. That is *society.* But a number of people congregated together to talk small talk and sup, is *not* society. It excites and fatigues, without giving any real pleasure." Clearly, these activities seemed superficial to Julia who had followed Fanny Wright's attempts to emancipate America's slaves and Elizabeth Fry's efforts to educate continental authorities on the proper treatment of female prisoners.

In time, Julia began to create her own activities, the most deeply self-satisfying of which was her assistance to women. Even as Elizabeth Fry wrote, "I have found in my late attention to Newgate a peace and prosperity that I seldom remember before," so did Julia find release and fulfillment in the help she brought to a number of afflicted or in some way needy women. All these subsequent relationships—with Minna Meyer, Clara Ranke, Mrs. Fauche, and others—were not so much a search for companionship, as a desire to exert beneficent power, to be really useful to others. She had failed to follow Elizabeth Fry in the path of prison reforms. Perhaps, at least in a small way, she could help the women who lived in the prisons of the everyday world.

The first in a long line of recipients of Julia's favors was Minna Meyer, daughter of some old Hanover friends. Hers were the problems of the single girl without prospects. She was young, and her family was not wealthy. She would have to earn her bread, most probably as a governess. Julia wanted to give the girl a start in the world, some instruction, some shaping, a chance for advancement. Like Jane Austen's Emma before her, she warmed to the task of molding a pliant Minna into a more self-sufficient young "lady." She wrote Frau Meyer:

> If you would confide your dear Minna to my care this winter, she could easily find a suitable position in the spring—it would be advantageous to be seen and known—and this winter she could perfect herself in *English, French, and music* —three important points for education—young people who are capable of teaching *these three things* are much sought for here. If you can make up your mind therefore to part with Minna this winter, pray, *send her to us*—and I will endeavour to promote her advantage in every way in my power.

Even more deeply, Minna would become the daughter for whom Julia had ever longed.

But Julia's most heartfelt concern was the plight of unhappy wives, of whom she knew several. Mme. Fauche, the consul's wife from Bruges, who now lived separated from her husband in Paris, had long been an object of

Julia's sympathy. Now Mme. Fauche's daughter was distraught: her prospective father-in-law, a German professor, wanted to force his son to withdraw his offer of marriage because Monsieur Fauche had circulated bad reports about his wife's reputation. Since the Schusters were from Hanover, Julia asked Minna Meyer to help. Thus, along with Mrs. Trollope, Julia rallied around her beleaguered friend and involved herself in repairing the complex marital negotiations. First, she tried to help by sending portions of a letter from Mrs. Trollope, a good friend of Mme. Fauche, to Dr. Schuster.

> Mrs. Trollope writes: I have known Mme. Fauche from my earliest childhood and know her conduct to be most *exemplary* as a wife and mother. Her husband is a heartless dissipated man, who treated his wife in a shameful manner, neglected his children, and squandered his money, at last. Mr. Tomkinson (a man of great respectability, and large fortune—the father of Mme. Fauche) forced his daughter to leave her husband and settled £ 200 a year upon her— upon this she has lived and educated her two daughters and a son who died in a decline last year, just as he had the prospect of being settled comfortably— *the mother has conducted herself admirably through all her trials* and is a very superior woman.

Then, in a gesture which was for her some effort, Julia went to Dr. Schuster personally, convincing him of the absolute innocence of Mme. Fauche. As she told Minna: "I think I could convince him of Mrs. Fauche's innocence if I were to see him, but perhaps . . . someone who knows him might have the same effect. . . ." Eventually the marriage took place. That its outcome was not a happy one was perhaps the crowning irony of the whole affair. Wanting to help her friend's daughter, Julia had merely assisted in making Mary Fauche Schuster one more trapped and unhappy wife.

Clara Ranke, born Graves, was another English wife of a German historian, whose marriage seemed to Julia repressive and unhappy. Miss Graves had brought a large dowry to her husband, but in her case, money had not resulted in power. The new Frau Ranke began bearing children and being unhappy almost at once. Two years after her marriage, when she and her infant son were quite sick, the Garnetts asked Julia: "Is he—Ranke—much grieved at the illness of the babe? I hope he will sympathize with the poor mother on this occasion." Julia's descriptions of Ranke to Harriet were of an "unfeeling, selfish man." Most perplexing was his wife's toleration of her oppression. As Harriet once told Julia, "It is fortunate she has not sense enough to be aware of his defects." References to Ranke's tyrannies abound in the letters of the period. "Poor Mme. Ranke, how much she is to be pitied —what a wretched character Ranke must be." Soon, Julia's defense of Mme.

Ranke became a cause of alarm to the women of the circle, who implored her to be "more prudent" at least for her friend's own sake:

> Many things have already been repeated to him as coming from you, & he knows your opinion of him full well. This of course mortifies him, & [her mother] dreads his forbidding his wife from seeing you, which is a great comfort ... to poor Clara. Therefore do not, dearest Julia, speak of the man anymore, as the poor wife will be the sufferer. ... Speak not of his meanness or unkindness to his wife to any one.

Clara herself found a solution to her oppression in a deeply religious resignation. She was convinced of her own sinfulness and saw all her sorrows as an inevitable part of the Christian life. When she lost a child, she wrote: "At such moments one feels the full blessed power of Christianity. ... I feel my sweet smiling child is accepted through our Saviour's merits into glory and that I am mother of an angel in Heaven." When she grew homesick for Ireland, longing for her family and even for mail, she consoled herself with the thought that "the home, if it exists, is not on earth. ... " When, after years of living a life solely in accordance with her husband's wishes, however unreasonable, she fell sick, she wrote: "My weak vessel I fear will not last very long; but as long as I can creep about & do all my household business I shall be thankful." As she told a friend, "It is the will of God to leave me still here, until I may be more perfect through Christ." Gradually, she grew seriously weak, completely paralyzed with a mysterious ailment which, from this vantage point, seems the body's rejection of a tyranny which the mind had accepted in the name of Christ. She went through periods of being unable to move her hands and feet, unable to cut her own meat, or get anything she wanted, even within view. She saw all the specialists, from Berlin, from London, the Swiss mesmerist Rugetsky and the French magnetizer Szapare. Finally, she had to be fed and washed: she couldn't even turn the pages of a book. She told her brother and sister: "I seemed to have ears all over my body, to have crickets singing and dancing in my backbone, to feel the house and everything about me continually shaking, never to be in a comfortable position, always longing for change, seeing fire before my eyes, burning heat or freezing from cold." She concluded: "Happy I shall be, when I shall be a butterfly. When will that be?"

Contributing to her illness was Clara's sense of uselessness. With her educated background, she, like Julia, always thought of achievement in intellectual terms. She had vaguely expected to be of assistance to her husband, or at least to share in his work. Thus, she conceived the idea of translating his history of Serbia into her native English. Indeed, she threw herself into

the work, finishing a few chapters before bringing it to her husband's attention. With his typical unfeeling attitude, Ranke ordered the project halted
and announced his intention of securing professional services for this task.
Not only did Clara have to stifle her wishes, but she was also forced to comply
with her husband's request that she write her family in order to find the
proper translator. It was no wonder that her frail body took refuge in illness.

In the midst of her sufferings, she sought an occupation of sorts by composing poetry. Here, at least, her efforts would not interfere with her husband's
field. Her major poetic compositions she called "Stars of My Life," brief
poems about the famous and notable people who had, across the years,
populated her Berlin drawing room. Bettina von Arnim, Alexander von Hum-
boldt, the philosopher Friedrich von Schelling, the brothers Grimm, Ludwig
Tieck, August Schlegel, Felix Mendelssohn, Giacomo Meyerbeer, and Robert
Wilhelm Bunsen, among countless others. Friends, too, were memorialized—
Pertz, Julia, Julius Mohl (husband of Mary Clarke), the Danish sculptor
Thorwaldson, and Florence Nightingale. Although there is no poem directly
on her husband, one of the "Stars" concerns her parents-in-law, whom she
compares to two streams which, between them, produced a powerful river,
while themselves remaining all the while entirely insignificant. When she
thinks what it was that grew out of this source, she meditates for hours on
the picture, feeling the mystery which had blessed her life through the lives
of Leopold's parents.

Despite her illness, in these years almost all of Clara's energy was devoted
to her poems, which she reworked, and translated into German, Italian,
Spanish, Portuguese, French, Alemanish, and Dutch, and with the help of
friends into Hungarian, and Finnish! Her obsession with these remembrances
of friends eventually matured into a desire to publish the poems "in 2 volumes, containing the English original and the German translation." But once
again, Leopold von Ranke forbad Clara to undertake this project. Whether
he thought it inappropriate that anyone else in his family, especially his wife,
should take to the pen and win fame, or whether he found something offen-
sive in some items, is unknown. Clara, of course, obeyed. But, in the last act
of her life, she dictated a letter to her daughter hours before her death in 1871,
and returned to this long-cherished project. Leopold, she told her brother
Robert Graves, had now relented and let her publish excerpts from the poems
—but only if she used her own money. As her dying wish, she entrusted the
task to her English family, and she closed with a last expression of her
frustrated life. This new possibility seemed like a dream come true. Unfortu-
nately, the poems remain uncatalogued and unpublished.

Julia's assistance to Clara Ranke had been well-meaning, but in the end,
she herself became too weak to provide much concrete help. After 1849, they

were incapable of meeting, except by means of the brief notes they continued to exchange. Julia told her sister: "[Clara] is much attached to me—& would be happier if she could oftener be with me—but we are both too weak for visits." But Mme. Ranke's unthinking acceptance of a Christianity which saw a woman's lot as suffering, placed her beyond mere earthly assistance. In any case, unconsciously, her body provided a solution—a lingering illness which permitted her to escape the rigors of associating with her husband and children and gave her time for poetasting. In fact, she outlived all the women who had frequently worried lest their next exchange should find her dead. In the year of Julia's own death (and nineteen years before Clara finally died), Harriet asked: "How is poor Mme. Ranke? You perhaps will not find her alive on your return & she has so little happiness in life that one ought not to regret her death." In some manner, Julia's concern, her daily notes, their infrequent outings, the sustaining power of her friendship, had helped Clara Ranke keep soul and body alive. In her later years, as if in mute remembrance of her debt, she called herself Hermann's "Mutter," and enjoyed daily visits from Julia's favorite son. "My son Hermann," she wrote her brother in 1859, "is engaged to a nice English girl of 17, Emma Wilkinson." Having chosen an English wife himself—thus repeating the pattern of both his mother and Clara Ranke—Hermann asked the latter to be godmother to his first child. Although the Ranke family referred to him as their mother's "adopted son," Clara made no such distinction. She told her brother, for example, upon the birth of Hermann's child, "I am a grandmamma." Thus she repaid, as best she could, the friendship of Julia.

Julia also worried about her sister-in-law, Betty Pertz, who had remained in Mrs. Meyer's charge when the Pertzes left Hanover. Betty's fate loomed as an example of what happened to women who lived useless lives. Julia frequently expressed concern over her sister-in-law's "melancholy state of mind," advising Mrs. Meyer to place Betty "for the winter at least in some quiet respectable family, where she may be amused and occupied without being excited or contradicted. . . . Active occupation is absolutely necessary for her—and she is always most desirous to make herself useful." Julia had tried hard to "bear her company," but found that "she always depresses my spirits, for I have the wish to make her comfortable & happy—& find it impossible to do so." She had "wished her to pass her life with us—but she was not happy with *me.*" Julia saw Betty's restless state as troubling: "Poor girl, I fear she will scarcely find a situation in which her mind will be tranquil —& this thought makes me often sad."

These dramatic struggles of other women—for advancement, security, dignity, indeed for sanity itself—along with her own for usefulness and selfhood, contrasted starkly with the liberal education of her youth, born of ideas coming out of the French Revolution. What she was seeing and experiencing was a whole variety of inhibiting factors—some personal, some social. For Julia herself, marriage had clearly been the precipitating factor in the change she noted, as she once permitted herself to recall the old days in America, when she had played chess with the President of Columbia College and made innocent jokes amid the merry circle of Brunswick:

> We were gay, gay and careless of the moment. We did not dream of sorrow— or of the loss of the friends we had. They were with us, they were well, and we were happy—and we are so *now*—but it is a different kind of happiness. The illusions of life are vanished. We know that we *have* suffered—and *shall* suffer. That this world is *not* (what in my early youth I thought to find)—*one long day of happiness,* but the knowledge comes gradually upon us, and therefore we are not oppressed by it. We are calmer too. We live, or ought to do so, more for others. Is it not so . . . and is this not the most sweet and satisfactory sort of happiness?

Julia seemed somewhat unsure of the answer to her own question. Service to others had been her chosen vocation; had it really produced a happiness worth the costs?

> I am moved to think of gone-by days—of what I *was,* and *am,* of my *past* and *present* happiness. From a free bred (not *born*) American girl, I am become a sedate German matron, the wife of a German scholar, and of a good and amiable man. I am the mother of three promising boys. But I am neither young nor strong, and who knows how long I may be permitted to enjoy the blessings that I possess? I am separated too from all my early and much loved. . . . How often have I changed my home, my friends, my habits. I have been separated from my mother, from my sisters, and have not had it in my power to be of service, or to return to them the kindness that I have experienced from them. This is a subject of continual regret.

What could be salvaged? For women who had not the strength, courage, or luck to be world-movers, the ideal of service persisted: "We live, or we ought to do so, more for others. . . . Is this not the most sweet and satisfactory sort of happiness?" Julia had made a lifelong devotion to husband, children, family and friends. And although her wistful phrasing made what should have rung out boldly like an ideal, sound instead like a hesitant query, she had ever been faithful to that life lived for others, even while she had long sought to make that ideal into a satisfying personal occupation.

In the summer of 1844, Julia made the last of the significant female friend-ships of her life. In contrast to most of the other relationships, Julia Smith needed nothing from Julia Pertz. She was neither seeking to enter marriage, nor fleeing from it. She needed no boost or start in life. Julia Smith was an older single woman of some means, one of the large and lively Smith family who, as one member put it, "never thought of anything all day long but our own ease and pleasure." Julia Smith's sister Fanny, after a stormy and unsuc-cessful love affair, had married William Henry Nightingale III. Miss Smith was a maiden aunt to the two girls born to the Nightingales, Parthe and Florence, each named, somewhat romantically, after the foreign cities in which they were born. Julia Pertz at fifty and Julia Smith at sixty were instantly drawn to one another. By the fall of the year they met (Miss Smith had come to Berlin with a letter of introduction), their letters made manifest a deeply shared bond upon which Miss Smith remarked: "You are so *in* me, so little connected with my past and I fear with my future too, and yet you are so strong and vivid in my present inward life, you sometimes seem to me like a dream." Like many of her other friendships, this one was sustained largely through letters.

Julia seemed neither to need nor really to want to see her correspondents. Julia Smith's last comment provides the key to her friend's apparent lack of interest in actual meetings. After all, she and her women friends were in truth unconnected in terms of both past and future. The past was too far away: as Julia Pertz had painfully discovered, it was inaccessible, gone. Their futures were not their own, tied as they were to families and responsibilities. Yet each of them saw the other "strong and vivid" in what Julia Smith called the "present inward life." Here, in this dream-like space, the women met, talked, shared ideas and thoughts. Here they existed for one another in a reality which would never prove disillusioning. It was the only space they had wrested free for themselves. Unlike Virginia Woolf's room of one's own, it was not physical territory, but the neutral ground of the letters.

Over the next eight years, the two Julias wrote to each other regularly, providing a lively record of both their personal lives and women's concerns in their rapidly changing world. Two issues seemed of particular importance: employment opportunities and public education. Women like Julia Pertz and Julia Smith had been well educated, but only by benefit of the chance of social class and enlightened parents. Now such women were trying to provide education as a matter of course for all women. Julia Smith told Mrs. Pertz about the efforts of her friend Lady Byron, for example, who was using her wealth, position, and time to found schools and orphanages. She was "really undeniably useful." USEFUL. It was becoming the new watchword of the times, a goal for women more important even than good looks, marriage, or sexual fulfillment. Even those once "redundant" single ladies were finding meaningful occupation more accessible. Such women, wrote Miss Smith, "may find enough to do in England with the thousands of little un-ABC'd who crowd upon us—and so the poor single ladies may fancy themselves useful," which, she added with characteristically rough frankness to Dr. Pertz's wife, "is a pleasant illusion not so easily had in Germany." Although both of them were products of the older world, which had started so well and ended with so many limitations, and in a sense their fates were sealed, they were curious about the future and its emerging new types of womanhood, who were trying, via education and occupation, to find something more in life than the usual woman's lot.

Some of their friends—like Mary Clarke—although of their generation in age, were in temperament and lifestyle more like that "new" woman. Mary, of the fascinating conversation and salon life, was clearly a woman who had answered the call of the self and not of service to others, and yet, she had lived an undeniably "useful" life. Miss Smith admired her heartily:

> What a capital person Miss Clarke is; I really hardly know her equal. She has built up such a superstructure of agreeable and animating and companionable qualities on her original foundation of benevolence and good sense, her sympathies are so true & wide and her resources so various, it seems to me as if no person in any circumstances of need would come to her in vain. She has such peculiar ways of her own that one is a good while before one learns that she can do the same kind of things that everybody does in addition to what she alone can do, but so it is, one may count on her for the common as well as the uncommon. I have enjoyed her conversation immensely in this bit of time we have had together. It seems to me she had put more ideas into me than any or all persons together [whom I have seen since I came to England]. She has set me speculating on the great advantages of that free life she has led wherein heart and mind both seem to have had free play & abundant exercise. To be sure she has not learned the housekeeping accomplishments, but she has learned to be happy without them & if she had wanted them, she would have learned them too.

Indeed, a year later, when the fifty-seven- year-old Miss Clarke unexpectedly married her old friend Julius Mohl, Miss Smith, along with everyone else, was surprised. Still, she was sure, knowing their previous relationship, that Mr. Mohl would not "force upon her any new life or new habits, but only revivify and strengthen all her old interests and be at once a support & an occupation to her." And in fact, in external framework, marriage did not change Mary Clarke's life. She simply exchanged one companion for another, continuing to reside (after her mother's death) in her old house, fitting up her mother's room as a library for M. Mohl. It would seem as if he made the most changes, not she, who remained the center of her remarkable salon. There was little to fear in marriage for one so already confirmed in habits of independence as was Mary Clarke.

Interested as Julia was in these women and their fates, her own life suddenly took a dramatic turn of its own. In November 1847, after several months of feeling poorly, Julia fell seriously ill with influenza, which sapped her remaining physical reserves. For weeks she was confined to her bedroom, unable even to read or talk. Despite the best of care, her recovery was agonizingly slow. With her children grown, she was now alone most of the time. Her husband, in these difficult months, was increasingly busy and preoccupied. Mornings were devoted to the Royal Library and afternoons were for visiting and proceeding with the Folio editions of the *Monumenta Germanica.* The eighth volume had just gone to press, and six young men were assisting Pertz in the "great labour." In addition to his other responsibilities, he was now lecturing at the Royal Academy and even published late in this year a talk on the discovery of a fragment of the eighty-ninth book of Livy! He was also approaching the end of his biographical study of Stein, called by Julia "for some years the *evening* occupation of my husband." Julia stayed in her rooms, too ill that Christmas even to come down for the festivities. She visited no one and confessed to Miss Smith: "I was rather too much alone. My good husband came as often as he could and my boys during the holidays. But I was all day alone & I had no one to whom I could say 'Que la solitude est belle.' " Even though her husband postponed the Christmas tree lighting until January 1 so that she could participate, she was not up to it, and was "forced to go to bed & give up all thoughts of the celebration." She subsequently busied herself studying Italian, mastering the language well enough to read Tasso's *Jerusalem.*

As the winter neared its end, Julia's health was still poor, and she looked forward to warmer weather to complete her cure. Instead, the winds of March brought news of the Revolution in Paris, and within a few days, of similar uprisings in Milan, Munich, Vienna, and then, outside her own windows in Berlin. It was a shocking development, for which nothing had prepared Julia. Paris, yes, was always dangerous, and the Italians were prone to excitement; but her Berlin had seemed the last place in the world for revolution. With its strong monarchy, powerful army, efficient civil service, it had exuded stability and order. While the king was not a tyrant and had been personally benevolent to many, his government, too, crumbled under the same pressures erupting in countries with weak or tyrannical rulers like Louis Phillipe and Metternich.

The revolution in Berlin followed the general pattern. Peaceful demonstrations turned to violence through the panic and over-reaction of military authorities; armed guards opened fire on the people, and in the resulting fracas, blood was spilt on both sides, barricades were built, and a night of confusion and noise ensued. Because the Pertzes lived in the center of Berlin, they were caught in the midst of the turmoil. Weakened in health and spirits, Julia suffered something resembling a nervous breakdown. Her letters of these days are shocking and staggering. She reported that the revolution was a "universal plot against the monarchy and the whole order of civil life." She wrote of foreign spies who were paid to inflame the mob. She maintained that only prompt action by the military saved the town from being burned to the ground and from a general massacre. The whole populace lusted after "mischief, sedition, murder and destruction." When the King withdrew his army and peace was restored, in Julia's eyes the situation was worse than ever. Sedition and agitation turned to public discussions, newspapers printed vulgar caricatures, and placards appeared, even on the streets outside her house. A letter written a few weeks after these events, summarized her nearly apocalyptic view:

> I was happy in Berlin—my husband had such an honourable position there. Well, the revolution has upset everything—our friends and companions are leaving the city—the poor have no work—who can work at this moment? People do not know if they will be here tomorrow—if they will be alive tomorrow—they shout—they quarrel—the revolutionaries (that is to say those who have nothing to lose and everything to gain) wish for a republic—the fathers of families and honest men wish to retain the monarchy, and reestablish order and business. But those who shout are listened to—especially those who pay, and there are those who pay well for republican shouts, hoping to build themselves a triumphal arch on the ruins of the palace of their king. I too have suffered much from this revolution, dear friends—I have never seen my husband so crushed—he who has such an even temper and such a strong character, —and such a happy disposition. It is 20 years since I was married, and it is the first time that *together,* and surrounded by our children, we have not felt happy. How can we be so when all around us are suffering? Ah! who can look about him today, who can read the newspapers and think of the events that have followed one another with such alarming rapidity . . . without sorrow and pain? And how will it end? Alas, that is a question that all the world asks, and that God alone can resolve.

Her friends were shocked by these letters, so unlike Julia, and so very different from other accounts of the events in Berlin. Harriet saw the revolutions as a "wild and glorious dream." She told her sister: "Germany will also be a great and happy country, these days of horror will pass away." Although she deplored "the blood that has been shed," she acknowledged "the good that has been done. . . . The clouds will pass away and a glorious sun will arise for the world." She added, pointedly, "Are you not pleased that King Ernest [of Hanover] has been obliged to yield?"

For her part, Julia Smith, too, tried to reason with her friend:

> You are an English woman & surely you know that up to a certain point . . . all these means of expressions are safety valves. People talk themselves out, & the discontents which, pent up and concentrated in silence would become bitter & strong, allowed to evaporate in words, do no harm at all. . . . You, who were born & bred under liberal institutions, who have long seen the people in possession of power, & using it on the whole well, why should you be in such an agony of fear when you see them about to gain possession of what surely *you* will not deny to be their just right, namely to enjoy a portion in their own government. . . .

> My first and last word to you, dear friend, is *"Hope & Trust"* & encourage your fellow creatures in good by supposing them to be well inclined, do not provoke them to evil by blaming them too soon.

A few days earlier, Julia Smith had concluded another lengthy letter, designed to still Frau Pertz's fears, with a typical phrase: "What wonderful times we live in. . . . These last four weeks have had a century of history crowded into them. . . . Surely it is a fine privilege to live in these times for those who can interpret them in some measure rightly. The old routine is broken up & mankind *must* think & feel & search out new ways. We may hope that the world is better prepared to do so than it was a half a century ago & I believe nowhere better able to do so than in Germany." But Julia Pertz would heed no such advice, and was roused to rare anger by such attempts at cheering her up: "You in your quiet peaceful happy English home," she wrote Julia Smith, "have no idea of what we have suffered here; you do not know what it is to rise in the morning without hope and go to bed without security. . . . You do not know what it is to live under the government of a hired mob, paid by foreigners." And she told Minna Meyer: "Who can tell what the next day may bring? We are living on a volcano and no one can say *when* the irruption will take place or *who* will be buried in its ruins."

Her most pressing concern was for her husband and her family. To Harriet, she had written that Mr. Pertz would lose his position under the new regime, and they would all be out on the streets. Apparently, this anxiety grew ever more pronounced in her letters. Harriet wrote back of Julia's "dreadful state of alarm." She feared a "brain or nervous fever." She hastened to soothe Julia: "Why should he lose a place that cannot possibly have rendered him obnoxious in any political light? A literary & learned employment only & one he is peculiarly formed to fill honourably." Throughout the spring, Julia worried. She wrote of the need to economize and the horror of living under a popularly elected assembly. This latter remark brought back Harriet's reply: "Nothing would ever reconcile me to living and bringing up sons in a despotic country; I never said so when I thought it was your fate to do so, dear Julia; but pray teach your sons there is something nobler in living under freer institutions." To Julia, however, events seemed poised on the brink of a new reign of terror, and she wrote that she and her sons would end up eating only dry bread.

She was so upset that her husband finally forbad her to read the newspapers. This did not, however, prevent her from writing constantly of the horrors of revolutionary events and correcting Harriet's opinions. To this her sister remonstrated: "How little you can really care, dear Julia, about the great events passing in all countries when with papers on the table in the library, you never read them. You may know the local events of Berlin, but how can you know what is doing elsewhere?" Julia, however, would not be moved and returned repeatedly to her charges that the whole revolution was led by communists and terrorists. Her own fears were that the worst was still to come, that even the Royal Library would be attacked.

Almost as if in confirmation of these fears, Berlin did experience another outbreak of violence—precipitated by the King's repeated postponement of actions to fulfill his promise of representative government. But Julia saw events as a fulfillment of all her predictions of disaster:

> The papers will have told you [she wrote Harriet on June 26] of the violent skirmish of the 14th; it was frightful to witness & to *hear*. From our Library Balcony we saw the whole—the storming of the arsenal & the torches (by favor of whose light the guns & balls & armour were stolen) gave a fearful splendor to the scene. Oh—it was a terrible night. The citizens [National Guard] fired several times—2 men were killed & 5 wounded—we heard the firing of the guns —we saw the people flying on all sides—rushing past our house—roaring, screaming, threatening vengeance with their fists. . . .
>
> We fled into the Library (which has iron doors) [from their adjoining residence] —George collected some money & papers, which he concealed partly about his person, partly in the library (our silver we keep there always now)—we brought some beds—we thought to repose there if repose were possible—we calmed the

servants & endeavoured to be calm ourselves. In a moment a large barricade was built under our windows—and loud cries of "Hauser auf"—break the doors open—were heard. George said "NO! They may break them, but we will not open them." At last, an Hotel opposite to us opened the door, & in a moment the people marched in & appeared again with boxes & tubs & boards & I know not what beside. I covered my eyes with my hands. I almost groaned aloud—the scenes of the 18th and 19th [of March] were again acting before me. . . .

Towards 3 in the morning the people dispersed—a company of soldiers came & many of the guns were retaken—many more were sold the next day for a few Groschens (pence)—the barricades were taken down—(no one knew against whom they were erected)—and an appearance of quiet & order returned.

Terrified by these scenes, Julia decided she would have to take refuge away from the library with her sons.

My poor husband could not accompany us—*his duty kept him here*—it was a hard struggle—I left him with a beating & bleeding heart—under what circumstances might we meet again? or we might *never* meet again—but I went. My housemaid has an uncle [and had offered] some furnished rooms in his cottage should we be forced to fly, some time before—I did not then think I should have been induced to accept her Hospitality—but on hearing that all lodgings were taken (a lady had given 5 dollars for a bed in that night of terror) I determined to drive to her house. I packed some linen & clothes together & set off with my boys & maid. How sad I felt.

I could not enjoy the quiet of the little room—I heard always shooting & hooting & reports came, exaggerated of course—the Palace had been stormed—the King was fled—the Republic proclaimed, and my boys would not bear it. They returned to their father—and I was alone. But George came the next day—the attempt had been made—but it had failed & all was again quiet *for the moment.* I stayed 8 days—and now I am again here. . . .

It is said that a desperate trial is impending. . . . *it is a civil war* as in France. The best citizens acting with the Gov't for the cause of order & legality—against the lower classes who are starving. . . . and have joined the democratic party in the hope of getting pay & plunder. A butcher threatened Mde. Grimm some days ago with the words "*Your* house shall be one of the first that is plundered—it is marked down already." (She had left him because his meat was bad)—and the poor people have been promised plunder by their leaders as a reward for their active assistance.

Such is the state of things dear Harry—but do not let dear Mamma know it— it would alarm her & keep her awake at night—and after all, things *may* turn out better, and as you say good may come of evil at last. Do not be uneasy dear Mother & sisters. We shall probably have left Berlin before the revolt.

The bloody scenes in Berlin, however, were minor in the face of the new outrages in Paris, the rebellion of the mobs against their own republican revolutionary government, in the spectacular June Days. At the first news of the fresh insurrections, Julia wrote: "My dear Harriet: I think of the pain this will cause you. Your disappointment is greater than mine, who had only *fears* from the first. Alas! are they not all justified? The bright and glorious dream has ended in a very sad reality of misery. . . . What elements for discord! And all in the name of 'la Patrie et la liberte.' Oh, that I *could* believe in the virtue and patriotism of [the] mass[es]."

Julia could not help gloating a little over the correctness of her own views:

The accounts from Paris are terrible—what a scene of blood and confusion. . . . For the present I am of opinion that force and strength (moral & physical) can alone prevent the effusion of blood. As I observed I believe in my first letters (which you termed toryism dear Harry) it *must* end in anarchy, or military despotism and here also and in Austria & in Italy.

Whatever one might think of her political opinions, Julia was remarkably accurate in her predictions. By late August she could report, "The people who roared for a Republic, now sue for a *Dictator.* They have felt their helplessness, their incapacity to govern *themselves."* They want someone "to save them from the mob—from the reign of terror—which would have raised its bloody standard throughout Europe, had the faction *triumphed* which overturned the Gov't and has well nigh ruined France." Her own prejudices were strongly fixed:

Law and Order must finally triumph. Berlin is much changed . . . and *not for the better.* Vulgarity and vice walk without shame or fear, and irreligion and immorality are openly professed and defended. Mr. Held (the Democratic Hero of the day) declares openly that *religion and morality are prejudices of the majority. . . .*

If it comes to a conflict, it will be a frightful scene of confusion, blood and anarchy —but I am *thoroughly persuaded* that the good cause will prevail. . . . Oh what blood and misery have these wild theories of Louis Blanc occasioned; but thank God his reign is over, and he is condemned by the voices of all good men.

For her part, Julia was determined to stand by the forces of order.

> On the virtue and discipline of the Army depends the *fate of Prussia* and perhaps that of Europe—for the present struggle is that of civilization or Barbarism—but I must not touch on this theme—its interest is of an all too painful nature.

After such events, Julia was indeed at her wit's end. Time and again her letters lose control. Even as she poured out fear, confusion and terror, she apologized to her correspondents for the stridency of her tone:

> I with cholera and revolution around me—in the impure moral and physical atmosphere of this wicked town in which the very trees preach rebellion, atheism and immorality (placards are posted on all the trees Under the Linden), is it to be wondered at if my letters are infected by the air I breathe and that you and I take different views of the world and of the scenes acted in it.

Aware that she was losing balance, she frequently tried to catch herself: "But why do I write this? I cannot alter things—cannot avert evil by dwelling on it." Scene after dramatic scene was followed by her resolve to stop—"But I must speak of other things"—only to have the narrative resume almost at once.

Harriet saw how the revolution had changed her sister. Julia who had always striven for greater personal freedom, had now become strangely conservative. "Dear Julia . . . you are a most kindhearted, amiable, generous tory —and as such I love you with all my heart; tho' I regret the change that living in a despotic country has wrought in you. . . . You once thought and felt as I do—& the world is become wiser and more Liberal than those days. . . . When strangers express tory opinions such as yours, I only smile—but I feel pained when they come from you, who once felt as I do." Indeed, the revolution seemed to have driven home to Julia, Sismondi's old lessons about acceptance and inevitable suffering. Caught up in these turbulences, Julia wrote Mme. de Neuville, who had fled Paris, "sometimes it seems to me that Europe—that the world—will perish—that God's patience is exhausted, and that to punish mankind for its perversity he allows them to tear one another to pieces." The struggle between the warring classes of her society occupied her every waking thought, and the outcome seemed clear: "I fear we are emerging in a state of Barbarism. The Roman empire had her decline—that of Germany—even that of Europe, may soon be the subject of some future Gibbon—written in America." Her letters, for the first time in her long correspondence, strike a newly resigned tone. She wrote Harriet: "God has ordained that this world should be one of suffering & we must bow to his will

& endeavour to prepare ourselves for one in which all sorrows will have an end."

By November, order had been restored to Berlin with the arrival of General Wrangel and loyal troops. Julia was enthusiastic:

> I feel so happy today. I long to shake hands with the whole world (with the exception of the *left* side of the national assembly—and *a few* democrats). . . . What an excellent man this general is; without bloodshed, without violence, to put down rebellion & anarchy! If anyone had foretold this 2 days ago, I should have looked upon him as an idle dreamer—and yet *it is all true*—and Berlin is spared the dreadful fate of Vienna, Paris, Naples, Milan etc. [where the revolutions had been suppressed by violence]. A weight is removed from my heart which has weighed heavily upon it since March. Praise be to God! & Gen. Wrangel.
>
> Tonight all honest people may venture out—only rogues & rebels have cause to fear & hide themselves.

But the revolution had its unalterable effects upon Julia. For the rest of her life, she withdrew further into herself and her circle of friends. Gone was her concern for public involvement, such as Elizabeth Fry's reforms. Politically, she became rigidly conservative. Her thoughts flew back to her own early experiences, but now these seemed to her quite different:

> We were very happy, dear friends, on the banks of the Raritan, and there we did not talk of revolutions, barricades, and the Organization of Labour [Louis Blanc's book]—of liberty, of equality—these did not concern us—but we were peaceful and free—not free as they are in Europe today to tear down all that is, in order to build on sand—and what can we hope from an edifice erected on such a foundation?

Julia's reaction was typical of that of a whole generation of women. Nurtured on the intellectual premises of the Enlightenment and, through the French Revolution and the economic developments of the early nineteenth century, accustomed to expect the actualization of their equality in practical terms, they were the potential vanguard of a feminist movement. The abrupt realities of 1848 had deeply shaken them. What if their intellectual demands were to inflame women to repudiate the virtues they still held dear: motherhood, duty, service, society? She had long ago broken with Fanny Wright over just such issues. Warned now by the lessons of 1848, Julia and many of the women of her class—the potential leaders of a feminist movement—drew back in horror and shock. The cause of a more active feminism would have to await the recruitment of a new generation of women, who had not gone through the traumas of these revolutions.

This is not to say that they lost their interest in the fates of women. Rather, they turned to individual solutions, not organized or political ones. Paradoxically, while embracing General Wrangel and his armed men, Julia would continue to watch and help women who were fighting their way through to new forms of female freedom.

After 1848, Julia sought to return to a close circle of friendship where freedom was inward, in both direction and effect. When her beloved mother died in November 1848, her first thoughts were of her sisters: "This is a heavy blow," she wrote a friend, "and my poor sisters lose their only object in life —the care of my aged mother who had filled their time and their thoughts since I left them 20 years ago." They must now be reunited. Now her mother's death had removed some of the old obstacles to a reunion. "If my sisters can not, *will* not come to me—I must and will go to them." But the old dream of sisterly community was not to be resurrected. Berlin was hardly a tempting spot for the Garnett sisters to live; in the aftermath of revolution, a severe influenza settled upon the city, affecting some 60,000 people. The health-conscious Harriet would not venture into such surroundings, and Julia, of course, could not live elsewhere.

Lonelier than ever, Julia settled back into the routine of her life, but was more determined than ever to create a circle of women and enjoy their friendships as much as her weakened health would permit. In the strife-torn city, she had found a new friend, Mrs. Helen Martineau, wife of Harriet Martineau's brother, who had come with her clergyman husband to spend a year in Berlin. During their stay, the ladies exchanged visits and notes, and after the Martineaus returned to England, their letters, different from those exchanged with Harriet and the sturdy, more down-to-earth Miss Smith, were redolent with the special language of female love, which bound together so many lonely ladies of the period. These communications did not convey ideas or debate politics. Julia's correspondence with Mrs. Martineau was an ongoing exchange of shared affection and heartfelt emotion. The younger woman told Julia upon her return to England, "Were I not Helen Martineau with husband and children, I would be your eldest daughter, or youngest sister and never leave you." When Julia grew too ill to write for a while, Mrs. Martineau confessed that she had "treasured up" Julia's letters "to read again and again when I would fain hear from you and cannot. Indeed, I have almost every scrap you ever wrote me, including those dear little notes that passed in the Behren Strasse." In a rare moment of introspection, Mrs. Martineau analyzed the special relationship between the two women:

Among all my friends I have nobody who stands to me at all in your relation —like a sweet elder sister, or an impossibly young mother. . . . I have no one just so much in advance of me as you in life's experience, with sympathies so true and a heart so young.

Such a relationship was one shared by many single women of the period. What struck them both as remarkable was that such love should be found between two married women. As Mrs. Martineau noted:

Unmarried friends, though never so good and true, cannot comprehend one's whole self: they either crave to fathom your heart's depths and envy your possessions, or they ignore its wonderfulness and think you are its slave.

To open up to each other the "whole self" and the "heart's depths" was the whole extent and purpose of their letters. To enjoy such feelings was sustaining, like eating good food.

Indeed, Mrs. Martineau's girls had formed their own such attachments with a young German girl, Gertrude Passow, whom Mrs. Martineau had invited to England, to spend a year as companion to her daughters. She told Julia: "It would bring out Bertha especially, and indeed all in their own degree. . . . I have not seen my gentle Isabella *ever* so bent on the fulfilling of a hope, and . . . Mary Ellen and one and all of the young ones are continually planning loving schemes for companionship. . . . There seems to me no limit to the mutual improvement that would be taking place. Music would be a great bond too & I should delight to hear Gertrude play . . . on our 'pet' grand piano." But such sweet satisfying evenings, such heartfelt feelings, such deep "bonds" were, alas, no part of Julia Pertz's present life in Berlin.

Her last illness was completely incapacitating, and even more than discomfort, she feared her increasing uselessness. Repeatedly, she regretted her inability "to be of some use" to her family and friends. She told Mrs. Martineau: "I have been a nonentity—a burthen to myself and friends—and worse, for I have caused them much pain and anxiety." She felt herself "condemned to total idleness." But however tiresome she feared becoming to her family, she never doubted her worth to her women friends. "I am dreadfully stupid," she wrote Miss Smith, "but I know that you will not be impatient, and that you will bear with me and love me, [in] spite of my emptiness."

Still, despite her illness, and still fearful of the attendant dangers of revolution, Julia was glad to see that a new, stronger kind of woman seemed to be emerging, not a by-product, as much as a more congenial form of the new world even then being born. Her continuing correspondence with Julia Smith was the principal vehicle of these vicarious hopes. With her friend, she eagerly listened for news of this new woman who would not, Miss Smith predicted, live "without getting hold of any one engrossing pursuit." Miss Smith was quite clear that her young nieces and friends needed to "early fly this Babylonian woe, as I consider the lack of pursuit to be." She who had herself suffered a "chopped up destiny," and who had watched the fates of the Garnett sisters and the ambivalent struggles of the warm-hearted Mrs. Pertz, sided unequivocally with change. She wrote Julia:

> I am glad to see all the young women of my acquaintance getting hold of some occupation or at least feeling the want of it. Few sit down contented now, with the life that was considered to do very well in my young days, made up of *a little* music and *a little* drawing and a good deal of visiting. I remember looking round upon the *little* world I lived in and making my *little* reflections, but alas, they did not prevent my falling into the snare.

Now, Julia Smith acknowledged that like most women, she could only improvise. The fault lay with her past education. "If [young women] had been fed with strengthening food, with Latin and Mathematics instead of romance, reading & music, they would have seen life and human beings more truly. . . ." As for herself, "Every book I read makes me feel my wants more than my enjoyments . . . makes me wish to begin at the beginning again and makes me hope and trust more and more that in some world or another, either the next we go into, or the next after that, or that next after that, opportunity will be afforded for a fresh beginning." To Julia she admitted that "If I had not been an Englishwoman I should have liked to have been a German *man*, . . . but the fate of a German *woman* does not particularly excite my envy."

Now in her later years, Julia Smith devoted herself to serve on a committee of a school for middle-class girls, and when the Great Exhibition opened, she became an avid booster. Maintaining that all women should visit it to "drink in knowledge at such a copious and rich source as it proved to those who really set about to profit by it," she herself had been a frequent visitor and found her experiences "well worth having for the rest of one's life." Many have regarded the Exhibition as a device for demonstrating England's progress—and so it was. But it also represented one of the few opportunities women had for learning in previously unavailable areas. Those who were most forward looking, drank in the taste of knowledge and blessed Albert and Victoria for having made it all possible. Wrote Julia Smith, "I never felt so loyal as this year."

But the real future, both Julias were convinced, rested with the young, and they avidly followed the development of their friends. Hilary Bonham-

Carter, another of Miss Smith's nieces, won their approval when, after a long battle with her parents, she set off for Paris in the winter of 1849 for a stay with Mr. and Mrs. Mohl, hoping to make great strides in her drawing. Perhaps in watching women like the two Julias, both of whom lived with regrets for what they had not accomplished during their lives, these younger women in turn resolved to do better. Certainly they appreciated these signs of approval, for not everyone supported them. Sarah Bayley, living contentedly with her sisters and the Garnetts at Hastings, found that Julia Smith's nieces, while "full of activity—romance—and yearning somewhat intemperately after reforms of all kinds," might end up producing only "intolerance and misplaced zeal." Indeed, Sarah told Julia Pertz confidentially, "your friend Julia [Smith] is not a little wild in the same direction." She pointed out the living example of a life ruined by such experiences: Frances Wright, now alone in the world, recently released from her sordid husband by divorce. The conventional Sarah was convinced that "her life has been a failure from the want of practical good sense."

Despite these warnings from old friends, Julia Pertz continued to encourage her young female acquaintances to break away from family and friends in order to lead lives of their own. When Helen Martineau invited young Gertrude Passow to spend a year with them in England, Julia was instrumental in bringing it off. She triumphantly wrote the waiting Mrs. Martineau:

> The last efforts I was able to make in Berlin, were employed in arguments to induce her to make a final decision in favor of England. I wished it for your sake, for the sake of your dear girls, and I wished it for dear Gertrude's sake—for I know the immense advantages she will derive from a residence under your hospitable roof. I told her it was her *duty* not to throw away such an opportunity of enriching her future life with stores of knowledge, and of every sort of interest. I pointed out to her . . . the value of the friendship of *such a family* as yours—such an offer I added, occurred in the course of life, only *once*—and to how few.
>
> I saw the feelings that were struggling in her bosom—the separation from her family and friends, the distance from home etc., but I saw that my arguments had made an impression—some days afterwards . . . she expressed to her Parents that she felt equal to the effort.

All kinds and stations of women were moving away from the old ideal of service and self-sacrifice. One of the Smith family's old Nannys had left the security of the large Smith brood for a farm in Sussex where, Miss Smith supposed, "she is learning to fatten pigs and to make cheese." Despite the obvious decline in gentility, she was at least working for herself. Pointedly, she drew a parallel with Barbara Smith, another of her nieces who was training for a career: "She and Barbara are perhaps the only two girls I know who will not find themselves at a loss for positive occupation; their great native energy, and the large liberty they have always enjoyed contribute much to this end." Barbara Smith, later Mme. Bodichon, would eventually write an influential book on *Women and Work* (1859) in which she insisted that occupation was one of woman's greatest needs and rights. In a culminating passage, she explained: "I believe more than one half the women who go into the Catholic Church join her because she gives work to her children. Happier by far is a Sister of Charity or Mercy than a young lady at home without a work or a lover. We do not mean to say work will take the place of love in life; that is impossible; does it with men? But we ardently desire that women should not make love their profession." Julia Smith would heartily approve of those sentiments.

Julia Pertz, finding it too late to change herself or her fate, delighted in this correspondence, so hopeful and forward looking. On a trip to Dresden, taken out of family obligations, she had arrived too ill even to leave the hotel room, and so settled down to read while her family went visiting. She chose a relatively new book—*Jane Eyre.* To her young friend Minna Meyer, now herself a governess, Julia described her vicarious delight in this new heroine, whose breezy sense of freedom was so refreshing. She wrote: "This book helped me to pass my time very agreeably, although a great sufferer. It forms a new Era in Novel literature. . . . The book is certainly clever and singular, especially when you consider that the authoress is a young lady 25 years of age." To a generation of women who did stay in their places, and who did *not* advertise, about whom no one took notice, the proud declaration "I care for myself" rang like a bell of prophetic liberty.

At almost this same instant—as Julia Pertz, feeling useless and ill, read *Jane Eyre,* and her German friend Gertrude Passow set off for a year in England, and Miss Smith's niece, Hilary Bonham-Carter began her artist's routine in Paris, a young lady who had recently given much trouble to her parents by not settling down to the life they had chosen for her was returning with some friends from Egypt, where, it was fervently hoped, she had profited from the instruction of antiquity and learned her place in the immortal scheme of things. That young woman, another of Julia Smith's many nieces, was Florence Nightingale. Miss Smith had arranged for her niece to meet Mrs. Pertz, thus providing Florence the pleasure of knowing her friend, and Julia a rare glimpse of the living future. But the encounter between these two women was to be only a brief and formal one. Mrs. Pertz was too ill to speak at length to anyone, or even to descend the stairs to meet the party, which came to her as she lay upon her sofa. Fearing the effects of fatigue and excitement, she later explained to Miss Smith how painful was the realization that she was "too weak to give pleasure to others—to enjoy the society of clever and amiable persons." Indeed, she added, "I deeply lamented this when Miss Nightingale and Mr & Mrs Bracebridge were here."

This brief meeting was symbolically the convergence of two worlds. Florence Nightingale was a young woman on her way to a life of personal goals and occupation which had not proved possible for women of an earlier generation; Julia Pertz was a representative victim of that generation. In the year of our Lord 1850, only the truly remarkable woman could hear and respond to calls from any God beyond that of the family. All those silent sisters had stayed at their posts, devoted in service to mothers, sisters, husbands, children, but not, as yet, to causes. Surely one of the motivating factors in Florence Nightingale's life was her determination to avoid a fate like that visible in the wasted frame of the woman she had come to Berlin to meet. Much later, in reflecting upon her experiences, Florence wrote a passionate complaint against the life of women in the nineteenth century: "I see so many of my kind who have gone mad for want of something to do. People who might have been so happy." Aware of "the petty grinding tyrannies supposed to be exercised in convents," she realized there was "no tyranny greater than that exercised by a good family. And the only alleviation is that the tyrannized submits with a heart full of affection."

Julia herself would never have uttered such words. But Florence Nightingale continued to be angry on behalf of all those who had sacrificed their lives for family duties. In a later, suppressed work, "Cassandra," Miss Nightingale painted an imaginary scene in which a dying woman, very much like Julia Pertz, spoke to her family of mourners a truth the women of this circle had sensed but could not have articulated themselves:

> "Oh, if you knew how gladly I leave this life, how much more courage I feel to take the chance of another, than of anything I see before me in this, you would put on your wedding-clothes instead of mourning for me."

> "But," they say, "so much talent, so many gifts! Such good which you might have done!"

> "The world will be put back some little time by my death," she says; "you see, I estimate my powers at least as highly as you can, but it is by the death which has taken place some years ago in me, not by the death which is about to take place now."

> And so is the world put back by the death of every one who has to sacrifice the development of his or her peculiar gifts to conventionality.

"My people were like children playing on the shore of the 18th century. I was their hobby horse, their plaything; & they drove me to and fro, dear souls, never weary of the play themselves, til I, who had grown to woman's estate & to the ideas of the 19th century, lay down exhausted, my mind closed to hope, my heart to strength.

Free—free—oh! divine freedom, art thou come at last? Welcome, beautiful death!"

A year after Julia's death, Florence Nightingale had won her own battle with her family and had become head of a small philanthropic nursing home. That winter, the Crimean war broke out, insuring the subsequent unfolding of Miss Nightingale's destiny. She would be one of the first to cheat the oracle which had always pronounced woman's fate as relative, her personal occupations unimportant.

But Julia Pertz was beyond choosing either the old or the new worlds; the end of her days was fast approaching. By spring 1852, she no longer could descend the stairs, and gave up hope that fresh air or drives could alleviate her ills. She was suffocating—both in spirit and in body—choking, half-crazed with the ever-rising phlegm which she relieved with an incessant cough which made conversation impossible. Even meals, which could take as long as two hours, became trials. Sitting in an armchair given her by Mr. Pertz, she sighed to her friends, "Mine is a weary sad life." Slumbering and coughing away the days, she tried to make herself believe that "God's will be done." She prayed now for patience: "After all, we must submit to God's will, and to do so with cheerfulness shall be my study."

In her last months, she drew even closer to women. She managed one more visit to Mrs. Ranke. The two invalids took a drive to the Charlottenburg rose gardens, after which they exchanged their usual affectionate but melancholy notes. She told Clara: "The roses we saw in bud were fast fading and in a few days they will be gone—so is it with us, dear friend, we are born to grow, flourish, fade and die." Anticipating her own approaching death, Julia made generous offers to finance the trip of a female companion who she thought would brighten the life of Clara Ranke. Indeed, she had always believed the company of female friends essential: "I wish I had such a friend to whom I could say, come, but to a stranger I have not courage to apply." She was still hoping for a visit from Julia Smith or Minna Meyer. As she explained to Mrs. Ranke, "She could be to *me* what I trust and believe Miss Russell [the prospective companion] will be to *you*. We both need female friends, for we both suffer from weak nerves and are both unable to perform unassisted the duties of our station in life." Out of the question now was the one woman who had offered, twenty-five years ago, to come whenever the need arose. The young Frances Wright had told Julia, "Thou hast only to write to thy

Fanny, come and take me to thee, and she will come—were it from the end of the earth to its other farthest extremity." But Julia had not written to Miss Wright (now the divorced Madame d'Arusmont) since the years when scandal had surrounded her name, and now, surely, it was too late.

Then, unexpectedly, a new female correspondent appeared. Addressed as "highly honored and dear mother" by an unknown young lady, Julia was at first unpleasantly surprised by what she called a "strange affair." Her son George (without notifying his parents or even introducing them to the young lady) had suddenly engaged himself to Hedwig von Pallandt. But Julia was softened by the girl's affectionate letter. After all, the long-desired daughter had at length appeared, and her first letter soon became a treasured piece; the spring before her death, Julia translated it into English, "that I might have the pleasure of reading it in my native tongue, and as I do so, I could cheat myself in the belief that my little Mary—the daughter whom I lost so soon—was restored to me. Hedwig calls me *teur Mutter* and I feel like a Mother towards her." But alas, that joy was never to be. In the few months of life left to her, Julia never met Hedwig, the girl whose promise George had so precipitously obtained, who had written to Julia "with filial heart."

In July 1852, Julia's condition worsened and she made a last desperate effort to recover her health, planning a trip to Soden, where that classic remedy, change of air, was expected to work miracles. On July 9, Julia set out with her husband and a maid on a long railway journey. The same railroad which had driven her friends and sisters from Hastings, dissipating its charms and rural character, now carried Julia to the end. En route, the Pertzes stepped off for a moment at Frankfurt, and in one of those incredible coincidences of life, met Julia Smith on the platform. Julia wrote her sister, "Was it not a strange accident that brought us in the same day to the same place?" This brief encounter was to be their last meeting.

After ten days of "taking the waters," Julia collapsed. The trip had been a terrible failure. Julia had planned to return by way of Hanover to see the Meyers, but she suffered a bad relapse. As she told Minna, she tried not to despair, but it was difficult to be sanguine. "I have neither moral or physical strength . . . both have been broken by . . . *four* years of intense suffering. My poor children—their home is now anything but a cheerful one—& I am a source of constant anxiety to my excellent husband—but God's will be done! I will try to submit to his decrees with resignation, but I am often in a very unhappy state of spirits." Characteristically, her thoughts had turned to the impact of her illness upon others.

In the end, she felt she could try the longer route home via Hanover, but once again the rigor of travel proved too much. Later, Minna would recall Mrs. Pertz's visit, as told to her by a younger sister:

At that time I was no longer living at home and thus did not see the noble sufferer. Since she was feeling so ill, she did not want to accept the invitation of our parents, but planned only to spend the night in a hotel in Hanover on the return trip from Soden. But because of some royal visit or some other celebration, all the hotels were filled and one evening a carriage drove up to our parents' house: Pertz climbed down out of the carriage and asked if our parents could put him and his sick wife up for the night, since they could get no other accommodations. Naturally, the beds were immediately made up and Emily remembers still today how much the poor woman was suffering. And indeed, she was not to live much longer. The mortally ill Julia returned to Berlin and by September was dead.

How many such women there were! Devoted to family and friends, weaving the social fabric tightly with their rounds of visiting and kind notes, binding themselves and their circle together in a language and a ritual of sisterly love. Above all, they sought to be useful—sewing, collecting, entertaining friends, tending the sick, helping young girls, teaching their children, assisting their husbands' endeavors, all the while seeking to find something purely their own. In the end, many of them discovered it in writing. Unlike anything else in their lives, it bore no relationship to their marital or domestic status, and it had rewards.

Women had been making their impact in this way throughout the century. That the pen was mightier than the sword, some women knew. Mrs. Trollope had penned her many novels, ruling the circulating libraries from the Orkneys to Land's End. A young woman from Haworth parsonage had transformed the face of English fiction with a single book. Harriet Beecher Stowe's novel was even now seeding the American civil war. Mrs. Browning's *Aurora Leigh* was the best seller of the age. Miss Mitford's *Our Village* had made her a celebrity and saved her family from ruin. Young American women like Kate Field were even now "making a great spring" in literature. Mrs. Fry had unsettled centuries of tradition with her prison reforms. Miss Martineau had turned the government upside-down with her political-economic stories. Frances Wright, in spite of personal failures, had tried to change the world, and her first fame had come with a book. Even Florence Nightingale had won her greatest triumphs, not while pacing the wards of hospitals, but in her room, quietly assembling the massive statistics out of which she wrote the reports which moved the entrenched bureaucracy of an entire army.

At first glance, it seems that the Garnett sisters left little in the way of such monuments to fame. There were no memorials besides Fanny's collections of corallines, pressed seaweed and shells, and Harriet's two unpublished novels and a host of anonymous translations. Of Julia, all that remained were some locks of "precious hair" and a collection of letters which she had preserved over a lifetime. But through her letters and those of her many correspondents, Julia had secured a kind of immortality for them all. Here, indeed, in the pages of Julia's treasury of letters, was the genuine experience of "unimportant, eventless" lives, which contained truths gotten at authentically. Here were records of remembered life, of pain and suffering, striving, small successes and failures. Faded flowers pressed between the pages of some long-forgotten book, the letters are the genuine records of the thoughts and feelings of these early nineteenth-century women.

Unconsciously, Julia knew that their words were the final witness to their experience. In the last year of her life, her communication with her friends, even those living nearby, became almost totally epistolary. She told Clara Ranke of the urgency with which she now pursued her correspondence. Because her family was far away and her difficulty in speaking so intense as to make visiting an ordeal, her letters were the only remaining bond with others. "I feel a pen more useful now, than I ever felt it to be, when those I loved were within reach of me." Even in the lives of these ordinary women, writing had wrought a kind of salvation. In their hours of correspondence, words had bound together their seemingly separate lives and helped them to see their experience as meaningful. None of these women, from the most insignificant to the most prominent, had written memoirs. They had left no records of their own. Yet here in letters, untroubled by ideas of propriety or public image, Julia and her friends had put down their private struggles with destiny. Their need to express themselves and to report on one anothers' lives, even to a limited circle of friends, was vital to each of them, and permits us the reconstruction of their history.

In that reconstruction and evaluation, Julia's role is central. To preserve the letters had been to pledge faith, to swear witness that these existences had importance, even beyond their own times and places. In the letters, the images of the sisterhood of women shine clear across the years. For Frances Wright, sisterhood had meant a bonding together for mutual action. For Harriet, it had meant a fulfillment in the single state. For both of them, physical proximity was the key. Now Julia discovered that sisterhood had a larger meaning and could still work even though women lived isolated domestic lives, even though they were geographically separated. In saving these letters, she had discovered this saving truth, honored the women of her circle, and fulfilled herself in a vocation of preserving the documents of a shared experience which had given meaning and value to all their lives. Like the griots of Africa, whose oral preservation of tradition permitted a modern writer to rediscover his roots, Julia had preserved the means through which the experience of this circle did not vanish, but was passed along, stored and relayed, so that other women might recognize something of who they are. Julia's sisterhood thus extends into a future where both its aspirations and its failures can be of value to others.

The story of yet another member of the circle remains to be told, that of the professional writer Frances Trollope. With the others, she had felt the heartfelt joys of the relationships with women, as well as the strong appeal of Fanny Wright's quest for useful activity. Indeed, that attraction, by circuitous routes, had drawn her out of the domestic sphere into a career as novelist. Her lifelong friendship with Harriet and Julia sustained her in hard times, and later she was to provide them once more with an ideal woman to energize the aspirations of the sisterhood. Alas, when Julia died, and Dr. Pertz sent to her friends for letters, Mrs. Trollope had to admit she had kept none and had destroyed the letters of a lifetime. Instead, her record of the circle of women was stored in her creative imagination. In the decade of her seventies, when all her hard struggles were over, she would have a word for the importance of sisterhood in the last novels of her life.

REFERENCES

PAGE

142 "Truly I have suffered . . ." JGP to Frau Rehberg, 9 January 1829, GPC.

143 "I might sometimes regret . . ." S/JGP, 8 February 1829, GPC.

143 "It is for you . . . " S/JGP, 3 May 1829, GPC.

144f. "When I first knew you . . ." S/JGP, 8 March 1829 and 17 March 1833, GPC.

146 "Well do I understand . . ." S/JGP, 17 March 1833, GPC.

148 "If I had a child . . ." HG & MG/JGP, 13 & 14 January 1836, GPC.

148 "that a mother's love . . ." HG/JGP, 19 December 1835, GPC.

148 "and so goes on . . ." MG/JGP, 18 December 1833, GPC.

148 "I am sorry . . ." HG/JGP, 22 June 1834, GPC.

149 "Her appearance is just . . ." JGP/HG, 6 April 1840, GPC. Eight years later, Julia Smith read a life of Mrs. Fry and wrote her impressions to Julia: "She was . . . a large & high minded being, attached to her religious creed & peculiarities without overvaluing them or wanting to convert any body to them. Berlin is often mentioned, & her success there is represented as great. I should like to know if her labours have left any permanent effects there. . . . She really was a wonderful woman—not only asserting the principle that criminals were to be treated with a view to their reformation, but also carrying it into practice & producing within her lifetime proofs & successes which carried all objections before them." JS/JGP, 16 February 1848, GPC.

150 "Could a married woman . . ." Information on Elizabeth Fry from M. Phillips & W. S. Tomkinson, *English Women in Life and Letters;* and Mrs. E. R. Pitman, *Elizabeth Fry;* and Margaret Tabor, *Pioneer Women.*

151 "fearful distance . . ." Jessie Allen Sismondi to JGP, 2 January 1842, GPC.

152 "Dr. Pertz has paid . . ." JGP to Mrs. Taylor, 28 April 1842, GPC.

153 "I have found . . ." Elizabeth Fry, quoted in Phillips and Tomkinson, *English Women,* pp. 325–30.

153 "If you would confide . . ." JGP to Mrs. Meyer, 29 August 1842, GPC.

154 "Mrs. Trollope writes . . ." Quoted in JGP to Minna Meyer, 23 July 1845, GPC.

154 "Clara Ranke, born Graves . . ." Information on Clara Ranke from letters in GPC and from Gisbert Bäcker-Ranke, "Leopold von Ranke und seine Familie" (1955), and "Rankes Ehefrau Clarissa geb. Graves-Perceval" (1957), pp. 1–23.

154 "Poor Mme. Ranke . . ." HG/JGP, 5 October 1845, GPC.

155 "Many things have already . . ." HG/JGP, letter of 1846, GPC.

155 "At such moments . . ." All quotations in the paragraph from letters of Clara Ranke to several correspondents, quoted by Bäcker-Ranke in "Leopold von Ranke und seine Familie," especially pp. 45–50.

157 "How is poor Mme. Ranke? . . ." HG/JGP, 7 August 1852, GPC.

157 "Betty Pertz . . ." JGP/HG, 20 October 1842, GPC.

157 "bear her company . . ." JGP/HG, 16 December 1842, GPC.

158 "We were gay . . ." JGP to Fanny Colden, late 1843, GPC.

159 "You are so *in* me . . ." JS/JGP, 30 September 1844, GPC.

160 "What a capital person . . ." JS/JGP, 14 April 1846, GPC.

161 "for some years the *evening* occupation . . ." JGP/JS, January 1848, GPC.

162 "I was happy in Berlin . . ." JGP to Madame de Neuville, 5 June 1848, GPC.

163 "You are an English woman . . ." JS/JGP, 8 and 9 April 1848, GPC.

163 "What wonderful times . . ." JS/JGP, 24 March and 4 April 1848, GPC.

164 "Why should he lose . . ." HG/JGP, March 1848, GPC.

164f. "The papers will have told you . . ." JGP/HG, 26 June 1848, GPC.

166 "The accounts from Paris . . ." JGP to Minna Meyer, 1 September 1848, GPC.

166 "*Law and Order* . . ." JGP to Minna Meyer, 1 September 1848, GPC.

167 "I with cholera . . ." JGP/JS, 4 September 1848, GPC.

168 "I feel so happy today . . ." JGP/JS, November 1848, GPC.

168 "We were very happy . . ." JGP/JS, November 1848, GPC.

169 "Were I not Helen . . ." HM/JGP, 14 May 1849, GPC.

170 "Among all my friends . . ." HM/JGP, 7 April 1851, GPC.

170 "I am dreadfully stupid . . ." JGP/HM, 14 August 1849, GPC.

171 "I am glad to see . . ." JS/JGP. These letters begin 23 June 1844 and continue regularly until late 1852, when Julia Smith learned of her friend's death. She wrote an account of her friendship with Julia and sent copies of Julia's letters to Dr. Pertz for his projected monograph.

172 "The last efforts . . ." JGP/HM, 14 August 1849, GPC. Miss Passow was in England from October 1849 to October 1850.

173 "Barbara Smith, later Mme. Bodichon . . ." Quote is from Barbara Bodichon, *Women and Work,* p. 27.

173 "This book helped me . . ." JGP to Minna Meyer, 23 December 1850, GPC.

174 "I deeply lamented this . . ." JGP/JS, 21 October 1850, GPC.

174 "Oh, if you knew how gladly . . ." Florence Nightingale, "Cassandra," part VII, printed in Strachey, *The Cause: A Short History of the Women's Movement in Great Britain.*

175 "The roses we saw in bud . . ." JGP to Clara Ranke, 20 June 1852, GPC.

176 "a new female correspondent . . ." Letter from Hedwig von Pallandt to JGP, 6 June 1852. Julia translated the letter into French and English and shared it with her sisters.

177 "At that time . . ." Minna Meyer, letter of 1909, GPC.

177 "Harriet Beecher Stowe's novel . . ." In 1852, recalling Harriet's earlier attempt at a slavery novel, Jessie Allen Sismondi discussed Mrs. Stowe's novel with Harriet: ". . . talking of clever women reminds me of an American lady. I am reading *Uncle Tom's Cabin* with intense interest. You have read it long ago I daresay. . . . Uncle Tom reminds me of your tale. Why do you not finish it? and try its fate? The American repugnance to colour is the next trait to slavery and ought to be written down. Mrs. Stowe has an awakened mind on the subject and I think every book approaching it will be seized on. Do try it—Confined as you are now, what a pleasing occupation it will prove. Only think of Mrs. Stowe making more than 10,000 pounds in two months by her tale. Such a sum was never made before in so short a time in the whole history of literature—even by large works and to look at that little book and weight it against what it has brought in is something marvellous—it gives me a higher opinion of the human nature at this period. . . ." GPC.

178 "I feel a pen more useful now . . ." JGP to Clara Ranke, November 1851, GPC.

Frances Milton Trollope

CHAPTER SEVEN

Frances Trollope

*E*ven with women—as the world has found out—it is possible both to write a book and make a pudding; to study deeply art or science, and yet understand that not inferior art and science of how to keep house with economy, skill, and grace. Incredible as it might appear to the last generation, some of our best modern authoresses have been also the best of wives and mothers; or, failing this natural and highest vocation, have led a most useful life, deficient in none of the characteristics of genius, except its eccentricities and follies.

Mrs. Craik, **"Genius," in *About Money*, 1887**

*T*he first responsibility of a 'liberated' woman is to lead the fullest, freest, and most imaginative life she can. The second responsibility is her solidarity with other women.

Susan Sontag, ***Partisan Review*, 1973**

I have always thought and felt that I was not quite an ordinary character.

Frances Trollope, *The Life and Adventures of a Clever Woman*, 1854

THE FACE of Frances Trollope looks out from beside the title page of the fifth edition of *Domestic Manners of the Americans*, the first and most famous book she ever wrote. The artist, her protégé Hervieu, has given the portrait a triple focus. The face, compassionate but strong, is full of experience, but bears a pleasant expression withal. It is the intelligent face of an understanding friend. Her femininity is emphasized by her style of clothing. She is dressed richly, proudly proclaiming her financial success, in a stately hat covered with fine feathers and curlicues. An elegant lace shawl is draped carelessly over the shoulders. The vee of the large collar draws the eye downward to a hand laid firmly upon an open book. Her posture and gesture testify to the occupation which had spelled her destiny. Frances Wright had once posed herself for a portrait by Hervieu, standing beside a horse, as if to announce her appearance as a new, feminine knight. Julia's portrait had been a domestic pose, in a soft cap and pearls, her life's function engraved beneath in the epigraph, "She lives and loves." Frances Trollope appears before the world as author, though her face and apparel indicate a blending of that dominant role with others equally important.

Had anyone asked her to identify the major focuses of her life before she reached the age of fifty-three, she would have answered, husband, children, friends, probably in that order of importance. Thereafter, the reply would have added the ingredient of work. The constant factor in the long equation of her life was her motherhood, but it was balanced by other, equally strong preoccupations. While many women of her time were seeking new kinds of self-fulfillment, Frances Trollope was that rare individual who successfully blended the conflicting demands of inner and outer—the needs of others as opposed to individual goals. In her circle of friends, in the years between 1800 and 1850, she was a unique combination of mother and worker. Like some mythical creature, she seemed to them a marvel, one of whom they sometimes disapproved, but whom, in the end, they unabashedly admired. The amplitude of her life provided them with a sense of possibility. Frances Wright had striven for great goals, but her personal life had been unsuccessful. Harriet had achieved satisfying relationships, but had failed to find the public achievement she so desired. Julia had been consumed by her wifedom and motherhood. The woman who could enter the male world of endeavor, be a good wife and mother, and maintain her bonds and supportive relationships with women had done the really difficult thing. Mrs. Trollope lived this triple existence, despite the cultural and philosophical stances of the time which had ever tried to limit woman to a single sphere. The roots of her accomplishment ran deep; they had been forming and strengthening for more than half the lifetime of Frances Milton Trollope.

They first set themselves down in the soil of Nashoba in 1827, when she followed Frances Wright to America, moved half by desperate finances and half by a restlessness longing to express itself in some meaningful action. But her arrival at Nashoba was not happy. After a grueling trip up the Mississippi by steamboat to Memphis, and a fifteen-mile ride through the dense forests, they saw the colony, and Mrs. Trollope's first impression can best be gathered from her own words: "One glance sufficed to convince me that every idea I had formed of the place was as far as possible from the truth. Desolation was the only feeling—the only word that presented itself." The wilderness lay all about; the settlement boasted but a few shacks. Mrs. Trollope shared Fanny Wright's bedroom, which had no ceiling, and the floor of which consisted of planks laid loosely in piles which raised it a few feet from the earth. Rain poured in through the wooden roof, and the log chimney caught fire "at least a dozen times in a day." Yet Frances Wright, according to her shocked friend, stood in the midst of all this desolation "with the air of a conqueror." The school, to which Hervieu had come as drawing master, had not yet been built. While there were books, and one or two professors engaged, nothing was as yet organized. Hervieu wept in rage and grief. The food was poor, and there was no beverage but rain water. There were wheat bread and rice, but there was no meat but pork. Later, Mrs. Trollope commented sarcastically on Frances Wright's ability to make a meal of Indian corn bread and tepid water, meanwhile smiling "with the sort of complacency that we may conceive Peter the Hermit felt when eating his acorns in the wilderness."

But when Mrs. Trollope recognized the ravages of malarial fever on the faces of Camilla and Richeson Whitby, she feared for her frail children, and determined to leave as soon as she could muster the money and throw together a new plan for survival. Her hopes of finding Henry work as a tutor at Nashoba were over. Rudely shocked by Nashoba's primitive living conditions, and frightened by its pestilential swamp climate, she left it within ten days, abandoning all the furniture she had brought, as well as her small investment. Still hoping to cement Henry's future at least, she sent him to the cooperative school of William Maclure at New Harmony, Indiana, where students could earn their way by manual labor. Mrs. Trollope had met Maclure upon her arrival in New Orleans and been impressed with him. But Henry was unequal to the necessary physical exertions, and once Mrs. Trollope had settled her family in Cincinnati, she borrowed money from Hervieu (who had also left Nashoba in disgust) to bring her ailing son to Cincinnati. There he tried again, offering his services as tutor to young gentlemen, but he had no answers to his newspaper advertisement as Latin teacher.

After her departure from Nashoba, Mrs. Trollope was completely cut off from family and friends. Her husband, angry and humiliated, had sent no replies to her desperate letters begging for money to return home. Not wishing to hurt the Garnetts, whose attachment to Fanny Wright was strong, she decided not to write them about the feelings which had prompted her abandonment of the colony. Her decision to head up river to a healthier climate had been impulsive, and further removed her from everyone she knew. What was she to do next? For the first time in her life, in her forty-ninth year, she was truly on her own, in a strange land, with three children to support, and no immediate means of earning a living. For a while, she depended solely on Hervieu, who was frantically painting portraits of local notables to earn enough money for food.

But she was strong and healthy and did not like taking her younger friend's money. Unaware of the American proprieties which decreed that women should shun the sullying marketplace and business world, she went to work for the Western Museum of Cincinnati which, in an attempt to avoid bankruptcy, was expanding its serious scientific displays, with shows featuring oddities, freaks, and wax figures. Although lacking business experience, Frances Trollope was clever and ingenious. The cultured Englishwoman devised an exciting and novel attraction with the so-called "Invisible Girl," a mysterious sibyl who delivered responses in Latin, Greek, and French to the questions of paying visitors. The new display was well reviewed by the Cincinnati papers: "The responses of the invisible maiden are very pertinent and amusing. She answers with great readiness; and the curiosity is increased by the utter inability of the hearer to ascertain whence the sound proceeds. Many have exercised their skill to find out the secret, but in vain." At last, it seemed, Henry Trollope had found a momentary niche and Frances a way to exploit her son's linguistic talents so recently and more straightforwardly offered. For eight solid weeks, Henry held forth at the Museum, and the Trollopes were, for a time, solvent. Then the Invisible Girl gave way to another of his mother's ideas. As a young woman she had read Dante while hemming sheets. Now, she came up with the scheme of a tableau of Hell, the famous "Infernal Regions," a representation in wax of Dante's *Inferno,* complete with dramatic scenes and images of horror and terror. Its chief thrill was the hidden electrical machine which shocked spectators when they touched 'he displays. Mrs. Trollope's idea saved the Museum and was still packing them in fifty years later, long after she had left Cincinnati and America forever. After only a few months, she had discovered the popular vogue for being deliciously terrified, and had quickly determined to give the public what it wanted. Such would be her method for success when she later became one of the best-selling novelists of the forties. But her association with the Museum, while it brought some money and did seem to help Henry utilize his talents, was not enough to build him a secure future. Soon she thought she knew enough about America to try an even more ambitious project for survival, one which would place Henry for life in a solid and profitable career. Once again, her own interests and projects were inextricably bound up with the lives of her children.

During her first months in Cincinnati, Frances had been surprised by the cultural and recreational malaise of the city. Its major amusements were phrenology lectures, temperance societies, and ladies clubs. The most stirring event within recent memory had been a nine-day long debate on the existence of God, which, in her own count, left the numerical amount of Christians and infidels in Cincinnati exactly what it was when it began. More disturbing, there were no public places, outside the churches, where citizens of both sexes could meet to enjoy elegant entertainment or seek enlightenment. America seemed to lack places for women to mingle at ease in society, as they had at La Grange and in the Paris salons of Mary Clarke and the Garnetts. Brilliantly sensing the possibilities, both for Cincinnati and for Henry, Mrs. Trollope proposed to add a new dimension of life to the city, and designed, built, and began to superintend the Bazaar, a structure whose conception was as bold and imaginative as the woman herself.

Dubbed by its early critics "a great omnigatherum establishment, somewhere between Noah's ark and the tower of Babel," it was America's first shopping–culture mall. The complex multi-level structure included a coffeehouse, a bar-room, apartments, elegant boutiques akin to today's museum shops, open-air panoramas for viewing, exhibition galleries for art shows, an orchestral hall, and a splendid ballroom, complete with Cincinnati's first gas lights, its walls emblazoned with life-size murals of prominent citizens and events in American history, painted by the ever-present, faithful friend Hervieu. But the marvellous project failed, partly out of some unavoidable bad luck, and partly because Mrs. Trollope's unorthodox, unfeminine manners and associations had offended Jacksonian America's exalted, if limiting, concepts of the role of woman. She was too outspoken, learned, and bold mannered, walking unaccompanied, even at night and in rough weather, in "those colossean strides unattainable by any but Englishwomen." Her housekeeping was untidy and sporadic, her children ran free, and her friendship with Hervieu was socially unacceptable. Such blatant defiance of the proprieties of life in the self-conscious "Athens of the West" persuaded its townspeople to brand her a dangerous deviant, a "wandering Huzzy who chose to build bazaars." Given the chance to boycott her idea, Cincinnatians were secretly glad to find the means of expelling the disturbing element from their midst. One lady put it this way: "It should be understood that when Mrs. Trollope came here, she was quite unknown, except inasmuch as that she was a married woman, traveling without her husband. In a small society . . . it was not surprising, therefore, that we should be cautious about receiving a lady who, in our opinion, was offending against *les bienséances.''*

Within six months the extraordinary building was put into receivership (it subsequently housed an odd assortment of functions, beginning with a mechanic's institute and ending with a brothel) and all Mrs. Trollope's few remaining personal belongings were seized to pay the workmen and the outstanding debts.

In a series of letters, Mrs. Trollope told Julia the story of the collapse after she recovered from a fever of nine weeks which had brought her close to death. She told her friend that she was as well as ever now, "but very much thinner—and very much older—so do not be frightened when you see me." In these darkest hours of her life, when both health and work seemed on the verge of collapse, she needed to re-establish communication with her women friends. Next, Henry fell seriously ill. "No sooner was his physician dismissed and we thought him recovered, he fell again worse than ever—again we recovered him, and after about six weeks interval, he took the ague and fever so severely that he soon looked like a walking corpse. Every one said that his

native air was all that was left to try for him, and you will easily believe . . .
I decided that come what may, he should have it." As she described the
collapse of the Bazaar, her thoughts centered upon Henry's failed future.
"Guess what I must have suffered at finding that all the pecuniary efforts poor
Trollope had been making to place him well, and permanently, at Cincinnati,
were utterly thrown away!" Still, she was not one to live in regrets, and she
tried to see some good in all the debacle: "Spite of sickness, embarrassment,
and sorrow, I still am in good spirits, and full of hope for the future—Henry
was far from steady, and I flatter myself that he is much more likely to
become so, after all he has suffered. He proposes, if his health is restored, to
apply with dilligence [sic] to the law, the profession his father originally
wished him to adopt." If Henry could rise from these ashes, all might yet be
well.

Despite her silences to them, the Garnetts had continued to write, even
though she could not for a whole year bring herself to describe the disasters
of her American ventures to them. As she told Harriet in the first letter she
wrote, "If I have not written fully before, it has not been owing to any want
of confidence, but from the feeling, oppressively strong, that in telling you
all I have seen, and all I have heard I should be giving you the greatest pain
—but you ask for it, and you have a right to my fullest confidence, for you
are an old, loved, and tried friend."

Once the correspondence was re-established, Mrs. Trollope poured out her
troubles in letters to Julia. Alas, there was no money left to buy even Henry's
return fare to England, and he was very ill. Again, Hervieu stepped into the
gap left by Mr. Trollope's silences. Mrs. Trollope told Julia how they had
found the money to send Henry home. "Had it not been for our excellent
friend Hervieu, my situation would really have been dreadful; but his kindness has been unfailing, and I avail myself of it at this moment without
scruple, knowing that eventually he will be no loser in a pecuniary light, and
that having it in his power to be useful to us is the greatest pleasure he could
have." For herself, when she contemplated a return to Europe, it was the
reunion with the Garnett circle that moved her most: "God grant that my lot
may place me where I may sometimes see you—for the longer I live, and the
more I travel, the stronger is the feeling that you and Harriet are unequalled
in all the qualities that I love and honor most." When she permitted herself
the luxury of dreams, she thought of a meeting with her friends. "Would it
not be a pretty scheme for us to meet at Geneva some year or two hence? Oh
what a meeting it would be! What questionings! What answerings! What
delightful 'outpourings of the spirit.'" More than anything else, she had
missed such consolations during the three and a half years of her stay in the
United States.

She had not, however, been idle after the collapse of the Bazaar. In reflecting upon her experiences thus far, Mrs. Trollope had made two important discoveries. First, the support of her family obviously depended upon her own efforts. More important, she must find an occupation which did not take her away from that family. The answer lay in writing. During the long months of her struggle to survive in Cincinnati, she had kept notes of her experiences. To some makeshift school notebooks belonging to her son, she confided her most intimate reactions. When she turned to those journals with the thought of writing a book, she found they contained an embryonic account of life in the western United States. With the determined enthusiasm which always characterized her actions, she boldly proclaimed her new career to Julia.

> As soon as I had decided that Henry could not continue in Cincinnati, I determined to leave. . . . It is in no respect an agreeable residence, and I have long ago written everything about it that I think worth putting in *my book*.

Thus she announced to her friends the book which she hoped would make her fortunes.

Then, at last, she, the girls, and Hervieu returned to England (Mr. Trollope sent them the fare in response to his wife's threat to throw herself upon the mercy of his family), but she found affairs in worse disorder than when she had left. The only good news which awaited her was a letter from Julia. Mrs. Trollope replied, "How delightful . . . to find a letter from you on my arrival! dear Julia, it made me feel for a moment as if you and Europe were the same —and that I was indeed come back to you. Would to Heaven I were! how much I would give to talk to you, to consult with you." When she looked about her, despair almost overwhelmed her. She told Julia, "God knows what will become of us all." The rest of her letter makes clear that concern over the children's futures was still central in her thoughts.

> Tom is doing very well at Oxford—Henry and Anthony are perfectly without destination—They are both excellent scholars—but latin and greek are very *unmarketable*. We are living at a miserable house on the Harrow Weald farm. . . . My dear children are *all* devoted to me—I never saw *more* attached or affectionate children—This is my greatest comfort.

In the midst of these unsettled and harrowing conditions, she readied her completed manuscript for a publisher who, on the recommendation of Mary Russell Mitford, consented to read the pages of this unknown author. Despite such bleak prospects, she immediately set to work upon a novel of American life. There was no time to wait for acceptances or reviews. If her family were to survive, survival would depend upon the productivity and skill of her pen.

Her fundamental energy, that unnamed mysterious power which had propelled her through the desperate days in America, had been the devotion of her children and the love of her friends. Now she threw herself into the demanding work of writing. Like a storage battery capable of running on alternating and direct currents, she stayed in touch with several sources of power for the rest of her life. Her work. Her children. Beyond those, the sustaining circle of correspondence with friends. Although it was clear that her Harrow social life was over ("My friends all declare themselves delighted at my return—but if I can give no more parties—I shall not long count many friends"), her regrets were few could she remain close to the Garnetts and Julia, whom she told, with a little bravado, "This I should care nothing about, could I see my dear boys placed in situations where their talents and good conduct might enable them to gain their board." Of late, the greatest sufferer must surely have been Cecilia, who had grown into a handsome young woman. How could she meet a young man, how could she blossom and grow as women should, given the Trollopes' miserable surroundings. Mrs. Trollope told Julia, "My girls are nice creatures Julia—would you let Cecilia pay you a visit if any possibility of sending her occurred? and would you make her learn german—it might be very useful to her." If not marriage, perhaps work. The girls, too, must see to their futures. Mrs. Trollope could ask favors of her real friends in these hard times, without worrying about pride.

In that fall of 1831, she was still in the dark about the fate of her book. In the anxious weeks before its appearance, she wrote Julia, "If the delays of the law are tormenting, those of booksellers are at least equally so." There was cholera at Harrow, and living conditions continued crowded and miserable. Then, at last, the book was out, bringing more success than anyone had ever dreamed. Overnight, Frances Trollope had made the topic of "domestic manners" important. Certainly, she could speak with some authority upon that subject. She reported "the happy termination" of this "troublesome publishing business" to Julia.

> That is to say, the book is out, is highly praised in the *Quarterly*, and the sale is going on well. Murray says that Washington Irving declares it is all an abominable fabrication got up in London by someone who has never visited America. I suppose that I shall be most heartily abused by all who hold the theory that America is a pattern country.

The book sold out its first edition quickly, and suddenly there was money at Harrow once again. In its disposal, Mrs. Trollope took firm charge.

These tangible fruits of her labors, she determined would be used for the benefit of her children and a trip to see Julia. Her first goal was to return the family to its pretty farmhouse, Julian Hill. She told Julia: "I mean, if possible, to get back to my dear Julian Hill. It will *I hope* be vacant at Michaelmas and I think that with my little *gains,* and steady economy we may be able to get on there again very well. All the dear children wish it. . . . They will have a comfortable and quiet room to study in—and we must make the most of the means for improvement which we have here." This she clearly did. As her son Thomas Adolphus later recalled, "The return of my mother, and the success of her book, produced a change in the condition and circumstances of affairs at home which resembled the transformation scene in a pantomime that takes place at the advent of the good fairy." There were new curtains and a pillow for everyone's head. To such comforts, she added other "luxuries": a quarter of a pound of green tea, a half a pound of fresh butter, and a *wax* candle. Anthony, too, later recalled this refurbishing process, and of being once more surrounded by "moderate comforts." Both her sons testified to her special ability to brighten their living quarters, no matter how difficult the situation.

Next, she investigated the possibility of making a German tour for a publisher, which would, of course, include a visit to Julia in Hanover. As she explained to her friend:

> I have a longing Julie, to see you, & your husband, & your children which at times almost overpowers my efforts to occupy myself—how much I have yet to tell you! to you, the only living being to whom I could tell all I have seen and known—Shall I tell you of a bright vision which often floats before my eyes between sleeping and waking? I will—*If* my book should take and *if* it should be favorably received . . . I should offer the publisher to travel into Germany —to visit the watering places etc., & to write a volume of gossip of all I should see. . . . But observe my dear friend, these thoughts are at present only moonshine—when one is rather in the dark however, even such borrowed light is worth something.

Her metaphor is telling. In her dark times, it had been the sustaining power of friendship that had brought light. Repeatedly, she returned to the theme of needing to see her friends. "Oh for wings Julia! If I were but just going to take my coffee with you tonight—how willingly would I be whipt tomorrow if that could purchase it." When she thought of the prospect of a reunion, she cried, "Pray for me if I am disappointed—for I know not how I should bear it."

But bear it she did, for the trip to Germany was not immediately possible. For one thing, her available money was already gone. She had made a fourth (and final) attempt to set Henry on some path leading to a career, enrolling him in a program of legal studies. But first, before beginning such hard work, the companion of her sufferings in America would have a much-needed vacation, a walking tour around Exeter. She hoped that the exercise and the fresh air would complete the recovery of his health. Henry was delighted and, as he made his way, clinking his hammer "on every rock from Ottery & Exeter to the Landsend and the Lizard," wrote a regular series of letters to his mother in which his devotion to her and his pride in her success are clear. He knew whence the money had come for his tour, and told his mother from Taunton: "All hail to the £400—to the receiver thereof & to the writer therefore. Why, really, this is capital. . . . I should ask questions of you did I not fear that I should have no answer, concerning the sale of the last edition of the *Domestic Manners* and of your approaching 4th edition." He knew she was already at work on *The Refugee,* her "good Yankee story," and wrote, "How I long for your novel to be out. I shall now ask for it wherever I go." His deep love for her he sometimes presented in jovial fashion, as when he addressed her as "my most venerable and much venerated she parent," but his wish that she were there with him to share his pleasures came through clearly, as he described one particularly beautiful sunset and its Words-worthian ambience: "I can't describe it. I never saw anything like it before & probably never shall again. Oh mother, how I longed for you as I gazed on all that passed beneath my feet."

The trip culminated in one bright incident that brings into sudden focus the way in which Frances Trollope had successfully blended her roles as mother and worker in the eyes of her approving children. Henry had come upon the ruins of Buckfort Abbey, the finest of its kind in the western country, and had gone in search of a closer view.

> I was told I could not without leave from a Captain White R.N. who resided on the spot. I hesitated—I was very dirty.

Still, he could not resist.

> I sent in my name, begging admittance. The gallant captain came out himself & not only showed me the mines but asked me to dine, took me to his *dressing room* where I washed and shaved and put on a coat and waistcoat of his.

The reason for the captain's unusual hospitality had become immediately clear to the young Henry.

> To your fame, oh illustrious mother, do I owe this honor—this dinner—not to mention ruins—tea—conversation—and cake.

How his hard-working mother must have enjoyed that letter!

To her old friend Mary Russell Mitford, she was always quite frank about the kind of benefits she sought from her literary success; personal fame had never been her object:

> I never felt less in good humour with people in my life than I have done since I have been so be-puffed and be-praised. I am, however, thankful for the MONEY I have gained by it; it has been very useful to us. My dear Henry is to be immediately entered at the Temple by means of it—so VIVE LA PLUME!

She continued to be on the lookout for further literary work, but was unsure about where to turn next. She asked the more experienced Miss Mitford, "What does one do to get business with the mags and annuals? Does one say, as at playing ecarté, 'I propose,' or must one wait to be asked? Remember dear, that I have five children." Such questions could not be made of men.

Even as she had turned to a successful literary woman for help, she now made herself part of that sustaining network of women by putting her new literary fame at the service of Harriet Garnett. Having read her friend's novel, she anticipated the problems in getting it published. She herself had tried unsuccessfully to place Harriet's "sweet story" with a friendly firm. She told Julia, "It is *beautifully* written, full of deep & genuine feeling, and has but one fault—it is too short—not but that it is complete, but it is too long for an article in an annual—& too short of a volume by itself." Along with the advice she freely offered, Mrs. Trollope admitted to a hope that Harriet join her in some kind of writing partnership. "I long *too* to have her near me— I think we should be so very happy scribbling away together." Even in her new profession, so private by nature, Mrs. Trollope envisioned the sisterhood of women as a potentially important factor. Her hopes that Harriet succeed stemmed on the one hand from a genuine admiration of her friend's talents, and on the other, from an appealing mental picture of cooperation and support within a male-dominated and highly competitive profession. She told Julia, "I *long* for Harriet to enter the lists—I am so sure of her ultimate success —There is something so sweet, so delicate, so true to nature in her manner of writing, that I cannot doubt it. Would it not be delightful for us to be in

London together reaping our gold and our laurels?" When Harriet's work found no takers, Mrs. Trollope's annoyance was clear. "I have had much vexation and disappointment respecting dear Harriet's compositions—There cannot be the shadow of a doubt as to her power of writing—but the difficulty of starting is very much greater than anyone would believe who had not tried—I would have her revise her tales *most carefully*—with all their merit there are evident marks of their being carelessly written but that rather shows her power to be greater than less." Clearly, Mrs. Trollope was attempting to function as mentor to Harriet, who stood at a crucial point in her struggle for a career. That Harriet did not heed Mrs. Trollope's good advice in this matter of length and persistence, was the key to the ultimate collapse of her literary hopes.

Finally, in June 1833, Mrs. Trollope made the long-anticipated journey to Germany where she did stay with the Pertzes in Hanover. But pressed as she was for money, the trip had to be filled with hard work; indeed, a complete travel book was ready upon her return: *Belgium and Western Germany in 1833.* By then, the next of her life's great trials was almost upon her. Even her substantial earnings had not been enough to stop the financial catastrophe which was imminent at Harrow. Soon the bailiffs were at Julian Hill, seizing everything, for the Trollopes could no longer meet either their rental payments or bills. The family fled to Bruges, where Mr. Trollope's creditors could not present their demands. There they found housing at once through the good offices of another of Mrs. Trollope's close women friends, Mme. Fauche, the consul's wife. In their rented lodgings at Chateau d'Hondt, Mrs. Trollope set about making the bare, empty rooms habitable. Later, her eldest son recalled how the house, "taken unfurnished, speedily became under my mother's hands a very pleasant one." Mrs. Trollope herself described the process by which she transformed that dwelling into a home.

> Each of us have already learned to fix ourselves in some selected corner of our different rooms, and believe ourselves at home. The old desks have found new tables to rest upon, and the few favorite volumes that could not leave us, are made to fill their narrow limits in orderly rows that seem to say "here we are to dwell together."

She continued, telling her Harrow friends, "in order to *make believe* that it is furnished, ingenuity is obliged to do the work of money—and I am plotting and planning from morning to night how to make one table and two chairs do the work of a dozen." She was as sensitive to the duties and beauties of ordinary life as she was to become to the twists and turns of the plots of the many novels she would soon turn to composing. She had rescued from the auctioneer's block "some china, and a little glass, a few books, and a very moderate supply of household silver," and out of such slim ingredients made surroundings in which her children could again feel themselves at home. With characteristic understatement, Anthony later commented upon his mother's domestic energies, remarking that the house in Bruges was "the third that she had put in order since she came back from America." After *Domestic Manners* had made her fame, she had thought to provide income primarily through writing travel books. But the expenses of her German tour (and subsequent ones to Paris and Vienna, with their attendant two-volume accounts) proved uneconomical. The profits barely covered the costs incurred.

Moreover, it soon became apparent that her family included at least three seriously ill persons; indeed, when she faced the obvious signs, all three of them were dying: Henry, Emily, and Mr. Trollope himself, who had given up the struggle for solvency and taken to his bed with wracking, wasting head-aches. With the responsibility for lengthy nursing in her hands, travel was absolutely out of the question; she decided to turn her abilities to the writing of novels, which could be done in the quiet and necessary seclusion of home.

By the spring of 1834, Henry was desperately ill. As Mrs. Trollope told Julia: "He is grown pale and thin beyond what you can imagine and has a cough that tears him to pieces." Still, the doctor held out hope. "He thinks [Henry] will recover [from] the attack upon his lungs. All this has certainly kept me in a state of mind not favorable to writing." By summer, conditions had not improved. The interval of time had been "one of the most painful" of her life. "During great part of the time, I have been suffering from the dreadful apprehension that I was going to lose my dear dear Henry—and even now, though I speak of this misery as being past, I am far, very far from being at ease respecting him."

Then, Henry's health worsened. She told Tom, "My life is a very sad one, but I keep up as well as I can. And I write too,—though I scarcely know how I *can* do it." But necessity moved her to try. Had she broken over Henry, she would never have emerged to any of her later successes. During that cata-strophic winter of 1834, her character and habits of work were formed with finality. In those months were fashioned her will and the key to her working life. Amid scenes of poverty and sickness, the writing of novels began and went on. Her son Anthony, who was to inherit his mother's strength of character as well as her unusual working habits, recalled how "the doctor's vials and the ink bottle held equal places in my mother's rooms." He marveled then, as we must now, at her incredible power of dividing herself into two parts, keeping her mind clear and fit for the duty of contriving elaborate plots and exciting characters, and her strength and spirits equal to the task of nursing the suffering and dying. As Anthony later commented, "I have written many novels under many circumstances; but I doubt much whether I could write one when my whole heart was by the bedside of a dying son." It was demanding and exhausting work, and she managed only by dosing herself with strong green tea on alternate nights so that she could stay awake to write. While some of the novels written under these conditions suffer from wildly improbable plots, it is truly wonderful that she managed to write them at all.

Compartmentalization had become the secret of her working life. She described her method to Tom early in December:

> This is my night for writing,—not letters, but novel; so do not wonder at my scrawling with more rapidity than precision. . . . In spite of everything I go on with my book. . . . Poor Henry grows daily more *exigeant* as to my time. It is so hard to refuse him in his sad state when he wishes to have me with him. But I do get on, though not so fast as I wish.

Apparently Tom had remonstrated with his mother upon her spartan working habits, for she had to tell him,

> "I *do* take care of myself, dear Tom;—all the more because my children wish it. My working nights are far from disagreeable, and I sleep the night after, like a top."

Still, she could not conceal all her suffering.

> "Henry is *very* bad. Poor dear, dear fellow! It is heartbreaking to watch him."

During these months she learned to transform her experiences into fiction. The wild sorrow she felt when she realized that Henry would probably not recover vanished during the hours she spent writing, when, with an economy born of despair, she used his trials as novelistic material. While Henry was dying his difficult death, Mrs. Trollope wrote *Tremordyn Cliff,* the story of a young earl who dies of hemorrhaging. The story surely bore the traces of her current preoccupations. The heroine is the strongest character of the book: dominating, determined, and clever, she is better qualified to rule than her brother the earl, who is tender, soft, and girlish. In this unusual and probably unconscious reversal of the traditional sex roles, Mrs. Trollope was telling the story of her own heroics. During this dreary Belgian winter of suffering, the indomitable character of Frances Trollope was born. Her five children, in turn, occupied the center stage of her life, playing out their personal dramas; she was both audience and participant in their stories. Henry had been only the first; the lessons she learned during his ordeal would last forever.

But, as her daughter-in-law's biography of her makes clear, she did not brood over the memory of Henry. "There were others to be thought of. There was her husband, whose health was rapidly failing; there was Emily, delicate and fragile, and already showing unmistakable symptoms of the terrible disease which had carried off her brother; there was her elder daughter Cecilia; and there were her two dearly loved boys. She must be up and doing." And indeed, this neat synopsis spelled out the lines of her subsequent life.

After Henry's death, Mr. Trollope's health worsened. Although he was just sixty, he looked at least twenty years older. This once proud and prosperous barrister had thought to protect his wife and family always, but life had brought instead the bitter disappointment of a failed inheritance, professional and financial ruin, and slowly debilitating illness. The old courtship letters reveal his character: learned, quaint, hesitant—full of surprised love of her bright, fun-loving personality and awe before her prodigious energies. Even then, he had been almost constitutionally unable to show tenderness or affection to those he loved. In later years his irritability of temper had worsened, making Tom "fear his reason was, or would become, unhinged." He had become increasingly morose and morbid during her years in America. After her return, she sturdily shouldered the roles of breadwinner and nurse as he declined into a semi-invalid state. What none of them connected by the bonds of love could have known was that Mr. Trollope was mortally ill, probably with a slowly advancing brain tumor. As Tom later recalled, "he had suffered very distressingly for many years from bilious headache, which gradually increased upon him the whole of his life." Tom thought his father's nervous system had been shattered by the large doses of calomel he took to cope with his pain. As Tom wrote: "He became increasingly irritable; never with the effect of causing him to raise a hand against any one of us, but with the effect of making intercourse with him so sure to issue in something unpleasant that, unconsciously, we sought to avoid his presence, and to consider as hours of enjoyment only those that could be passed away from it." His children gradually learned simply to keep away.

Mrs. Trollope took another approach and encouraged her husband to try writing. It was the only salvation she knew. When he took up a hopeless, pedantic project of writing an Ecclesiastical Encyclopedia ("a complete history of the Church, containing a full and compendious explanation of all ecclesiastical rites and ceremonies; a distinct and accurate account of all denominations of Christians from the earliest ages of Christianity to the present time"), she was glad just to see the way activity had improved his outlook. As she remarked, "I cannot express my delight at his having found an occupation. He really seems quite another being; and so am I too in consequence." But though his temper improved under the healing powers of his new occupation, his daily physical ailments and sufferings continued. Mrs. Trollope had lived so long with his condition that when the end came, it hit her with a dull shock. Even her daily habit of writing, which she had sustained under the most terrible conditions, she could not for a time resume. As she told Bentley, "This melancholy and unsuspected event—for I believed all danger over—has rendered me very uncapable of working." Although the Garnetts thought that "Mr. Trollope's death will be a great relief to all his family," Mrs. Trollope truly mourned the passing of the man to whose fiercely upright and serious character her own sunny temperament had long ago been drawn. But even the luxury of grief was not permitted her for long.

Emily, her youngest daughter, now bore alarming signs of the consumption that had killed Henry. After Mr. Trollope's death, Mrs. Trollope moved from the damp climate of Bruges to a pretty country house at Hadley, hoping to nurse the frail girl back to a health which it was clear she had lost. The boys were away, and Cecilia was once more sent forth on a visit to protect her from contagion. The truth was kept from her, and she was told that Mrs. Trollope's old friend from Harrow, Lady Milman, "felt herself to be growing very old and feeble, and wished to have her dear young friend with her once more before her death." Even as she had sheltered Tom from the news of the bankruptcy proceedings at Harrow because he was taking final exams at Oxford, so too here, she tried to keep Cecilia free of the cares she would once again encounter. This time, the nursing was briefer and easier. As Frances Eleanor Trollope recounts the story, "Emily's sweet temper and unselfishness to some extent lightened her mother's hard task at this time. She was never irritable, never exacting about engrossing her mother's society, as Henry had been." The reason is not far to seek. She had lived through that Belgian winter with her mother and knew clearly that the two parts of her mother's life must go ahead, the one unimpeded by the other, as nearly as possible. The eighteen-year-old Emily "fully recognized the necessity of certain hours of seclusion, if literary work were to be done at all." By the spring, Emily was dead and *Jonathan Jefferson Whitlaw* was finished.

Once again, Mrs. Trollope had written her sufferings into the text of a novel. This slavery story, so full of the doings of strong women, also features the especial trials of slave mothers, who must stand by and watch while their children suffer, and yet are able to do nothing. In one particularly affecting scene, when a young slave girl is about to be stripped and beaten, her mother grabs her two younger children and retreats to the forest, "in the hope of placing herself and the little ones beyond reach of hearing the groans which she knew would soon be wrung from the innocent being she left." Mrs.

Trollope stepped into the narrative in her own voice, to plead understanding for the mother "when she hurried from the scene of her child's suffering." "She," the author remarks, "might have carried with her an anguish the bitterness of which no mother blessed with the power of protecting her offspring can conceive." This book, the first treatment in fiction of the slavery issue, is all the more powerful because it is the product of a real mother who had been equally powerless to prevent the loss of yet another beloved child.

In the fall of the following year, Thomas Adolphus provided Mrs. Trollope with her next trial, albeit not one involving hopeless nursing, for the sturdy Tom seemed to have inherited his mother's strong constitution, and indeed, would live well into his eighties. His was a crisis of will and discipline. In the autumn of 1837, Tom contemplated giving up his hard-won mastership at Birmingham in order to join his mother on her travels. Indeed, Tom had been called away from his mother's side in Vienna to take the position, and as she told Julia at the time, "it was rather a hard struggle, poor fellow, between interest and inclination." That struggle his mother had long ago won, as all must who hope to leave their mark upon the world. But by year's end, Tom was bored, and longed to join his interesting mother, whose first letter to him during this crisis clearly indicated her position: "Your friend has left you, and you are dull. But think you that at my age, when the strength fails and the spirits flag, I can go on forever writing with pleasure?—You know what heavy, uphill work I have hitherto had; and may pretty well guess what the effect on me would be, of sanctioning your throwing up a certain maintenance, before I have cleared myself from the claims that still hang upon me." Someday she hoped he would be her companion, but there was first much work to be done. "Give me the great comfort of knowing that you have sufficient strength of mind and resolution to stick to it for a little while." When a second letter from Tom produced no recantation of the idea, she wrote again, repeatedly setting before him her principles and the way in which his intention to throw up his job was cutting in upon valuable time she needed for her novels. She told him, "I have sometimes thought as I have sat pen in hand meditating upon the state of mind which must have dictated such a project instead of giving my attention to my heroes and heroines, that I must have misunderstood you." But, when she reread his letter, she found it "so clearly set down that *you have almost made up your mind to quit Birmingham* that it has turned me faint and heart sick." At the end of the letter, she ceased making severe admonitions and concluded with advice as to Tom's health: "Take regular exercise . . . above all things use cold water abundantly in the morning." Finally, she praised some of his recent efforts at writing, thus cushioning the harshness of her letter with the encouragement and solicitous advice of a concerned mother. Still, the message was clear: stay at Birmingham. Beware of enthusiastic and ambitious projects. Work hard and endure, for only in the sweat of the brow will success be earned. It was the kind of message that only such a mother could give, and it is not surprising that the twenty-seven-year-old Tom obediently remained at his post.

That Christmas, she called all her surviving children to her, telling Tom, "I have worked so hard, that I think I may try to give my children a merry Christmas with a safe conscience." She looked forward to seeing them all, and especially to those daily walks with Tom "as in days of yore." She told him, in a revealing aside, how the sustaining love of her children had provided her with the energy for continuing work: "I do truly believe that so many pages in proof of my industry would not now be burthening bookshelves, had you not done me this good service at Harrow."

In the following year, there were momentous changes. Cecilia had fallen in love with John Tilley, one of Anthony's fellow clerks at the Post Office, where he now worked, and was preparing for her wedding and subsequent departure to Penrith, where she would live. Mrs. Trollope quickly fell in love herself with Cecilia's new husband who, as she told Julia, was "a very admirable person," and provided "all the minor matters of income, house, and so forth . . . quite as I could wish." She expressed relief to see that "*that* part of my business on earth has been very well accomplished." On her first visit to her daughter's home, she composed another novel called *One Fault.* Once again, it had its relationship to her family life. This novel was a study of a progressively deteriorating marriage caused by the husband's bad temper. The inspiration for her analysis of this trait was undoubtedly Thomas Anthony Trollope. In all her correspondence, there is only one guarded allusion to her husband's similarly difficult disposition, but it is telling. In an early letter to Harriet, she had explained her American trip as promising "frequent intervals of tranquility in the absence of Mr. Trollope," whose temper, she explained, was increasingly "dreadful." Here at Penrith, watching the buoyant spirits of the young Tilleys who, it seemed to her, had all the world before them, Frances Trollope hurried to complete her latest novel amidst an old woman's feelings of regret at the tragic fate of her own husband whom she had loved faithfully to the end.

Anthony, in his turn, now became a serious worry. For many years, he had not lived near his mother. Since October of 1834, he had been toiling away at his position in the London Post Office. The first seven years of that life were full of failure and dissipation. Indeed, once Mrs. Trollope's old friend Mrs. Clayton Freeling, who had found Anthony his position, brought him a rumor that he was in danger of being dismissed for unseemly conduct and, "with tears in her eyes, besought me to think of my mother." Ashamed before her above all others, Anthony concealed from his mother the desperate state of his life. As he remarked, "Who in such a condition ever tells all and makes a clean breast of it?" Twice, things were so bad that he was imprisoned for debt until he was anonymously bailed out. He did not inquire into his bene-factor's identity. It had been, of course, his mother. At twenty-five, he seemed to be going nowhere. Although he longed to write, he lacked courage. He had promised himself to venture a novel, and "no day was passed without thoughts of attempting, and a mental acknowledgment of the disgrace of postponing it." As he watched his mother's industry, success, and good fortune, he could think only of his own deplorable state. "I hated the office, I hated my work. More than all I hated my idleness."

It was to be Mrs. Trollope's greatest triumph that she brought Anthony out of that "sickness unto death" and provided the world with a great novelist to boot. Filled with self-hatred, Anthony fell ill with a mysterious ailment for which the doctors could find no cure. Indeed, Mrs. Trollope had sum-moned to help two girls who participated in mesmeric experiments, a strange episode called by some of her biographers "absolute folly." Instead, it re-vealed her awareness that Anthony's illness was primarily psychological, quite beyond physical medicine. When both science and the occult failed her, she brought him through in the only way she could—by participating in the sadly familiar task of nursing throughout most of the summer and early autumn of 1840, and by writing. This time, as if to demonstrate to Anthony the secret resources of her strength, she produced two novels, laying out before him both her fertile imagination and her Herculean energies. Both novels had their analogies to Anthony's present state. One concentrated on those who thirsted for literary fame (*Charles Chesterfield*) and the other ex-posed the flimsiness of the lionizing coteries of London (*Blue Belles of England*). It saddened her to see how Anthony had made himself sick with longings for such success; her books were a living demonstration to him that all was possible merely with steady application to the task. These two books are as much a sign of her maternal concern for her youngest son as were the hours spent at his bedside during their months of composition.

And Anthony, as he lay recuperating, cannot have failed to follow with interest the installments of his mother's accounts of London life. Many of the characters in his later novels show the impact of Frances Trollope upon the writing career of her youngest son. Gradually, Anthony recovered, extricating himself from his fateful idleness. He discovered the art of compartmentaliz-ing, mastering his mother's "power of dividing herself into two parts, and keeping her intellect by itself, clear from the troubles of the world, and fit for the duty it had to do." Two years later, when he began his own literary productions, he unconsciously followed her example. Much later, he con-fessed his mother's influence, acknowledging that his grasp of the human character had been enlarged by his special "sonship." Beyond her heroic breadwinning, Anthony owed his mother a threefold debt: his rigorous and disciplined writing habits, his prevalent realism, and his understanding of the multifaceted female character. The seeds of his greatness had been sown in the London of 1840–41, as Anthony observed his mother working steadily amid distractions, transforming her experiences into the stuff of fiction, and embodying that sense of triumph which she brought to so many of her female characters. His debt to her was beyond measure.

Having buried her husband and four of her seven children, and supervised the successful maturing of the remaining three, Mrs. Trollope doubtlessly expected to be done with sorrowful losses. She had moved her residence to Florence, expecting no further pressing maternal cares. But in her seventieth year, she endured the most terrible trial of all, the death of Cecilia in the prime of her life. After a rapid succession of five pregnancies, Cecilia's strength was but fragile. In 1847, John Tilley wrote Mrs. Trollope that the doctors had ordered Cecilia to spend two years in Italy to recover her failing health. But a year later, all attempts to effect a cure were given up there, and Mrs. Trollope sent her daughter home to England so weak that she had to be carried from bed to sofa. The doctors told Tilley that her case was hopeless. Cecilia, buttressed by the example of her mother's behavior of the past, composed herself and directed her husband to write her mother the truth about her condition. The Garnetts marveled at Cecilia's serene acceptance of her death sentence. "She has prepared her husband herself for this event, and behaves with the noblest fortitude and resignation expressing no pang at all she quits—yet no woman ever loved a husband and children more fervently than she does. Mr. Tilley had written to Mrs. Trollope that if she wished to see Cecilia again she must come immediately to England." The Garnetts were certain that Mrs. Trollope, in her advanced age, could not be expected to brave the difficult winter weather and the tumultuous revolutions then paralyzing Europe for a trip to see her dying daughter.

But Mrs. Trollope had already set out on the long and solitary journey, truly "a dismal trial to my strength of all kinds." Tom, now married, could not come, as his wife was in poor health. Mrs. Trollope arrived on March 10, exhausted but grateful to find she had not been too late. She prepared for her fourth and last deathbed vigil, marked as were the others, by tireless nursing, watching, and the ever-allotted number of daily pages. The habits of a lifetime could not be changed, even though the pressing needs of the past were over. Indeed, the writing process was a necessary buttress as she watched her daughter lying on an early deathbed. The children were cared for by friends and relatives, while the grief-stricken husband and anguished old mother waited for the end. During her solitary hours, Mrs. Trollope sought to find the circumstances to continue her ritual of writing. She told Tom:

> The difficulty of finding a quiet half-hour here to write, is incredibly great. Sometimes I feel in absolute despair on the subject. John Tilley is *very* kind, but he has no power to help it. Cecilia sleeps in the back drawing-room, and has the doors open day and night into the other, so I cannot work there. At night (the only quiet time), although I am sorely tired, I *would* try, had I fire. But this I cannot have, because the fire in my room is laid for the morning, which is the only moment I can command.

She fretted over work not done, even as she agonized over her daughter's state. "To write more than a page at a time, is pretty nearly impossible. And even so, I scarcely know what I am writing." By April, Cecilia was dead. Mrs. Trollope told Tom: "The last month has been the most suffering period of my existence." But the balance of tasks, as ever, had saved her.

She never forgot the pain of Cecilia's death. When she herself died fourteen years later, aged eighty-three years and seven months, her last intelligible words, as recorded by Tom, were "Poor Cecilia." In these last years, her ties to her children had finally slackened; her role as mother was no longer dominant. Cecilia was gone, and most of her young children were soon to follow her. Tom and Anthony were married and occupied with their own lives. In a last flowering of creativity, Mrs. Trollope rounded out her prolific writing career with a curiously innovative series of novels unabashedly glorifying independent, strong women. Now she had time to reflect upon the strengths that had carried her through. In these last novels, she celebrated herself and the sisterhood of women that had been such an important factor in her long life.

Recently, Carolyn Heilbron has observed that women writers, with few exceptions, "do not imagine women characters with even the autonomy they themselves have achieved." The autonomous self, in this definition, is one that is not ancillary, not described by a relationship as wife, mother, daughter, or mistress. This critical insight suggests that the most persistent problem facing the woman writer is to discover for her female characters some identity which is strictly their own.

In a series of books centering around the picaresque Widow Barnaby character, Mrs. Trollope long ago experimented with a potentially autonomous heroine, albeit in the comic mode (*The Widow Barnaby*, 1839; *The Widow Married*, 1840; *The Barnabys in America*, 1843). Her widow is a middle-aged woman who is ready to pack her bags on a moment's notice to explore life's possibilities. Different from the usual "suffering angels," neither wilting nor spiritual, the widow was in the words of one reviewer, "showy, strong-willed, supple-tongued, audacious, garrulous, affected, tawdry, lynx-eyed, indomitable in her scheming, and colossal in her selfishness." In all her many hilarious adventures, the widow's prevailing interest is herself and her own survival. Indeed, her identity is so much her own, that in the end, her third husband adopts her name, calling himself Major Barnaby in compliment to the superiority of his wife!

In the last novels of her life, Mrs. Trollope returned to this subject of female independence, this time in a more serious and realistic mode. Her interest in this theme was prompted by her own experiences and by the observations she had made of her circle of friends. Now her fiction turned ever more obsessively to a preoccupation with the problems of unhappy wives who must learn to achieve selfhood outside the marital bond. In the books written between 1851 and 1854, she included a whole gamut of dangerous, miserable, and exploiting marriages. In most cases, the heroines enter those marriages for the wrong reasons: social, familial, or financial. Each must learn to create an independent self in spite of an unsatisfying marriage contract.

In the first novel of this series, *Second Love, or Beauty and Intellect* (1851), there are several possibilities for marital trouble: a marriage undertaken out of a sense of duty, the incompatible marriage of a young wife and a much older man, and the marriage of a clever woman with a man not her intellectual or moral equal. Release and satisfaction are not won, as is Mrs. Trollope's clear point, by submissiveness to one's fate, but by the preservation of inner integrity. In the end, she rewards those who persevere with the deaths or disappearances of their respective spouses.

That same year, she completed a book (*Mrs. Mathews, or Family Mysteries*, 1851) about another reluctant and disastrous marriage, this time by a middle-aged woman who is perfectly happy and exceedingly capable of taking care of herself, but who marries to please her father, an old chauvinist who is worried about "what will become of [his fifty-year-old daughter] and her money, when she should no longer have any man belonging to her." Once the heroine consents to an apparently harmless match with her father's old friend, Mrs. Trollope takes an entire chapter to explain the woman's attempts to make a marriage settlement aimed at protecting her financial interests in case of disaster. The lady also warns her prospective husband about her sturdy habit of independence. "I am quite sure . . . that I could not be passively obedient to anyone." Still, despite all her precautions, Mary nearly loses everything. Her husband tries to exploit her, calling himself "master of the house," and making her life generally miserable. In the end he is apprehended in an assortment of crimes and conveniently dies, restoring Mrs. Mathews to single contentment and happiness.

Her next heroine (*The Young Heiress: A Novel,* 1853), after living for years with a Rochester-like hero in an illicit arrangement similar to the one proudly declined by Jane Eyre, is in her middle years discarded for a young wife. Apparently Griselda-like, she offers to stay on as a servant, while secretly vowing revenge upon the man who has ruined her life and that of her illegitimate son. To find in the end that she has murdered her old paramour by slow poisoning does not shock the careful reader who has followed the author's asides on the female character which manifests "a very strong and resolute power of self control . . . when circumstances call upon [women] to exert it. . . . This sort of passive power often very effectually supplies their want of strength, both moral and physical, in other respects." Self-control as passive power—in such devious but finally effective ways have women endured and triumphed in their difficult relations with men.

In *The Life and Adventures of a Clever Woman* (1854), Mrs. Trollope recounts the misadventures of another superior woman who makes a disastrous marriage. She begins as a clever, unmanageable, motherless girl who soon has enough of the restrictions of governesses and embarks upon the independent life in the great world of London. Realizing the uniqueness of her situation, she keeps a journal recounting her experiences and celebrating her own cleverness. Soon, for social and financial reasons, she falls into the marital trap like many a woman. Once again, Mrs. Trollope includes detail on marital and property settlements calculated to protect the wife from her husband's expressed maxim: "What belongs to my wife is mine; what belongs to me, is my own." After the marriage follows the battle for mastery, this one extreme, with the husband locking the wife in her room until the police finally rescue her. After her husband's eventual death, she has two further offers of marriage and, understandably, rejects both.

At one point in her journal entries (which alternate nicely with the exterior action of the novel), the new bride outlines the reasoning which has led her to the altar. Though the plot shows her to be badly mistaken, her justification here surely reflects that of her world.

> If I did not marry, my brilliant position in society would have been speedily converted, in the eyes of the world, into that of a disappointed old maid. This would have impeded, not to say destroyed, my still upward progress in society. I knew this, and I determined upon becoming a wife instead of an old maid.

In her heroine's extensive reflections on society's opinions of "old maids," Mrs. Trollope had touched on a subject which would lead, in her next novels, to further fictional investigation into the position of women.

In her earlier novels dealing with unsuccessful marriages, Mrs. Trollope sometimes ended by having her heroine make a more successful or compatible match. In the last novels of this series, she has her women refuse further relationships with men, in favor of something very much like sisterhood. The heroine in *The Life and Adventures of a Clever Woman* won't marry again, nor will Gertrude in that novel of 1855, having recognized that "her husband was a pompous fool, incapable of acting from rational motives; incapable of forming a rational opinion; and pretty nearly incapable of uttering a rational word." She comes to accept the fate "which had given her one of the dullest men that ever lived as a husband and companion" because she realizes an even worse one would have been to have married "a man who, with less of dullness, had a greater propensity to interfere with the opinions of his wife and who might have interfered more fatally still with the occupation of her time." Given these circumstances, she furnishes rooms to please herself, stocks a fine old library, and bears, happily, a daughter with whom, after her husband's death, she lives happily ever after. Thus the female community is underway.

Already seventy-five, Mrs. Trollope wrote only one more book, her thirty-fourth novel since she had begun her writing career at fifty-three. This last novel, *Fashionable Life: or Paris and London,* is a thinly disguised paean of praise for sisterhood as alternative and solution. A young heiress is unexpectedly rejected by a penniless suitor too proud to let himself be supported by a wealthy wife. To avoid temptation, he departs for Australia in the first volume, leaving the girl to wonder how she will manage her life and future, now that marriage is clearly out of the question. The departure of the impoverished young man, so clumsily motivated and managed as it is, surely betrays Mrs. Trollope's novelistic wish to make possible a celebration of sisterhood. The heroine must now think for herself. Her education, like that of many women, having been inconclusive in developing any one dominant interest, she turns to traveling, and embarks for a stay in Paris with her maiden aunt, "two single women, actually without connection or relations of any kind." When a new aristocratic female acquaintance with a young daughter suggests "entering into partnership," one providing money, the other rank, the female community begins in earnest.

The women, now four in number, are clear that it is precisely their collective single state that makes possible their agreeable living arrangements. The establishment begins and is soon as celebrated for hospitality as for elegance. The women lack neither "genuine liberality of feeling [nor] the unobtrusive and graceful expression of it." Indeed, as Mrs. Trollope comments, "If all people set about carrying out their own arrangements, and their own intentions, in as business-like and rational a manner as did the female co-partnership I am describing, there would be much fewer disappointments in life."

Repeatedly, throughout the middle sections of the novel, the author delineates the appeal of the female community, locating it primarily in a blending of disparate personalities among equals. "It would have been difficult, perhaps, to find any other group of four females who, while each was so essentially different from the others, could, nevertheless, constitute a society in which each should so delightfully contribute to the enjoyment of the rest." Her picture of shared happiness is always one of individual personalities in free expression of themselves. "How often did it happen to her, when deep in the perusal of some out of the way book . . . to have her philosophical train of thought interrupted by Aunt Sarah's merry laugh, while Annie was gamboling round her in some outrageously ridiculous *costume,* or mimicking some peculiarly comic Parisian peculiarity." This easy picture contrasts sharply with the restrictive male tyrannies of the other novels.

The women find themselves miraculously free from the "social slavery" which had heretofore permeated their lives. They all agreed that freedom was the keystone of their living arrangements. "They were . . . less hampered by the necessity of sacrificing their own inclinations . . . in order to do what others might deem necessary, than any individual of their acquaintance." Freedom among differences—this was the ingredient but rarely found in marriages of the period. The partners in this all-female family could share happiness and conversation at will and also withdraw at pleasure. As the author concluded her description of their mutual life, she pointedly added a generalizing comment: "Perhaps of all the goods the gods can give, the most precious is freedom of will and action."

This "perfect unison" of minds is temporarily disturbed when the youngest woman of the group falls in love. When there is financial trouble, and her prospective match is endangered, the women rally round their friend, making the necessary arrangements and bestowing the needed money. But clearly, the young couple will come to live within the sisterhood. The women make all the decisions without even consulting the young man. As one notes, "I much doubt if, in any matters of domestic arrangement, we would be likely to differ." And there is no difficulty, since none of the women can make up her mind "to passing the day without seeing her at all." It was as if the real life ladies at Harriet Garnett's Hastings community had arranged for Sarah Bayley and Mr. Kenyon to marry and move in as well. Curiously enough, two of the names of this fictional circle, Sarah and Anne, duplicate the names of Harriet's circle. And so the happy pair join the female community without "those tearful separations . . . which will often cause a parting bride to sigh, even at the moment when the dearest wish of her heart is fulfilled."

When, predictably, the marriage runs into trouble, and the young husband commits a melodramatic suicide, he is hardly missed by his wife, for the women go to work to interest the young widow in her infant daughter. It isn't hard to imagine Mrs. Trollope's reasoning, as she writes that "the strongest feeling of her nature, *maternal love*," has saved the girl. Yes, together with sisterhood and the machinations of "the whole of our female conclave, baby Clara included." Eventually another woman of the circle marries, but by this time, marriages really don't matter. Mrs. Trollope's point has already been made: salvation comes, not through men, but through sisterhood and mother love. In this late, last novel, the men of the plot are shadowy nonentities—the women stand out clearly, individualized, all most strongly motivated by love and concern for one another. Without mutual exploitation or pain and suffering, they have lived more successfully together than they ever have with men.

Indeed, like the worlds of so many other women of her time, the world of Frances Trollope's intimates had been primarily female. In youthful years, she was close to her selfless spinster aunt, Fanny Bent, and the Winchester schoolmaster's daughter, Marianne Gabell. Later, in London, she entertained Mrs. Edwards the bookseller's widow, and Mrs. Bartley the actress, who bestowed free tickets and spoke to the great publisher John Murray on Mrs. Trollope's behalf. Her Harrow friend Lady Dyer subsequently married a German nobleman, whose Bamberg castle was frequently offered to Mrs. Trollope as a refuge from her various troubles. With these women she shared her sorrows, anxieties, and joys, confident that they experienced emotions similar to hers. She deeply involved herself in the marital difficulties of Mme. Fauche and Rosina Bulwer. She followed the tragic fortunes of Camilla Wright and was forever fascinated by her sister. As a famous author, she was part of the supportive network of female literary friendships, primarily exemplified in her circle by Mary Russell Mitford and Letitia Landon. Abroad, she socialized with Lady Sevestre, Lady Normandy, the Princess Melanie Metternich, Madame Recamier, and Madame de Chateaubriand. Her emotional ties with Harriet Garnett and Julia Garnett Pertz were deep and lasting. She remained in close correspondence with them across her lifetime. These associations with literary, cultured, intellectual women had been an important part of her complex life. Their shared experiences and mutual affections helped shape her novelist's vision. And to her female friends, Frances Trollope was unique and central. As successful as she became, she never repudiated her womanhood and the claims of her women friends. When she left England forever, the letters of Harriet Garnett continued to express deep regrets about the departure of this incomparable friend.

Frances Trollope's successful life as mother, friend, and literary woman had not come easily. Indeed, it was possible primarily because she had solved what Florence Nightingale once isolated as the greatest problem of the nineteenth-century woman: the lack of her own time. Although Virginia Woolf later claimed that a woman, in order to write, needs a little money and a room of her own, Mrs. Trollope, had she been asked, would almost certainly have found these two only secondary. Certainly, she had never possessed either in abundance during her long life. What she did need, and learned to make for herself, was TIME. She created it, carving it out in large blocks from outside the parameters of the usual nineteenth-century female day, so pervasively occupied with the obligatory morning visits and afternoon calls which had sapped the energies of so many. Frances Trollope made for herself regular free periods from among the early morning hours of her days. As Anthony later noted, "She was at her table at four in the morning, and had finished her work before the world had begun to be aroused." Regular adherence to this practice enabled her comfortably to inhabit several worlds at the same time. She once told her publisher Bentley, "Since I have felt it my duty to write, I have devoted such a portion of each day to the occupation, as would enable me to keep my place before the public." To fledgling writers, the question of time was of supreme importance. She counseled her son Anthony to "lose no *idle* time, but give all he can." To Rosina Bulwer, who was trying to become a novelist, she wrote, "Give yourself quiet unbroken leisure to write, and I will readily stake my judgment on a brilliant success."

Time was the magic elixir which made individual creation, supportive friendships, and the activities of family life possible. While Florence Nightingale and others were sure that family life inevitably *"destroyed* the individual life," a notion which was to become almost an article of faith among a new generation of feminists, Frances Trollope, through her habit of compartmentalization, offered to her circle of friends, as she does to us, the possibility of living comfortably in the spheres of both domesticity and real work. When Tom's old Birmingham headmaster met the famous Mrs. Trollope, he noted in his diary some surprise at her diverse assortment of talents. "I expected to find Mrs. Trollope epigrammatic,—I found her clever, intelligent, and domestic." Apparently, that combination was rare enough to merit special notice. To mother a large family successfully, maintain significant connections with a wide circle of female friends, and write thirty-four novels and five books of travel was a large achievement indeed.

Those who had known her, even for short intervals of time, were always astonished at the intensity with which she inhabited her several spheres as mother, friend, and author. After Mrs. Trollope's death, her daughter-in-law,

herself a literary women of sorts, asked some old friends to send reminis-
cences and recollections she might use for a biography which she planned to
write. One of these is particularly illustrative of the combination of qualities
Mrs. Trollope stood for in the eyes of her women friends. It came from a
daughter of the large Drury family of Harrow days, who recalled how she was
once called home from school to meet a "little old lady . . . drinking tea." "I
think I heard something like this, 'Come and speak to Mrs. Trollope,' but I
am *quite sure* that the old lady in the black bonnet rose up, drew me lovingly
to her, and as she embraced me, said, 'You darling child'!"

> I was only allowed to stay at home a short time, and was then despatched back
> to lessons. But I was there quite long enough to fall in love with Mrs. Trollope.
> Children are seldom taken in; they seem to know intuitively whether the affec-
> tion shown them be genuine or not. I felt certain that this most delightful and
> affectionate stranger liked me. Her loving greeting and farewell made so deep
> an impression, that my little glimpse of the then famous novelist has never in
> the least faded from my memory. Of course I was then too young to understand
> the reason for the warmth of her manner. Childlike I took it to be entirely on
> my own account. But in after years, when I heard about the friendship [between
> her own mother and Mrs. Trollope in former years] which had so long existed,
> I realized that it was for the sake of another she had wished to see me, and when
> she saw, received me so kindly. And for that very reason I love her memory the
> more.
>
> After that, the name of Trollope fell on a responsive ear, and no sooner did
> I realize that my charming old lady wrote books, and that the books were stories,
> than I begged and entreated to be allowed to read some.
>
> I never saw Mrs. Trollope again. But from that day in my very early life to
> the present, the mention of her and hers, has to me always been associated with
> kindness, geniality, and intellect.

Kindness as a mother—geniality for friends—intellect for her profession.

Like Frances Wright, she had found the saving grace of occupation. Like
Julia, she had fulfilled the obligations of wife and mother. Like Harriet,
she had maintained her deep bond with the circle of women. Her success was
like that quest in the old fairy tales, in which the youngest son must achieve
three things, never one. While many other women of her time had found
one or another of life's prizes, Frances Trollope, convinced of the interde-
pendence of these goals, succeeded in balancing their conflicting claims to e-
merge in the end to the richly satisfying life she had earned. Her so doing taught and teaches other women that the quest is not a vain or hopeless one.

References

184 "Mrs. Trollope lived this triple existence . . ." For further information and documentation on the life of Frances Trollope, see Helen Heineman, *Mrs. Trollope: The Triumphant Feminine in the 19th Century.*

184 "one glance . . ." *Domestic Manners,* p. 27.

187 "It should be understood . . ." Quoted in Captain Frederick Marryat, *Diary in America,* ed. Jules Zanger (London: Nicholas Vane, 1960), pp. 261–62.

187 "In a series of letters . . ." Mrs. Trollope wrote six lengthy letters from America to Julia Garnett Pertz, as follows: 26 December 1827, on the Mississippi; 7 December 1828, Cincinnati; 27 April 1829; 20 August 1829; 12 March 1830, Baltimore; 11 April 1831, Alexandria, Virginia. They are all in the GPC.

187 "but very much thinner . . ." FT/JGP, 12 March 1830, GPC.

188 "If I have not written fully . . ." FT/JGP, 7 December 1828, GPC.

188 "Had it not been . . ." FT/JGP, 12 March 1830, GPC.

189 "As soon as I had decided . . ." FT/JGP, 12 March 1830, GPC.

189 "Tom is doing very well . . ." FT/JGP, 22 August 1831, GPC.

190 "This I should care nothing about . . ." FT/JGP, 22 August 1831, GPC.

190 "That is to say . . ." FT/JGP, 22 March 1832, GPC.

191 "The book sold out . . ." Frances Trollope, *Domestic Manners of the Americans,* 2 vols. London: Whittaker, Treacher, 1832.

191 "I mean, if possible . . ." FT/JGP, 27 June 1832, GPC.

191 "The return of my mother . . ." Thomas Adolphus Trollope, *What I Remember,* p. 162.

191 "moderate comforts . . ." Anthony Trollope, *An Autobiography,* p. 21.

191 "I have a longing Julie . . ." FT/JGP, 25 November 1833, GPC.

192 "a much-needed vacation . . ." Henry's vacation letters to his mother (26 July, 9 and 24 August 1832), Robert Taylor Collection.

193 "I never felt less in good humour . . ." FT to Mary Russell Mitford, 23 April 1832, in *The Friendships of Mary Russell Mitford,* I, 234.

193 "It is *beautifully* written . . ." FT/JGP, 22 March 1832, GPC.

193 "I *long* for Harriet . . ." FT/JGP, 27 June 1832, GPC.

194 "I have had much vexation . . ." FT/JGP, 16 February 1833, GPC.

194 "a complete travel book . . ." Frances Trollope, *Belgium & Western Germany in 1833: Including Visits to Baden-Baden, Wiesbaden, Cassel, Hanover, the Harz Mountains, etc.,* 2 vols. London: John Murray, 1834.

194 "Each of us have already . . ." FT to Colonel Grant, 3 June 1834, Morris L. Parrish Collection.

195 "the third that she had put . . ." Anthony Trollope, *Autobiography,* p. 23.

195 "He is grown pale . . ." FT/JGP, Spring 1834, GPC.

195 "During great part of the time . . ." FT/JGP, 13 July 1834, GPC.

195 "My life is a very sad one . . ." FT to Thomas Adolphus Trollope, in Frances Eleanor Trollope, *Frances Trollope: Her Life and Literary Work from George III to*

Victoria, I: 227. This biography of Mrs. Trollope by her daughter-in-law, who had access to many letters and papers which have since disappeared, is hereafter designated FET.

195 "the doctor's vials . . ." Anthony Trollope, *Autobiography,* p. 24.

196 "This is my night for writing . . ." FT to Thomas Adolphus Trollope, in FET, I:227–29.

196 *Tremordyn Cliff,* 3 vols. London: Bentley, 1835.

197 "There were others . . ." FET, I: 230–31

197 "fear his reason was . . ." Thomas Adolphus Trollope, *What I Remember,* p. 41.

197 "I cannot express my delight . . ." FET, I: 147.

198 "This melancholy and unsuspected event . . ." FT to Bentley, 7 November 1835, Robert Taylor Collection.

198 "Mr. Trollope's death . . ." MG/JGP, 22 November 1835, GPC.

198 "Emily's sweet temper . . ." FET, I: 256.

198 *The Life and Adventures of Jonathan Jefferson Whitlaw: or Scenes on the Mississippi,* 3 vols. London: Bentley, 1836.

198 "in the hope of placing herself . . ." *Jonathan Jefferson Whitlaw,* I: 214–15.

199 "it was rather a hard struggle . . ." FT/JGP, 17 January 1837, GPC.

199 "Your friend has left you . . ." FT to Thomas Adolphus Trollope, in FET, I: 285–86.

199 "I have sometimes thought . . ." FT to Thomas Adolphus Trollope, 12 September 1837, Morris L. Parrish Collection.

200 "I have worked so hard . . ." FT to Thomas Adolphus Trollope, in FET, I: 287.

200 *One Fault: a Novel,* 3 vols. London: Bentley, 1840.

200 "with tears in her eyes . . ." Anthony Trollope, *Autobiography,* p. 45.

201 *Charles Chesterfield: or the Adventures of a Youth of Genius,* 3 vols. London: Colburn, 1841.

201 *The Blue Belles of England,* 3 vols. London: Saunders & Otley, 1842.

201 "power of dividing . . . " Anthony Trollope, *Autobiography,* p. 25, p.

202 "She has prepared her husband . . ." HG/JGP, 22 October 1848, GPC.

203 "The difficulty of finding . . ." FT to Thomas Adolphus Trollope, in FET, II:140–41.

203 "Poor Cecilia . . ." FET, II:301.

203 Carolyn Heilbrun, *Reinventing Womanhood,* p. 71. The chapter is entitled, "Women Writers and Female Characters: The Failure of Imagination."

203 *The Widow Barnaby,* 3 vols., London: Bentley, 1839; *The Widow Married,* 3 vols. London: Colburn, 1840; *The Barnabys in America,* 3 vols. London: Colburn, 1843.

204 *Second Love, or Beauty and Intellect,* 3 vols. London: Colburn, 1851.

204 *Mrs. Mathews, or Family Mysteries,* 3 vols. London: Hurst & Blackett, 1851. Quotations are from I: 21ff., and 54.

205 *The Young Heiress: A Novel,* 3 vols. London: Hurst and Blackett, 1853. Quotation is from I: 110ff.

205 *The Life and Adventures of a Clever Woman. Illustrated with Occasional Extracts from her Diary,* 3 vols. London: Hurst & Blackett, 1854. Quotation is from III:190.

206 *Gertrude: or Family Pride,* 3 vols. London: Hurst & Blackett, 1855. Quotations are from I: 29–30 and 42–43.

206 *Fashionable Life: or Paris and London,* 3 vols. London: Hurst & Blackett, 1856.

206 "two single women . . ." *Fashionable Life,* I:207.

206 "If all people set about . . ." *Fashionable Life,* I:233, 236, and 242.

207 "How often did it happen . . ." *Fashionable Life,* I:247 and 248.

207 "Perhaps of all the goods . . ." *Fashionable Life,* I:275 and 289.

207 "those tearful separations . . ." *Fashionable Life,* II:271 and 277.

208 "maternal love . . ." *Fashionable Life,* III:169.

209 "She was at her table . . ." Anthony Trollope, *Autobiography,* p. 21.

209 "Since I have felt it my duty . . ." FT to Bentley, 24 June 1835, Robert Taylor Collection.

209 "lose no idle time . . ." FT to Rose Trollope, 7 August 1844. Robert Taylor Collection.

209 "Give yourself quiet . . ." FT to Rosina Bulwer, July 1840, in Louisa Devey, *Life of Rosina, Lady Lytton.* London: Swan Sonnenschein, Lowry & Co., 1887, p. 197.

209 "I expected to find . . ." FET, II:100.

210 "I was only allowed to stay . . ." FET, II:258–59.

your ... is at present out of the question. George is a very diligent musician, and plays very difficult musick. Hermann is very tall (as tall as his brothers) but is often ill in consequence I suppose of his growth. He will soon be 15 and George 18 in May – I thank God! that they are all three too young to go into the field – Charles was refused on the score of delicate health –

Farewell my dear Minna; again my affectionate thanks for your pretty letter – and I have also to thank your dear mother for a very sweet one from her. Heaven bless and preserve you and your dear family and friends! My Husband and sons often think of you and with the most affectionate interest –

ever your tenderly attached friend

Julia Pertz –

(To Miss Meyer) Berlin 5th April 1848

My dearest Minna – most affectionately do I thank you for your kind letter – in such times as these the human heart is keenly alive to all impressions, and the expressions of your affection and sympathy was very soothing to my excited feelings. We have suffered much dear Minna and we shall probably still have much to suffer – we are driving fast forward to a Republic I fear – to a French Republic, (that most odious of all human governments) with its mad dreams errors and crimes – our future is most fearful and uncertain – no one can say what the morrow may bring – War seems inevitable. We are pledged to defend Holstein and Schleswig, to make Poland independent, this involves us in a war with Denmark and Russia – England will seek her own advantage without caring for Germany, South Germany is opposed to us – and divided with itself – in our cities we have civil war and in the country plunderers and robbers – and to crown all these evils we must defend ourselves against France, who is almost compelled to invade Germany, in order to get rid of her roving Republicans and starving workmen. Heaven alone can avert all these evils and dangers! – we must bend ourselves and submit to the will of God – I am more resigned already to the fate that awaits us – not that I am more blind to the danger but I have schooled to face it with courage and resignation, and to bear up for my Husbands and childrens sake – May Germany arise with new vigour from the ruins of the old Monarchy! this is my prayer altho' I do not expect to live to see it – but our children may do so – and in this thought I will seek comfort and consolation – Most deeply do I feel for our amiable and unhappy King, he has been shamefully treated by his ungrateful subjects – who he loved so tenderly – I do not deny that the government has been in fault – that timely concessions might have avoided this great calamity, but the King was kept in ignorance of the state of the public mind – he acted to the best of his knowledge and judgement – he was deceived – but his intentions were good and pure as his own heart – he had been bred up with different opinions in an older school, and he was not aware of the change that had taken place in mens opinions – he has generous and elevated feelings, how can he be understood by a selfish and unfeeling world? – for such is the one in which we move – The King of Prussia is almost (I would find in my heart to write the only King in Europe who deserves to bear the title and I feel persuaded that the safety of Germany depends on the Imperial crown being placed on his head, but Bavaria, Austria, South Germany are opposed to it – each country will be first and virtue and patriotism must be sought for in a Dictionary, not in the hearts of men – such is my view dear Minna of the world – and of those who govern it – were men better and wiser, there would be no misuse of power – no revolutions, and if men would govern himself and his evil passions governments would have an easy task – would in fact be superfluous – but God has ordained that this world should be one of suffering and we must bow to his will and endeavour to prepare ourselves for one in which all sorrows will have an end – the enclosed letter is I fear of a very old date – Charles had undertaken to enclose it to you with a few lines of his own, but I find he has not done so – and I hasten therefore to send it with this note of mine. Charles' head is full of politics and thoughts of his future, alas! sad enough are the circumstances under which your brothers and our sons begin life! Charles will remain at home this

Hermann Pertz and Letter of Julia Garnett-Pertz

CHAPTER EIGHT

Conclusion:
Widening the Circle

ou tell me so prettily that my letters are delightful. . . . If you would practice . . . you would be infinitely my superior in this charming and good-natured accomplishment. It is one so peculiarly suited to our sex and for which most females have a natural talent that it is a pity when it is neglected. To a woman "whose noblest station is retreat," it is a never failing source of agreeable occupation to herself and of pleasure to her friends. . . . Therefore . . . let me impress upon you whilst you are young to cultivate your talent for letter-writing and you will soon like it when you find by constant practice you do it with ease and elegance. There is no subject however trifling or insignificant in itself which may not be rendered agreeable by the pen of a ready writer—and besides, is it not the bond which unites the absent? "They live, they breathe, they speak, what love inspire"—warm from the heart, even at the distance of 3000 miles.

MRS. SALLY COLES STEVENSON, **to her niece, 23 February 1839**

It was always a luminous point when one of these dear letters arrived in my governesses rooms in Celle and Hasperde. . . . I think you will keep the letters in reverence. I give them to you gladly—My eyes grow ever weaker and I probably will never again read them. And after my death, probably no one will have an interest in the letters.

MINNA MEYER **to Florence Pertz, 13 May 1909**

NOW THAT the mutual drama of these women's lives was over, it remained only for the script to be passed on to posterity, if it were to avoid the oblivion that had descended upon the lives of so many others.

After Julia died, many of her friends wrote to console Dr. Pertz and offer their recollections of his wife. While the physical Julia had succumbed to the maddening phlegm, persistent cough, and heart pains, many agreed that her spirit lived on in her letters. Helen Martineau claimed to see Julia solely in their correspondence, which seemed "the sacred history of her sweet suffering spirit." Though Julia had died as she had lived, separated from those both near and far, her essence remained clear and consistent: "I seem to see you faithfully, more and more refined and loving and beloved."

As he gathered up Julia's effects, Dr. Pertz came upon the collection of letters she had treasured across her lifetime. Aware of their value, he also saw in them a distillation of his wife's being. Soon the idea came to ask her correspondents for Julia's own letters. As he told Mrs. Trollope, "I should value them as most precious relics, since they are the genuine and beautiful expression of her pure elevated generous lovely being." Pertz had in mind writing a monograph on Julia's life. Had he done so, it doubtlessly would have resembled the cloyingly sweet conventional portraits of the time, such as the one of Clara Ranke, "Clarissa Ranke, ein christliches Lebensbild," presenting a pious, domestic picture.

But the task of procuring the documents did not prove to be an easy one. Dr. Pertz addressed himself first to Mrs. Trollope. Indeed, it had been a letter from Mrs. Trollope to Julia which had inspired Pertz's attempt at collection. He wrote:

> In my solitary hours I have been looking through letters and papers kept by my beloved Julia. Amongst them one has particularly touched me, where you write in May 1827 to Julia that her letter written about me showed that she loved me —the letter I carried to you from Paris. Now I should be very grateful to you my dear friend, if you would be so kind to communicate to me her letters kept by you, particularly that one. . . . Perhaps you would also feel inclined to write down or to dictate for me and our children reminiscences from your friendly intercourse with her and her family; you will certainly feel gratified in calling back so many proofs of her attachment for you and yours.

But Mrs. Trollope's "wandering habits" and large correspondence had forced her to "the resolution of keeping *no letters whatever*—and this resolution I have adhered to so strictly that I have not a single letter in my possession." Mrs. Martineau and Miss Smith declined to send Julia's letters (thus indicating in what importance they held them), but instead copied portions of them to comply with Pertz's request. Harriet Garnett, her sister's major correspondent over twenty-five years, had destroyed all of Julia's letters, believing as she did, that their correspondence had been a sacred bond which no other eyes should violate. Indeed, she had often questioned Julia about whether her sons read the letters, "for it would be a great restraint to think they read what I say to you. Tell me truly if they do & if you always burn my letters, for a sister may say many things which she does not wish her nephews to see. You know how sacred I consider a letter, & I always write as I should speak to you if quite alone with you." But Julia, for whom the letters had been life itself, could not bear to destroy them; in this one deception of Harriet, she kept her faith with posterity.

Actually, the project Dr. Pertz had in mind was primarily a memorial to Julia, in which the thousands of letters she had received would play no part. It was her correspondence alone which was to be perpetuated. When the letters started to come in, Pertz gave his youngest son Hermann the task of copying them. A year earlier, in one of those acts which seem at first purposeless and later fraught with meaning, Julia had given her son the gift of penmanship lessons with a Mr. Büzel, hoping to surprise his father with "his beautiful writing." Perhaps she thought to prepare him for a life of helping Pertz in research activity after she would be gone. At any rate, his newly won skill made Hermann the natural choice for a posthumous amanuensis. In Pertz's first Christmas letter to the Garnetts after his wife's death, he told Harriet how he, Hermann, and some of Julia's women friends, had marked Christmas day with a touch of Tennysonian melancholy, by visiting Julia's tomb, which they sadly adorned "with garlands wound by themselves." Alas, Madame Ranke was to have come, "but the air being somewhat fresh, her husband would not allow her." As Pertz added, "She is still very suffering. Hermann visits her twice a week." During those regular visits, the boy was able to speak English with Frau Ranke for, as his father explained, "his English is already very much improved in consequence of his copying about 70 letters (contributed by our friends here and at Hanover) written by his dear mother, which he placed upon the Christmas table prepared by him and Charley for me."

In that first Christmas without Julia, Pertz gave Charles, George, and Hermann his usual serious, scholarly gifts ("Lord John Russell's edition of Thomas More's Diary and Correspondence, and Bartlett's Sicily"), but added a sentimental touch: each son received a gold medalion framing a lock of Julia's hair. To Harriet, he painted a shining domestic scene, whose brightest, unextinguished light, would always be Julia.

> I live in the recollection of Her who adorned life with her sweet presence, and in the confident hope of meeting Her again at the termination of my earthly career. Fulfilling my duties makes the days glide imperceptibly away and I enjoy the company of my dear sons, who bear Her likeness and try to give me satisfaction.

But alas, despite Dr. Pertz's assiduous gathering and Hermann's loving re-copying, the project of framing a life of Julia came to naught. By the time the next Christmas rolled around, Professor Pertz had pledged his troth to another Englishwoman, Leonora Horner, making the project of writing a life of Julia both impractical and somewhat indelicate. As Julia Smith had once prophetically written to Julia, when discussing Niebuhr's life, "I suppose it is always rather an awkward relationship to two wives or two husbands, tho' the one is dead and the other living—because one cannot somehow manage to wish for the dead one to be alive again in this world." Soon, the boys were addressing Leonora as "dearest Mother."

Only Hermann, who was closest to Julia, perhaps because he had transcribed her letters and thus understood her best, never forgot his mother's memory. Like his father before him, he married an Englishwoman, for whom contact with family and friends was largely epistolary. She grew to understand his preservation of the thousands of letters for which Dr. Pertz had no further use, and also cherished a tradition of respect for the whole collection. Hermann's devotion to his mother was lifelong. When he died of pneumonia at an early age, in a last sentimental gesture, he asked that his mother's portrait be set at the foot of his bed so that he could watch the quiet, sweet face of Julia in his last moments of life.

Hermann's daughter, in turn, received the collection of letters and even tried to round it out further. Fifty-seven years after Julia's death, Florence Pertz was preparing the correspondence of her grandmother for some vaguely perceived posterity, and wrote to one of the last living members of Julia's circle for some missing letters. What her intention was in this re-gathering project is not known. However, Julia's old friend Minna Meyer sent the remaining correspondence in her possession to Florence Pertz, along with a letter which is both the end and the beginning of the story of this circle of women.

My dear Florence:

Enclosed you will find the letters of your treasured grandmother which you requested. In them you will discover her warm and loving spirit and also her pious resignation in times of the most serious suffering. There are not many letters missing; shortly after the death of his treasured wife, I sent several of them to your dear grandfather and I no longer recall whether or not I received all of them back again. In those days he planned to write a life-sketch of his deceased wife and requested letters from me. I believe that life-sketch was never written, however, since your dear grandfather married soon thereafter.

The first letter is from Bremen in the year 1840, where I was spending the winter; then in the winter 1842–43 I was in Berlin, at a time your dear grandmother was still healthy. In 1849 I traveled to Berlin to take care of her, and early in the spring or summer 1850, came back with her sisters. It was very interesting for me to read through all these letters once again; it was as if I were again living in the old days. It was always a luminous point when one of these dear letters arrived in my governesses rooms in Celle and Hasperde. . . .

The last letter which she wrote me was from Soden. —How much I should like to discuss all of this with you in a conversation. I think you will keep the letters in reverence. I give them to you gladly—My eyes grow ever weaker and I probably will never again read them. And after my death, probably no one will have an interest in the letters. . . .

Accept these as a friendly remembrance of your

Minna Meyer
13 May 1909

The entire correspondence, treasured by the women of the family, eventually passed to Florence's niece, Cecilia Payne-Gaposchkin, who also transcribed and catalogued the letters, even offering them to some male scholars—to whom they seemed lacking in the kind of importance worthy of any historical accounting.

Finally, they were put at my disposal when I was writing a biography of Frances Trollope. Reading through the thousands of pages for letters by and references to my subject, I found there the moving story of an entire circle of women whose collective life history seemed still important today. My sense of identification with those women of the past paralleled that of Ruth Benedict, who, on the brink of self-discovery, spent a difficult winter in which she had set herself a task upon which to concentrate, hoping just to get through the long days. She told only her diary of her solution: "My pet scheme is to steep myself in the lives of restless and highly enslaved women of past generations and write a series of biographical papers from the standpoint of the 'new woman.' My conclusion so far as I see it now is that there is nothing 'new' about the whole thing except the phraseology and the more independent economic standing of recent times—that the restlessness and groping are inherent in the nature of women and this generation can outdo the others long since past only in the frankness with which it acts upon these."

Ruth Benedict never completed or published those "biographical papers." Yet working on them had given her a sense of communion with other women. She discovered that her gropings and restlessness were not unique. That sense of sisterhood, even across centuries, was powerful enough to release her from her restless incarceration in the domestic life and to allow her great achievements as a world-renowned anthropologist and writer. To a similar extent, as the women of this circle read of the strivings of their sisters, they too made steps forward, however hesitant. They could not act with so much "frankness" as did Ruth Benedict. But their reading and writing of letters, and the concomitant formation of the epistolary female community assisted them as their collective reach, while exceeding their grasp, helped create a world where the next generation of women could strive together still further toward a destiny larger than that ever achieved by any of these "restless angels."

REFERENCES

PAGE

215 "I seem to see you . . ." HM/JGP, 3 April 1852, GPC.
216 "In my solitary hours . . ." Georg Heinrich Pertz to FT, 2 November 1852, GPC.

216 "wandering habits . . ." FT to Georg Heinrich Pertz, 14 November 1852, GPC.
216 "for it would be a great restraint . . ." HG/JGP, 4 November 1848, GPC.
217 "His English is already . . ." Georg Heinrich Pertz to HG, 19 January 1853, GPC.
217 "I live in the recollection . . ." Georg Heinrich Pertz to HG, 27 January 1853, GPC.
217 "I suppose it is always . . . " JS/JGP, 5 September 1852, GPC.
218 "Enclosed you will find . . ." Minna Meyer to Florence Pertz, 13 May 1909, GPC.
219 "My pet scheme . . ." Ruth Benedict's Journal, printed in *Revelations: Diaries of Women*, eds. Mary Jane Moffat and Charlotte Painter, pp. 155–56.

BIBLIOGRAPHY

Armstrong, Judith. *The Novel of Adultery*. New York: Barnes and Noble, 1976.

Auerbach, Nina. *Communities of Women: An Idea in Fiction*. Cambridge: Harvard University Press, 1978.

Bäcker-Ranke, Gisbert. "Leopold von Ranke und seine Familie." Ph.D. Dissertation, Bonn University, 1955.

Bäcker-Ranke, Gisbert. "Rankes Ehefrau Clarissa geb. Graves-Perceval." *Historisch-Politische Hefte der Ranke-Gesellschaft* 21 (1967).

Bald, Marjory A. *Women-Writers of the 19th Century*. Cambridge: University Press, 1923.

Banks, J. A., and Olive Banks. *Feminism and Family Planning in Victorian England*. New York: Schocken Books, 1965.

Basch, Francoise. *Relative Creatures: Victorian Women in Society and the Novel*. New York: Schocken Books, 1974.

Beer, Patricia. *Reader, I Married Him: A Study of the Women Characters of Jane Austen, Charlotte Brontë, Elizabeth Gaskell and George Eliot*. New York: Barnes and Noble, 1974.

Bentham, Jeremy. *The Works of . . . published under the superintendence of his Executor, John Bowring*. New York: Russell, 1962.

Bodichon, Barbara Leigh Smith. *Women and Work*. New York: C. S. Francis & Co., 1859.

Boykin, Edward, ed. *Victoria, Albert and Mrs. Stevenson*. New York: Rinehart & Co., 1957.

Branca, Patricia. *Silent Sisterhood: Middle-Class Women in the Victorian Home*. London: Croom Helm, 1975.

Branca, Patricia. *Women in Europe Since 1750*. London: Croom Helm, 1978.

Bridenthal, Renate and Claudia Koonz, eds. *Becoming Visible: Women in European History*. Boston: Houghton Mifflin, 1977.

Butler, Josephine E. *Memoir of John Grey of Dilston*. London: H. S. King & Co., 1869.

Cabell, Julia Mayo. *An Odd Volume of Facts & Fictions, in Prose and Verse*. Richmond, Virginia: Nash and Woodhouse, 1852.

Calder, Jenni. *Women and Marriage in Victorian Fiction*. New York: Oxford University Press, 1976.

Cott, Nancy. *The Bonds of Womanhood: "Woman's Sphere" in New England, 1780–1835*. New Haven: Yale University Press, 1977.

Craik, Dinah Maria Mulock. *About Money and Other Things. A Gift Book*. New York: Harper & Bros., 1887.

Craik, Dinah Maria Mulock. *A Woman's Thoughts about Women*. New York: Follett, Foster & Co., 1864.

Crenshaw, Mary Mayo, ed. *An American Lady in Paris, 1828–1829: The Diary of Mrs. John Mayo.* Boston: Houghton Mifflin Company, 1927.

Crow, Duncan. *The Victorian Woman.* London: Allen & Unwin, 1971.

Davidoff, Leonore. *The Best Circles: Society, Etiquette, and the Season.* Totowa, New Jersey: Rowman and Littlefield, 1973.

Douglas, Ann. *The Feminization of American Culture.* New York: Knopf, 1977.

Ellis, Sarah. *The Women of England: Their Social Duties and Domestic Habits.* New York: D. Appleton & Co., 1843.

Fuller, Margaret. *Woman in the 19th Century.* Boston: John P. Jewett & Co., 1855.

Gilbert, Sandra M. and Susan Gubar. *The Madwoman in the Attic: The Woman Writer and the 19th Century Literary Imagination.* New Haven: Yale University Press, 1979.

Gittings, Robert. *The Nature of Biography.* Seattle: University of Washington Press, 1978.

Gorsky, Susan. "Old Maids and New Women: Alternatives to Marriage in English-women's Novels, 1847–1915." *Journal of Popular Culture* VII (1973), 68–85.

Greg, William Rathbone. *Literary and Social Judgments.* Boston: James R. Osgood, 1873.

Harrison, J. F. C. *The Early Victorians: 1832–1851.* London: Weidenfield & Nicolson, 1971.

Hartman, Mary S. *Victorian Murderesses: A True History of Thirteen Respectable French and English Women Accused of Unspeakable Crimes.* New York: Schocken Books, 1977.

Hartman, Mary S. and Lois Banner, eds. *Clio's Consciousness Raised: New Perspectives on the History of Women.* New York: Harper & Row, 1974.

Heilbron, Carolyn. *Reinventing Womanhood.* New York: W. W. Norton & Co., 1979.

Heineman, Helen. *Mrs. Trollope: The Triumphant Feminine in the 19th Century.* Athens, Ohio: Ohio University Press, 1979.

Hufstader, Alice Anderson. *Sisters of the Quill.* New York: Dodd and Mead, 1978.

Keating, John M. *History of the City of Memphis Tennessee.* Syracuse, New York: D. Mason & Co., 1888.

Leranbaum, Miriam. " 'Mistresses of Orthodoxy': Education in the Lives & Writings of Late 18th Century English Women Writers." *Proceedings of the American Philosophical Society* 121 (1977), 281–301.

L'Estrange, Alfred Guy, ed. *The Friendships of Mary Russell Mitford, as Recorded in Letters from Her Literary Correspondents.* 2 vols. London: Hurst and Blackett, 1882.

Linder, C. A. "The Ideal Marriage as Depicted in the Novels of Jane Austen and Charlotte Brontë." *Standpunte* 96 (1971), 20–30.

Lockridge, Ross F. *The Old Fauntleroy Home.* New Harmony, Indiana: New Harmony Memorial Commission, 1939.

Marshall, Florence A. *The Life and Letters of Mary Wollstonecraft Shelley.* London: Bentley, 1889.

Marshall, J. F. "Les Dames Garnett amies de Stendhal." *Le Divan* (1949).

Martineau, Harriet. "Female Industry." *Edinburgh Review* 222 (1850), 293–336.

McGregor, O. R. *Divorce in England: A Centenary Study.* London: Heinemann, 1957.

Mérimée, Prosper. *Correspondance Generale,* ed. M. Parturier, P. Josserand, J. Mallion, vols. I-VI. Paris: Le Divan, 1941–1947.

Mews, Hazel. *Frail Vessels: Woman's Role in Women's Novels from Fanny Burney to George Eliot.* London: Athlone Press, 1969.

Milne, John Duguid. *Industrial Employment of Women in the Middle and Lower Ranks.* London: Longmans, Green & Co., 1870.

Mitchell, Julie. *Woman's Estate.* New York: Pantheon Books, 1971.

Moers, Ellen. *Literary Women: The Great Writers.* New York: Anchor-Doubleday 1977.

Moffat, Mary Jane and Charlotte Painter, eds. *Revelations: Diaries of Women.* New York: Vintage Books, 1975.

Moore, Katharine. *Cordial Relations: The Maiden Aunt in Fact and Fiction.* London: Heinemann, 1966.

Muncy, Raymond Lee. *Sex and Marriage in Utopian Communities: 19th Century America.* Bloomington, Indiana: Indiana University Press, 1973.

Musgrove, P. W. *Society and Education in England Since 1800.* London: Metheun, 1968.

Neff, Wanda Fraiken. *Victorian Working Women: An Historical and Literary Study of Women in British Industries and Professions 1832–1850.* New York: Columbia University Press, 1929.

Oakley, Ann. *Woman's Work: The Housewife, Past and Present.* New York: Vintage-Random House, 1974.

Olsen, Tillie. *Silences.* New York: Delacorte Press, 1978.

O'Meara, Kathleen. *Madame Mohl: Her Salon and Her Friends. A Study of Social Life in Paris.* London: Bentley, 1885.

Owen, Robert Dale. *Threading My Way.* New York: G. W. Carelton & Co., 1874.

Perkin, Harold James. *The Origins of Modern English Society, 1780–1880.* London: Routledge & Kegan Paul, 1969.

Phillips, M., and W. S. Tomkinson. *English Women in Life and Letters.* London: Oxford University Press, 1927.

Pitman, E. R. *Elizabeth Fry.* New York: Greenwood Press, 1969 [reprint of 1884 edition].

Quinlan, Maurice J. *Victorian Prelude.* Berkeley: California University Press, 1941.

Rees, Barbara. *The Victorian Lady.* London: Gardon & Cremonesi, 1977.

Reynolds, Myra. *The Learned Lady in England, 1650–1760.* Boston: Houghton Mifflin, 1920.

Rowbotham, Sheila. *Hidden from History: Rediscovering Women in History from the 17th Century to the Present.* New York: Vintage-Random House, 1973.

Rowbotham, Sheila. *Women, Resistance and Revolution.* London: Penguin Press, 1972.

Sandford, Mrs. John. *Woman in Her Social and Domestic Character.* Boston: Otis Broaders & Co., 1843 [5th edition].

Shorter, Edward. *The Making of the Modern Family.* New York: Basic Books, 1975.

Showalter, Elaine. *A Literature of Their Own: British Women Novelists from Brontë to Lessing.* Princeton, New Jersey: Princeton University Press, 1977.

Simpson, M. C. M. *Many Memories of Many People.* London: Arnold, 1898.

Spacks, Patricia Meyer. *The Female Imagination.* New York: Knopf, 1975.

Spacks, Patricia Meyer. *Imagining a Self: Autobiography and Novels in 18th Century England.* Cambridge: Harvard University Press, 1976.

Stenton, Doris Mary. *The English Woman in History.* London: George Allen & Unwin, 1957.

Stevenson, Sarah Coles. See Boykin.

Stone, Lawrence. *The Family, Sex and Marriage in England, 1500–1800.* New York: Harper and Row, 1977.

Strachey, Ray. *The Cause: A Short History of the Women's Movement in Great Britain.* London: Bell, 1928.

Tabor, Margaret. *Pioneer Women: Elizabeth Fry, Elizabeth Blackwell, Florence Nightingale, Mary Slessor.* London: Sheldon Press, 1925.

Thomson, Patricia. *The Victorian Heroine: A Changing Ideal.* London: George Allen & Unwin, 1956.

Trollope, Anthony. *An Autobiography.* London: Oxford University Press, 1961 [Reprint of 1883 edition].

Trollope, Frances Eleanor. *Frances Trollope: Her Life and Literary Work from George III to Victoria.* 2 vols. London: Bentley, 1895.

Trollope, Thomas Adolphus. *What I Remember.* New York: Harper & Bros., 1888.

Vicinus, Martha, ed. *Suffer and Be Still: Women in the Victorian Age.* Bloomington, Indiana: Indiana University Press, 1973.

Vicinus, Martha, ed. *A Widening Sphere: Changing Roles of Victorian Women.* Bloomington, Indiana: Indiana University Press, 1977.

Waterman, William Randall. *Frances Wright.* New York: Columbia University Press, 1924.

Wilson, William E. *The Angel and the Serpent: The Story of New Harmony.* Bloomington, Indiana: Indiana University Press, 1964.

Woolf, Virginia. *A Room of One's Own.* New York: Harcourt Brace Jovanovich, 1929.

Wright, Frances [Mme. D'Arusmont]. *Biography, Notes and Political Letters.* Dundee: J. Myles, 1844.

Wright, Frances [Mme. D'Arusmont]. *Views of Society and Manners in America.* Cambridge: Harvard University Press, 1963 [reprint of the 1823 edition].

Zeman, Anthea. *Presumptuous Girls: Women and Their World in the Serious Woman's Novel.* London: Weidenfeld and Nicolson, 1977.